# The Weight of Gold

*Attaining Your Potential
Through the Lens of the Bible*

*by*
Moshe Silver

 Mazo Publishers

The Weight of Gold: Attaining Your Potential
Through the Lens of the Bible

Softcover ISBN: 978-1-7360347-1-2
Hardcover ISBN: 978-1-7360347-0-5

Copyright © 2020 Moshe Silver

*Contact The Author*
E-mail: tikkun.olam@hotmail.com

*Published by*

Mazo Publishers
www.mazopublishers.com
mazopublishers@gmail.com

*Cover art by*
Marion Kunstenaar

54321

**All rights reserved.**
No part of this publication may be translated, reproduced, stored in a retrieval system, or transmitted in any form or by any means, electronic, mechanical, photocopying, recording or otherwise, without prior permission in writing from the publisher.

*– for D*

*When the world pushes you to your knees,
you're in the perfect position to pray.*

*– Rumi*

## Contents

The Author .................................................................... 7
Acknowledgements ........................................................ 8
Introduction .................................................................. 9
A Note to the Reader .................................................... 14

### Genesis ~ 17

Creation ....................................................................... 18
The Tower of Babel ..................................................... 25
Abraham ...................................................................... 31
Sodom and Gomorrah – The Sadness of God ............. 36
The Death of Sarah, the Trials of Isaac ....................... 41
Isaac and the Search for the Father ............................. 46
Jacob and the Fear of Living ....................................... 51
Jacob – The Struggle to Become ................................. 57
Joseph in Chains .......................................................... 62
Joseph Unbound .......................................................... 67
Joseph Revealed .......................................................... 72
The Death of Joseph and the Passing of an Era .......... 77

### Exodus ~ 83

Enter Moses ................................................................. 84
God Enters History ...................................................... 90
Hard-Hearted Pharaoh ................................................. 95
Seeing Is Believing .................................................... 100
Ten Words .................................................................. 106
We Will Do, and We Will Learn ............................... 110
Generous of Heart ..................................................... 115
Of Leaders and Locusts ............................................. 120
Erase Me! ................................................................... 125
The Consequences of Creation ................................. 130
A Full Accounting ..................................................... 136

### Leviticus ~ 141

Render unto God ....................................................... 142

Sacrifices of Love .................................................................. 147
The Still, Small Voice .............................................................. 151
Social Distancing .................................................................... 156
The Freedom to Choose ......................................................... 162
The Goat for Azazel ................................................................ 166
You Shall Be Holy ................................................................... 171
Whose Responsibility? ............................................................ 176
The World was Created for Me .............................................. 181
The Pain of Living ................................................................... 186

## *Numbers* ~ 193

To Choose or not to Choose ................................................... 194
Breaking Faith, Keeping Faith ................................................. 200
To Do Better ............................................................................ 205
To See or Not to See ............................................................... 210
The Great Undoing .................................................................. 214
"I Am Not a Man of Words" ................................................... 220
Of Prophets and of Fools ......................................................... 225
Rebel for the Sake of Heaven ................................................. 229
Nature or Nurture? ................................................................... 234
Full Circle ................................................................................ 241

## *Deuteronomy* ~ 245

Before the Future ..................................................................... 246
Hear, O Israel! ......................................................................... 252
The Beginning of Wisdom ....................................................... 258
To Truly See ............................................................................ 262
The Doors of Perception ......................................................... 266
Captivating Beauty .................................................................. 269
Remembering to Remember .................................................... 274
All On That Day ..................................................................... 280
Before the Great Sabbath ........................................................ 284
Songs of Innocence and Experience ....................................... 289
The Unbroken Circle ............................................................... 293

Excerpts .................................................................................... 298

# Yeshiva Chonen Daas
## Ramat Bet Shemesh

בס"ד

י"ט אלול, תש"פ
September 8, 2020

Dear Rabbi Silver,

Thank you for the opportunity to review your *sefer* **The Weight of Gold**. You have illuminated each parsha of the Torah in a way that brings the Torah to life whether or not one has a background in Torah learning.

This *sefer* is a wonderful aid for someone who wants to prepare a sermon that will immediately capture the attention of their audience. You have successfully blended Chazal and modern jargon in a way which delivers solid guidance that sheds light in today's world. These precious nuggets of Torah are a pleasure to read and share.

This sefer is well sourced and a reflection of your commitment to Torah and your overwhelming desire to educate others. May you merit seeing your *sefer*, **The Weight of Gold**, warmly received and well circulated amongst *Klal Yisrael*.

With Torah blessings and warmest regards,

*Rabbi Daniel Channen*

Rabbi Daniel Channen
Rosh Yeshiva
Yeshiva Chonen Daas

---

Nachal Refaim 34a Ramat Bet Shemesh, 99096, Israel
USA: 914-826-8686 Israel: 054-801-5821
Website: ChonenDaas.org Email: RabbiChannen@gmail.com

# The Author

Moshe Silver is a rabbi, teacher, and author living in Jerusalem. Throughout a career on Wall Street he taught Torah, meditation, literature and creative writing with students ranging from business executives to prison inmates. He continues mentoring colleagues and students, from Wall Street to a Jerusalem yeshiva. Rabbi Silver is available for speaking and teaching engagements and is a sought-after prayer leader and master shofar blower. Contact Rabbi Silver at tikkun.olam@hotmail.com.

---

*If I am the same today as I was yesterday,*

*then today was not worth living.*

*– Rebbe Nachman of Breslov*

# Acknowledgements

I offer this book with gratitude to God, who gives me life, and who has sustained me and guided me and brought me to this moment.

This book is the result of many years of learning from devoted teachers, of the loving support of family and friends, and of sincere criticism and occasional severe rebuke from those most important to me.

I am grateful to my teachers: Rabbi Shlomo Riskin, who set me on the path to a Jewish life; Rabbi Eliezer Diamond, who helped me on my way. Notably to Rabbi David Silber, and to Rabbi Dan Channen. To professors Michael Fishbane and Elisha Russ-Fishbane.

To those who encouraged and supported me as a teacher: To Rabbi Dov Peretz Elkins at the Princeton, NJ, Jewish Center; to Rabbi David Bassous and Congregation Etz Ahaim in Highland Park, NJ. To the memory of Laura Nadoolman, who launched me on the path to the rabbinate at the City Island Temple in the Bronx. To Greg Jeffers, who forced me off the ledge. To the beloved friends who shared hours of Torah study in our home in Princeton, and at Congregation Tefillat Kol Peh, first in Highland Park, now also in Jerusalem. To Rabbi Shlomo Channen and the students of Yeshivat Hashiveinu in Jerusalem.

To Martin Norregaard, who believed in me and encouraged me as a writer, and to Keith McCullough, who provided a platform for my writing, and who continues to prove that it's possible to run an ethical business on Wall Street.

Special thanks to Marion Kunstenaar for her enthusiasm and for providing the cover artwork, and to Deena Nataf, whose outstanding editorial work allowed this book to blossom.

It is no small matter to write a book. The hours of solitude and the long-term sustained focus extract a cost from those nearest to the writer. I am grateful to blessed with the love and support of my children and daughter-in-law. Most of all – first, last, and always – I fumble constantly to find words to express my gratitude for, and to, my wife Reza. May it be God's will that this book be worthy of all the love and support I have received.

# Introduction
## – *This book is for You* –

I wrote this book for one person. Now I turn it over to the rest of the world.

I have sought out universal human meanings from the central book of Judaism – the Torah – the first five books of the Old Testament, also known as the Five Books of Moses. I was prompted to do this at the request of a young friend of mine, a man outwardly as unlike myself as imaginable. He's in his early thirties; I'm in my mid-sixties. He's black and grew up poor and fatherless, an inner-city childhood where many a night he and his mother and brother slept in their car. I'm white, upper-middle-class, and grew up in an intact, professional family in an exclusive New York City neighborhood. He grew up running from bullies in the local public school; I attended New York's top private schools. He worked his way out of poverty and into an Ivy League college on an athletic scholarship. He was scouted for the pros before deciding on a career in finance. Meanwhile, I went to college in the United States and Europe, then to business school – then we both ended up on Wall Street, where our paths crossed.

He's a devout Christian, while I'm an Orthodox Jewish rabbi, yet when he was seeking answers, he and I formed an instant and lasting bond. My wife and I had sold our house in central New Jersey and moved to Jerusalem. One month later, I was on the phone with him, listening as, through his tears, he told me of the personal crisis he was facing, the chasm that had opened in his life.

We spoke frequently over the next several weeks, and with each conversation I heard the change as he embraced his path to redemption with the same discipline that had helped him become a world-class athlete. I heard his voice grow stronger from week to week. I heard the startling insights he shared with me – the humility with which he approached this work and the fearless honesty with which he shared his darkest, most troubling thoughts.

From my academic studies, I have learned to say, "Let me show you another way of looking at this." From the martial arts, I learned the importance of reading another person's energy. As a musician, I learned to listen more to others than to myself. From hasidic philosophy and Buddhist teachings and practice, I learned to ask, "How can I be of use?" And so first I listened. Then I asked.

"I'm here in Jerusalem," I said. "I can't head into Manhattan and meet you for coffee. I'm so far away," I continued, "how else can I be useful to you as you continue through your process?"

His response was immediate and enthusiastic. "You know that I read the Bible every day," he said. "But I only know what I've learned from my own reading and from the Christian teachers I've been around. It would be really helpful if you could give me a different perspective. Some Bible passages for personal growth from the Jewish point of view."

In traditional Jewish communities, the Torah is read in an annual cycle. Each week on the Sabbath, during the Saturday morning synagogue services, a portion of the Torah is read, in sequence, until over the course of the year the entire Torah is read aloud to the congregation. At the start of the new year, in the rejoicing after the end of the Jewish holidays of Rosh Hashana, Yom Kippur, and Sukkot, we finish reading the last verses of the Torah. Then the scrolls are rolled back to the beginning and the annual cycle starts anew.

Starting that very day, I began writing notes on the weekly Torah portion, keeping at it for the entire year until I had completed this new reading of the Torah. A Torah for everyone.

Practitioners of every religion insist that "We all worship the same God." Yet the exclusivity, the tribalism of organized religion, has done great damage throughout human history. More than a source of spiritual inspiration and fulfillment, more than a refuge and font of succor for suffering, religion has been the willing handmaiden of war, enslavement, racial hatred, and national divisiveness throughout recorded history.

*Introduction*

But what happens when, rather than looking for reasons to push others away, people seek each other out? The hasidic rebbes – whom you will see quoted often in this book – stress the need for love of one's fellow: "The greatest thing you can do in this world is to do something for another human being," said the great teacher Rabbi Kalonymus Kalman Shapira (1889–1943.) This specifically includes strangers, the Other. People not of our community. People not like us. The command to "love your neighbor as yourself" doesn't differentiate; it applies to everyone whose path we cross. Now, when I was blessed to be in the right place at the right time, I dug down to offer my own deepest thoughts in my own words.

My relationship to the Torah is that of an observant Jew – a rabbi, and a teacher and student of biblical text. It is also that of a modern skeptic, a literary scholar and writer of both fiction and nonfiction. To me, the Torah is at the same time the touchstone of my religious identity and a literary work, endlessly rich in meaning.

The project of writing this book absorbed that first year since coming to live in Jerusalem. It remains one of the greatest blessings in my life. That another person entrusted to me some measure of care of his soul. That he felt close enough to me to share his pain and struggle, and to respond enthusiastically when I offered my own words. Little did I imagine that telephone conversation would change my life in so many ways, setting me on my own course of inquiry, of relentlessly interrogating anew the Torah's text and my relationship to it. It has been a remarkable journey of self-discovery for me, for which I am immensely grateful.

And how is my young friend? you ask. Thank God, he has come through his dark night and is thriving. I am blessed to have played a part in this, but the credit goes to God, and to the young man who saw the challenge facing him and rather than running away, chose to grapple with it head-on. Rather than feeling sorry for himself, or blaming others, he took his responsibility squarely and faced it with remarkable candor and determination. I am blessed by the friendship that grew between us during the months as we spoke and corresponded over my weekly notes, blessed by all I have learned from him, and blessed to have played a part in his process of overcoming the obstacles in his life.

This book is a subjective approach to reading the Torah as a book that speaks to all humans, regardless of their faith – or even lack of faith. The Torah is chock-full of amazing characters: God, center stage, who must deal with the consequences of Creation. Abraham and his descendants who populate the book of Genesis. Moses and the Israelites who struggle through the Egyptian bondage, then forty years in the wilderness, through the books of Exodus, Leviticus, and Numbers. And finally, Moses himself, as narrator, teacher, and chastising parent, who takes over in Deuteronomy and gives the children of Israel an earful.

I have avoided calling God "He" and "Him." This book is most definitely *not* a work of theology. But whatever God may be – which remains utterly unknowable – it only confuses matters to portray God as a man. I have attempted to maintain a respectful distance from this ultimate mystery and to steer clear of a theological, human image of God – though the God who is a character in the Torah is rife with human qualities, not all of them endearing.

By way of disclaimer, the notions and theories, the orthodoxies and heresies in these pages, are all the product of my own thought. Please do not blame my teachers, nor the rabbis of the past millennia. The imperfections are my own doing; the perfection of the Torah and its teaching comes from God, by way of the text of the Torah and the words of the great rabbis.

To be invited into another person's soul is a blessing. It is also a burden. If we take seriously our task as a friend or a teacher – or as a spouse or a parent – we must recognize the enormity of the responsibility that rests on us. We affect other people's lives whether or not we are aware of it. As I embarked on this project – not yet realizing how all-consuming it would

*Introduction*

be – I found myself recalling a Grateful Dead song:

> *Now, I don't know but I was told*
> *It's hard to run with the weight of gold.*
> *Other hand, I've heard it said*
> *It's just as hard if the weight is lead.*

For over a year I have been running with the weight of gold, helping to bear the precious burden of another human soul. I take no credit for my friend's accomplishment, but I take profound joy in his success, and in the impact this has had on my life.

Now I turn this book over to you. It is not a traditional Jewish approach to the text of the Torah, though much in it is taken from basic Jewish sources. It is not an exhortation to become religious, nor is it a diatribe against religion. It is, rather, a call to engage, to examine our lives through the lens of this remarkable and eternal book. Life is a challenge every moment; let us take it up. As Bob Dylan writes, those who are not busy being born are busy dying. Each week, the Torah portion speaks to this: How do we deal with the challenges of being human? How do we confront the randomness of existence? How do we create and sustain a society founded on justice? How do we face the inevitability of failure, of loss, of pain and death? How do we relate to God – particularly at those times when God seems to refuse to relate to us?

Thank you for taking up this book. May you find something useful in these pages. May you be blessed to attain your full human potential. And may it be God's will that what I have written may in some measure help you to that end.

*Moshe Silver*
*Jerusalem*

# A Note to the Reader

As the core text of the Jewish people, the Torah has acquired a significant body of commentary since it first appeared in this world some 3,500 years ago. Throughout this book, reference will be made to some of the most important and best-known commentators, in order to clarify how the text is understood from a traditional perspective. The author will on occasion invoke the greatest rabbinic minds in history, only to argue with their interpretation. This is consistent with the way in which the commentators saw themselves and each other: all of them having something worthwhile to say, but each one acknowledging that they don't have exclusive ownership of the truth – no "hot line" to God. The only honest approach to studying the Torah is to accept up front that we can never know God's ultimate true meaning. That doesn't mean, however, that we cannot touch its outline.

Over the past 3,500 years, since the Torah first came into human hands, thousands of the most spiritual, most intelligent, and most dedicated people in human history have devoted their lives – and on many occasion given their lives – in the quest to understand what it is that God expects of us, and what God offers us.

The following are names that I shall refer to often in the course of this book. It is not my intention to give an exhaustive overview of rabbinic literature – indeed, this list omits some of the most important rabbinic commentators. My purpose is simply to introduce the main sources I cite.

*The Rabbis:* The Jewish teachers and sages spanning a period that begins with Ezra the Scribe, in around 480 BCE, and continuing until approximately 600 CE. The term "rabbinic literature" refers to post-biblical writings. These fundamental literary works of the Jewish oral tradition include the Midrash – a set of homiletical texts expounding on biblical passages written in the immediate post-biblical era but also continuing to be produced to this day; the Mishna – the compilation of

*A Note to the Reader*

Jewish Oral Law, redacted in Judea in about 200 CE; and the Talmud – an extensive set of rabbinic discussions analyzing the Mishna and spanning several centuries. The Jerusalem Talmud was compiled in the land of Israel in around 350-400 CE. The more extensive, and more widely influential, Babylonian Talmud was compiled around the year 500 CE and forms much of the basis for all further Jewish legal and ethical discussion.

*Maimonides:* Rabbi Moses ben [son of] Maimon is the prince of Jewish philosophy and one of the most important thinkers in history. Born in approximately 1135-1138 in Cordoba, in Moslem Iberia, Maimonides died in Egypt in 1204 and is buried in Tiberias, Israel. During his eventful and often difficult lifetime, Maimonides produced an unparalleled body of writing. He combined vast rabbinic knowledge with insights taken from Aristotle, whose work he discovered in Muslim Spain in Arabic-language paraphrases and translations, and also wrote extensively on medical issues – his writings on medical ethics are studied to this day. Maimonides served as court physician to Sultan Saladin, while also acting as the head of the Jewish community of Fustat, the capital city of Egypt. His writings provide a touchstone for the oldest rabbinic traditions of Torah knowledge; yet the intellectual rigor, the human and political wisdom, and the passion of his writing keep his work compellingly fresh – often startlingly contemporary.

*Hasidism and the Rebbes:* Taking its name from the Hebrew word meaning "piety," the Hasidic movement sprang up in the mid-1700's in what is now Western Ukraine. From there, it quickly spread through much of Russia and Central Europe. While the great Hasidic teachers – the "rebbes" – were deeply learned rabbis, many of their followers arose from the poorest Jewish communities, people whose abject poverty prevented them from aspiring to the great academies of rabbinic learning in Eastern and Central Europe. Hasidic teachings infuse traditional legalistic and text study with insights and practices drawn from Kabala, the Jewish mystic tradition. With their emphasis on ecstatic prayer, wordless spiritual song, and communal dance, Hasidic teachings encourage their followers to express their deepest emotional and spiritual yearnings, and to enter into a state of intimacy with the Divine.

*And beyond...* The study of the Torah remains at the core of Jewish religious identity and practice. These influences, and many others, continue to guide the rabbis and scholars of today. Unlike many areas of knowledge, dominated by an academic elite, Torah is the domain of all. To be sure, there are those who are more knowledgeable, those who have developed more profound insights. Those who are great teachers, as well as those who are at best mediocre students. But perhaps the most radical principle which the Torah itself enunciates is this: that the Torah is given to all of us – indeed, to each of us – and for all time. It is a book that God began to write. And as the Hasidic rebbes teach, it will never be complete until we have each made our own unique contribution to understanding its message.

---

On the opening page to Genesis, Exodus, Leviticus, Numbers and Deuteronomy, you will find a list of the Torah portions – in Hebrew, the *parshiyot* – in the traditional order, as read throughout the year in Jewish communities around the world. One portion is read each Sabbath in the synagogue; publicly, and in its entirety. The Hebrew title of each portion, or *parasha,* is listed, together with the chapters and verses. For the convenience of the reader, the chapters of this book correspond, in order, to the portions of the Torah as listed.

There are many resources available online for those interested in following the annual Torah cycle. For those just starting out, the author recommends beginning with traditional resources. Both www.chabad.org and www.myjewishlearning.com offer a clear and concise approach to the text, well-grounded in tradition.

Welcome to the study of Torah! May this be a blessing that will last a lifetime.

# *Genesis*

1 • *Bereshit*       (1:1 – 6:8)
2 • *Noach*          (6:9 – 11:32)
3 • *Lech-Lecha*     (12:1 – 17:27)
4 • *Va-Yeira*       (18:1 – 22:24)
5 • *Hayyei Sarah*   (23:1 – 25:18)
6 • *Toldot*         (25:19 – 28:9)
7 • *Va-Yeitze*      (28:10 – 32:3)
8 • *Va-Yishlach*    (32:4 – 36:43)
9 • *Va-Yeishev*     (37:1 – 40:23)
10 • *Miqqeitz*      (41:1 – 44:17)
11 • *Va-Yigash*     (44:18 – 47:27)
12 • *Va-Yechi*      (47:28 – 50:26)

# 1

# Creation

*And God said, Let us make man in our image, in our likeness...*

*– Genesis 1:26*

To write usefully about the mysterious opening section of Genesis – the first weekly Torah portion in the annual cycle – we must be open to uncovering what this text will show us about God. Throughout this book we shall try to follow the text where it leads us, rather than forcing the Torah to confirm the dogmas that surround us.

God creates the world with speech – what the rabbinic literature calls the "Ten Utterances" – *Let there be light, Let there be a firmament*, and so on. The one time God pauses is before creating the human where, rather than merely saying, "Let there be a man," God says, "Let us make man." God seems to need a moment to think it over before creating Adam.

Whom is God addressing, then, with the word "us"? The interpretation of God's invitation, "Let us make man," favored by the rabbis is that God is asking the angels to comment. And the angels bring a slew of objections: Humans will act wickedly; they will reject Your commandments; they will bring evil and destruction into the world; they will disobey You, and ultimately they will reject You entirely. Yes, says God. But they won't *all* do *all* these terrible things *all* the time. And anyway, I have decided to make them.

So the God of this aspect of Creation is the God who for some unknowable reason pauses before creating humans, perhaps because God needs to consider in advance the fact that, unlike every other aspect of Creation, humans are programmed to be unpredictable. Perhaps, as we shall see over and over as we delve deeper into subsequent passages of this remarkable book, no less unpredictable than their Creator. It may be our very unpredictability which most reflects God's likeness.

But it is also intriguing to read this verse as addressed not to the angels, but to us. To the reader. In seventeenth- and eighteenth-century English novels we come across phrases such as "gentle reader," or "dear reader." The Torah seems to be likewise inviting us to engage in the creative process, to make us active readers. "Let us make a protagonist," God says to us. "You and I," says the Torah. "Together, we shall make humanity in our image and in our likeness." Humanity as the central character, a protagonist that makes sense to us, the readers. Because the reader must fully identify with the characters in a book, otherwise the book will not thrive and its message will be lost.

The Torah is inviting our involvement. "I've made everything up to here," says God. "From now on, you and I will craft this narrative together." The story of humanity – and it begins to emerge here – is a shared creation, told jointly by God and by us.

What kind of person will we create?

## Adam and Eve

Let's begin with a key point that underlies so much that happens throughout the Bible: God has a hard time communicating clearly to humans. Indeed, the fundamental task of the Torah is to get us on God's wavelength. It's frequently unsuccessful, as we see in the defining first act of disobedience: Eve and Adam eating the fruit, which arises from a failure of communication.

God tells Adam that on the day Adam eats the fruit, "you will surely die" (Gen. 2:17).[1] From God's perspective, our death is the consequence of the eating of the fruit. To say that God exists outside of time means that God sees inseparably both the action and its consequence. But humans are time-bound,

---

1   Unless otherwise noted, all references in this section are to the book of Genesis.

and when the consequence does not occur simultaneously with the act, we don't believe they are connected. In this way, Eve – and perhaps Adam – come to disbelieve God's message. This disconnect, this type of communication failure, occurs repeatedly throughout the Torah. God is challenged to communicate in a way that we can understand, while we are challenged to see the world, and our actions, from God's perspective. It's not clear which of us has a more difficult task.

Our relationship with time necessarily gives rise to our freedom of choice: as we can't do more than one thing at a time, we must choose. And every act we choose leaves behind countless acts we will never be able to perform. If we follow the axiom that God can do only good – which the text itself will invite us to question – then it is precisely our quality of free choice that gives rise to evil in the world. Not by our choosing evil, but because it is impossible for all humans to always choose harmoniously, and this gives rise inevitably to conflict.

As arose between Cain and his brother.

## Cain and Abel

The Cain and Abel narrative lies at the heart of the biblical narrative. If God had to pause to consider all the ways in which humans might exercise free choice, then certainly Cain killing his brother Abel is the most unpredictable occurrence in the opening chapters of Genesis. In terms of narrative and literary themes, the trajectory of the Written Torah – and of much of the rest of the Bible thereafter – is a working-out of the story of Cain and Abel.

Cain is the firstborn of humanity. Cain and his brother Abel are the first human beings; the first people to be born of a father and a mother. Recognizing his status, and with the dawning awareness that he is able to feed himself by God's intervention through the process of growing crops, Cain thanks God with a gift. We can truly say that Cain invents religion.

But things don't work out as planned, because his kid

brother elbows his way in with a much nicer gift: the firstborn of the flock, fresh from the birthing season. The simplest reading of this story is that Cain brought his offering – spontaneous though it was – as an afterthought (4:3): "And it was at the end of the time period" (likely meaning the end of the season; the growing was done and the fresh produce had been eaten, and Cain brought only what was left over) "… and Cain brought an offering to God." And in the very next verse, "And Abel also brought." Although God does indeed favor Abel's offering, it seems that the issue is not the superior offering of the firstlings of the flock over the musty old leftover fruits. Rather, Cain eats his way through an entire year's produce and then decides it would be good to thank God. Abel, on the other hand, acts immediately. Before he even shears or eats from his flocks, the first thing he does is make an offering to God. What God seems to prefer is not the quality of the offering – though Abel's gift is superior – but the quality of the one bringing the offering. The latecomer, Abel, wins out over the enthusiastic Cain, who thought up the idea in the first place.

This is the traditional interpretation: Cain was selfish and gave God the leftovers; Abel was utterly selfless and gave of the very best. Cain grew vegetables and ate them; Abel cared for the sheep, even though God had not permitted humans to eat meat. Thus, Cain's activity was selfish, and Abel's was selfless. But there's a disconnect, because God tells Adam (3:17–19) that the ground is cursed for Adam, that Adam must toil and work the land all the days of his life: "By the sweat of your brow you will eat bread until you return to the earth, because you were taken from it; because you are dust, and to dust you shall return." Cain is merely doing what God foretold to Adam, tilling the soil to win his bread by the sweat of his brow. Seen from the perspective of God's own injunction, Cain's offering seems excessively generous; perhaps Cain's offering is an acknowledgement and acceptance of the paradox of existence, of serving a God both who brings us to life, yet who also causes our life to end.

"What are you so upset about?" God asks Cain. "Don't you know that you can improve if you try?" (4:6, 7). Cain takes God's words as a rejection; God has difficulty sending the right message in a way that Cain can grasp. God seems to be giving Cain a pep talk, trying to inspire him to higher achievement. But as all motivational speakers know, "It's not what you *say*, it's what *they hear*." There's no such thing as a message falling on deaf ears. The question is whether the message that is transmitted is also the one that's received. All Cain hears is criticism, and all he sees is God enjoying the savory stew prepared by his younger brother. Not for the last time, the second-born has usurped the place of the firstborn, a key aspect of the Cain/Abel theme running throughout the Torah. Abel brushes his brother aside, bringing God an offering from his flock. We shall see exactly this same story play out later when Jacob supplants his older brother by bringing their father Isaac a pot of lamb stew.

God's problems communicating with humans stem from God's expectation that we will do as God wishes. Meanwhile, it turns out that Cain's offering was not only about thanking God. When God doesn't get excited about Cain's offering, Cain is upset. When he sees that God is delighted with Abel's offering, Cain goes into an unquenchable rage. He is quick to act on his frustration and unfettered by notions of morality (see 3:7–21; the only thing humans have been troubled by was the sudden awareness of their nakedness). He rises up and kills Abel.

Both God and Cain are struck by the enormity of the deed. Cain suffers because he has discovered, too late, that he was responsible to protect and care for his brother, and that killing his own brother is an irreversible act. Cain is the first among us to confront evil. God, too, is suffering. In God's mind, notions of human good and evil are products of right or wrong choice: Don't eat the fruit. Don't turn nakedness from its pure, natural state into the state of lust and uncontrolled desire. But life and death are God's unique domain. God never conceived that people would slay one another: "Your brother's blood cries out to me from the earth!" God says (4:10). Cain's anguish is that he realizes he has done wrong. God is in shock over how easy it is for us humans to usurp God's most important role as bringer of life and death.

And now, for the first time, a human being suffers remorse and openly shrieks his agony before God, begging for help that he knows can never come. Unlike his parents, who pass the blame along to the next person, and then to the serpent (see 3:12–13), Cain steps up before God and wails acknowledgment of his act. He confesses his sin and asks, not for forgiveness – which he seems to recognize is impossible – but for some way of bearing up as he lives out the rest of his miserable life roaming the world.

Speaking technically, Cain experiences remorse, he confesses his sin before God, and he has learned the lesson and resolved that he will behave differently in the future. These are the prescribed steps in the process of returning to God as ordained by the rabbis. Cain, for all his mistakes – or because of them – is the first human to go through the process of repentance.

God has much to learn about the unpredictable nature of humanity. It is not until God meets God's own spiritual friend, Moses, that the full relationship between God and Creation will flourish.

There is so much here, and on so many levels, and it will reverberate again and again throughout the text. But if there is one lesson to be found on these first few pages of the book of Genesis, it is that none of us is wholly sufficient unto ourselves. It seems that even God in some way required something alongside God, or outside of God, or not-God – something to which, or to whom, God could relate. And all the attempts on the part of thousands of years of religious thinkers to "prove" that God is uniquely self-sufficient continually beg the question, Why Are We Here? Not why, from our point of view; why, from God's point of view. Why does God want us? Why does God need us?

If there is any purpose to life, then it must be that each one of us has a purpose. If there is more than one person in this world, it must be that each person has a unique purpose. And if someone near me seems to be fulfilling what I expected to be my purpose, it must be not that he is stealing my purpose – my blessing – but that I still need to search to fulfill my role in this world.

It's so basic, so fundamental – and so difficult for us to remember, much less to live by: Don't hold yourself to someone else's standard. Don't compare yourself to others; compare yourself to what your self is capable of. Our job is to devote our lives to realizing our God-given potential in light of our innate abilities, the circumstances surrounding us and over which we have no control, and our own ideas and ambitions.

Instead of being angry that God accepted Abel's offering, Cain might have said, "Wow! My very own brother – and God accepted his offering!" Cain might simply have said, "I'm so glad *someone* got it right!" Instead, Cain's focus and desired outcome was not on giving thanks to God. It was on God's giving thanks to Cain and praising him in acknowledgment of his giving thanks to God. It's so important for us to be clear about our motivation.

May we be blessed to be on a path of true discovery; may we find what it is within ourselves that can most be brought forth to change the world – and what it is within us that blocks that. And may we be able to clear away our ego and serve God and one another with a pure heart. For we serve God well when we strive to clarify our true purpose in life, and we serve God best when we serve others.

# 2

# The Tower of Babel

*Technology is a useful servant but a dangerous master.*

– Christian Lous Lange,
Nobel Peace Prize Address, 1921

Last week, God became upset that Creation wasn't working out according to plan. Filled with sadness and regret, God decided to destroy the world. Now we read the story of Noah and the Flood, which introduces the unendearing divine penchant for collective punishment, a theme that will surface repeatedly throughout the Torah.

In Genesis 7, God taps Noah to be the Last Man Standing – and to make a new start for all living beings while he's at it. There is an echo of the Cain–Abel narrative, in that one person or entity (in this version, it's all Creation except for Noah, his family, and a few animals) stays in place and is killed, while the other is sent out to roam. But the big picture of the Flood narrative is that it's a second Creation story, complete with birth from the great ocean, one of the core images of ancient Creation myths around the world.

There is much to be said on the story of Noah, but we will focus on the story of the Tower of Babel (Gen. 11:1–9), which appears after the Flood narrative. To dig through the many layers of meaning the Babel story offers, we need to approach the text in the original Hebrew. There is brilliant and profound wordplay throughout the verses, such that any translation prevents us from fully understanding this tale.

Genesis 11 opens with the verse, "And the earth was of one language and unified words." This is the most common understanding. However, the Hebrew is capable of many different translations, with vastly different meanings. Here, the word *unified* in the original also means "very few" – very few what? The word *words* also means "things" or "matters," or even "concepts."

In 11:3–4, the inhabitants of the Valley of Shinar "said to one another, 'Let's make bricks and burn them in fire,' and the bricks were stones for them, and the bitumen was mortar. And they said, 'Let's build a city and a tower with its top in the heavens and make a name for ourselves, lest we be dispersed across the face of the earth.'"

Of course, being dispersed across the face of the earth is exactly what does happen. It appears to be inevitable. God's first blessing to the animals, uttered on the fifth day, is, "Be fruitful and multiply" (1:22). In this week's reading, God blesses and commands Noah and his sons, "Be fruitful and multiply, and fill the land" (9:1). The consequence, if not the very purpose of the blessing/command to procreate is to cover the inhabitable places of the earth with living beings.

In the Hebrew, the word for bricks is used twice, first as a verb, then as a noun. Likewise, the word fire: "Let's brick bricks and fire a fire." Next, "the bricks were stones for them, and the bitumen was mortar." The word for *bitumen* is from the same Hebrew root as *mortar*, which in turn means "stuff" or "material." Thus, "the stuff was stuff," which completes the repetition pattern.

The language invites simultaneous transverse readings. The standard interpretation is that the people of Shinar all communicate perfectly and all agree on everything; they set out to make bricks and then to build a city, and then God decides to confound their plans by making them no longer able to communicate. A different, equally valid reading is that the people have one language, but very few words. Moreover, they don't yet have a notion of manufacturing, and they have never seen or made a brick before, and so the word *brick* becomes both a noun and the verb that describes making it. The fire becomes both the kiln and the act of firing up the kiln to bake the bricks. And when all is said and done, what have they made? "And the bricks were stone for them, and the bitumen [stuff] was mortar [stuff]."

There is rabbinic commentary that says there were no stones in that part of the world, so the inhabitants of the valley of Shinar have to invent a way to make them. Having hit upon a technology, they recognize that they have created something utterly new. Here we have the first description of the process of discovery, of the purely human creation of technology. Immediately before this, Noah builds the Ark following God as the Master Planner. God gives Noah all the instructions; not just the dimensions, but even a list of materials to use.

The inhabitants of the valley of Shinar have no such guidance. They hit upon a technological innovation so advanced that they struggle to describe it, and so they revert to simplistic language. This is common with new inventions: first, they are called by the name of the older technology which they will soon replace, and only later do they take on a separate identity. Think, Horseless Carriage. A computer computes. Silent movies gave way to talking pictures. Everywhere we turn, we see the transition as brand-new technologies come on the scene, ideas so startlingly novel that no one knows what to call them.

Holding a new technology in their hands, the people of Shinar dream of what they could do with it. It is their common language that allows them to plot and plan together. Once they identify the new technology and discover its potential, they begin discussing what to do with it, until they decide to build a city with a tower that reaches to the heavens.

Their activities attract God's attention, and God decides to come down to Earth to see what's going on (11:5). It's important to remember that God drove Adam and Eve from the Garden, not as punishment for eating from the Tree of Knowledge of Good and Evil, but to prevent them from eating from the Tree of Life (3:22–24). The implication is that humans can have either eternal life – which seems to be the way Adam was created – or God-like knowledge, but not both. Similarly, if God doesn't stop the people of Shinar, nothing will prevent them from accomplishing whatever they want. As language was the impetus for launching this project, God now makes language its undoing.

When an idea is new, no one knows what it is. There is no way to refer to a brick other than to call it a brick. But when bricks become part of a city, their character changes. People speak of their nostalgia for walking the cobblestoned streets of London and Paris, of striding the avenues of Manhattan and walking on the ancient stones of Rome. And each day as I walk the streets of Jerusalem, I wonder how often I am retracing the footsteps of the Prophets, of the great rabbis. Of King David and King Solomon.

What's so special about a stone? Once it's put together with others into the shape of a house, it becomes precious to those who were born and grew up there. Once houses are grouped into communities, they become precious to those who share the experience of living there.

The people of Shinar lose their way in the thrill of discovery. They were seeking to connect with God – in Aramaic, the name Babel means "Gate of God" – but their love affair with their new technology gets the better of them. The building becomes not a means to connect with God, but an end in itself.

As with the builders of the city that came to be called Babel, the builders of King Solomon's Temple made a name for themselves with their technology. But here's the thing: when we behold the remains of the Temple structure today, we spend so much time and energy wondering how they made the stone when we could have been wondering at even greater questions: How did God make those stones to begin with? Or that tree over there? How did God make the sky and the earth? And how about – Why did God make me? As with the builders of the Temple, the builders of the city that came to be called Babel made a name for themselves with their technology. They can all communicate clearly with each other, says God, and this is the best they can do? To try to elevate themselves alongside Me with their puny technology?

The story of Babel wraps up the first stage of Creation: God has created the world, has wiped it clean and tried to start over, only to learn that people are incorrigible: "I will no longer continue to curse the ground because of humanity, since the imaginings of the human heart are evil from their youngest days; and I will no longer strike down every living thing, as I have done." (8:21).

God has learned an important lesson about humans: that we are incorrigible. We don't change our behavior, even when we see how strikingly bad the outcome is for others, and even for ourselves. Exceptionalism Syndrome, it's called. We believe that *other people* shouldn't text while driving, because *they* will be distracted, making them a danger on the road. In surveys taken on traffic safety, something like 95 percent of respondents believed it was all right for them to text while driving, just not for others.

Are humans really that stupid? Even God is taken aback by the realization.

The people of Shinar created a technology to fill a need. They perceived that their inventions improved the quality of life, and soon the people of the valley were not thinking about bricks and mortar, but about cities and towers, and about becoming famous for what they had invented. Then they take it further. They want to be like God in some way. They want to build a tower that reaches up to Heaven. God created stones, they say. We did, too. God created a place for humans to live and called it the world. We built a place to live and we call it a city.

When we elevate our own accomplishments above our relationship with God, we are setting ourselves up for trouble. It's one of the easiest traps to fall into, because we work hard to succeed. And when our work pays off, we are entitled to a sense of accomplishment. And how easy is it for our pride of accomplishment to completely push aside our gratitude to God, our awareness that we must put God's agenda before our own?

How do we best show our gratitude to God, if not by constant acts of kindness, charity, support, and compassion toward other people? Toward each and every human being we meet – all of them created in God's image? If not by constantly striving to internalize the message of true humility: I did what I did, first because God gave me talents, second because God gave me opportunities, third because God has kept me alive and healthy for this long. My role? I suppose I was just lucky enough to follow the instructions.

How easily we fall in love with what we have done! With what we have made. Worse, with the objects we have received as a reward, as a consequence of our actions.

Keeping our eyes on the prize works in the short run: chin on chest, swing at the ball, keep hitting singles so you stay in the game. But we must lift our head from time to time and look for the greater prize.

You will be remembered not for the money you will earn in your career, not for the prizes and awards you amass. You will be remembered for the impact you have on the lives of those around you: your family, your friends, your coworkers, and those with whom you engage, whether in business or in daily life. And that impact comes first and always from how diligently and patiently you work on yourself. Life is a flood. By building your own ark, you make yourself the vessel to rescue others.

# 3

# Abraham

*One should be prepared at all times to review one's life and to start all over again in a different place.*

— Etty Hillesum

This week's Torah reading introduces the character of Abraham. Each year I struggle to say something useful about this portion without losing my patience with thousands of years of dogmatic teaching about the father of three great religions.

God tells Abraham, "Go forth from your land." My struggle is with the widely accepted interpretation that Abraham is special because God chose him. To which I say: God, if people achieve greatness only because You foreordained it, then You leave nothing over for the rest of us. If the greatness of our leaders is predetermined, then the Torah requires the rest of us to be mindless automata, blindly doing as we are told. Most insidious of all, it means that Abraham is not a role model; if God chose him, predetermined that he would attain spiritual greatness, then Abraham is not, in fact, great.

Greatness is attained through struggle, through meeting challenges. How is Abraham challenged if he is playing out the cards dealt from a stacked deck? If God created us in God's image, then we are meant to think, to create, to change the world each of us in our unique way. This becomes impossible if we are mere victims of fate.

There is so much to discuss about Abraham. I will focus on only one small piece. Early on, God tells Abraham (Gen. 13:16), "I will make your seed as the dust of the earth, such that if a man could count the dust of the earth, so shall your seed be counted." Later, God tells Abraham (15:5), "And [God] took [Abraham] outside and said, 'Look up to the sky and count the stars if you can count them.' And [God] said to him, 'So shall your seed be.'"

Which is it? Are Abraham's descendants like the dust of the earth, or like the stars of the sky?

A hint comes from the text itself. The dust of the earth is undifferentiated. God begins by creating the heavens and the earth. The upper world and the lower world. The pure spiritual world and the purely material one. What kind of person will you be, God asks? Will you be a spiritual person, like the stars of the heavens? Or will you be dragged down into the dust?

We know that the sand on the beach is made up of millions of tiny grains, yet they appear as an undifferentiated mass. But look up at the night sky. What do you see? As countless as the stars may be, each star appears separate from the others. Moreover, in one of the Psalms read each morning in the Jewish prayer service, King David says (Ps. 147:4), "He numbers the stars; He calls them all by name."

We are faced with a choice: we can be dragged down by our material selves, or we can rise up to our unique spiritual greatness. When we give in to the material – to our ego, to our appetites, to our fears and desires for pleasure – we become as the dust of the earth. Leaden, weighed down, and undistinguished. When we rise to embrace our spirituality, we set ourselves apart – and it is then that God will know us by name, for we will have risen to God's dwelling place.

This is the challenge Abraham takes on, and I refuse to accept that Abraham is capable of succeeding only because God foreordained it. If that is the way God operates, then we are all the dupes of an eternal cosmic joke.

Today's spiritual teachers do real harm when they insist on the unattainable greatness of our spiritual heroes. Whether it is Abraham or Moses, Joseph or David, whether Jesus or Muhammad – or Buddha or Gandhi or Martin Luther King, Jr. – each one of us is capable of attaining the same level of spiritual excellence, capable of becoming a true spiritual and moral leader. There is not much in life that is under our control. No one has a choice in being born female or male, or black or white. In being born healthy or sickly; being born to wealthy parents or into a life of utter poverty. But each one of us has the choice to behave morally or to behave wickedly. And make no mistake – and here is the harsh teaching of the great hasidic masters – there is no in-between. There is no such thing as a morally neutral act. Our every action is either moral, or it is immoral. Nothing we do – no smallest act or word – is devoid of moral content.

Consider the interaction between Abraham and his nephew Lot (Gen. 13:5–7). Abraham returns to Canaan from Egypt, rich with flocks and possessions. Lot comes along with him. The land cannot support them together, so weighted down are they with wealth. "And there was fighting between the herdsmen of Abraham's livestock and the herdsmen of Lot's livestock; and the Canaanite and the Perizzite were dwelling in the land at that time."

What's going on? The land is rich enough to accommodate two entire nations, the Canaanites and the Perizzites, yet when Abraham and Lot come on the scene there are not sufficient resources for them both? This is like the bad guy in the Western movie who says, "This town ain't big enough for the both of us!" The resources are there, but the will to cooperate is lacking – fatally so. Lot and Abraham must go their separate ways.

One of the greatest concepts in the world is articulated in the Torah as (Lev. 19:18), "You shall love your neighbor as yourself." This bears directly on our Torah text, and it is widely misunderstood because it is translated insufficiently.

First, the concept of "love."

Maimonides explains in his Laws of Repentance that this use of the word *love* means both less, and much more than having an emotional attachment to someone else. It is not friendship and good feelings between neighbors – though that is all to the good. Rather, it means that we are all responsible for protecting one another's interests. That we have an obligation to protect our neighbor's honor, their assets, and their well-being. That without this attitude of forceful positive engagement, our society will fail. And when we individually fail to engage actively in support of our neighbor, then we harm our society.

Second, to understand the word *neighbor*, we need to view it in the original Hebrew, which comes from the same root as *shepherd* and *pasture*. (The root word appears famously in the opening of the twenty-third Psalm: "The Lord is my Shepherd.") The biblical concept of neighbor is someone with whom you share pasturage, as among nomadic people who do not camp together but who come together to graze their flocks – a theme which will appear as a source of friction in the stories of Abraham, Jacob, and Moses. For this society to function, each person must take what they need while being mindful to leave over for others.

Are we like the dust of the earth, an undifferentiated mass, grabbing everything for ourselves with no thought for others? Or do we distinguish ourselves like the stars of the heavens, caring for our own but remembering the needs of others?

The Nobel Prize-winning economist Amartya Sen argues, with robust statistics to back his position, that throughout recorded history, famine has been a political phenomenon and not a result of natural forces. There is always food, argues Sen, but there is no political will to distribute it fairly. We shall soon come to the story of Joseph in Egypt and see proper management of the nation's food supply in action. But we have only to look to today's headlines to see story after story of food being wantonly destroyed in wealthy nations, while in nations beset by starvation the trucks full of grain stand within sight of the hungry masses, surrounded by heavily armed militias keeping the food away from those for whom it is intended.

What kind of world will we create? What kind of environment will we mold – for truly, our every action and word have an impact on our environment. The challenge that Abraham accepts is that of deciding to act morally in all cases and at every moment. This is staggering, but why else did God put us here?

Our obligation entails loving our neighbor. Caring for our neighbor's well-being is, at the very least, the key to ensuring our own – what the Dalai Lama refers to as "enlightened self-interest."

God urges Abraham to go out on his own – as the rabbis understand it, for himself, and for his own benefit. If, like Abraham, we strike out on our own, then God accompanies us. It is for this that each one of us was created; God relies on each of us to make our own unique contribution to the world.

Not to take from the earth, not to seek to take for ourselves at the expense of others. For then we become as the dust. And what is dust? The word first appears in the Eden narrative (Gen. 3:14) when God curses the serpent: "And you shall eat dust all the days of your life." Then to Adam (3:19): "By the sweat of your brow you shall eat bread until you return to the earth, for you were taken from it; because you are dust, and to dust you shall return."

Take selfishly and return to the dust, or strive to elevate yourself – and to elevate others as well. Look up to the heavens for guidance. Look to the stars for inspiration. Look to God's dwelling place. Because that's where you belong, too.

# 4

# Sodom and Gomorrah – The Sadness of God

*Let us here observe, that a religion that does not require the sacrifice of all things, never has power sufficient to produce the faith necessary unto life and salvation.*

– Joseph Smith

This week's Torah portion contains two important narratives: the destruction of Sodom and Gomorrah, which takes up chapters 18 and 19, and the binding of Isaac (22:1–19).

The portion opens with God telling Abraham that God intends to destroy Sodom and Gomorrah (18:17–21). This is introduced by a rare glimpse into God's mind. In an aside worthy of Shakespeare, God muses (18:17–19), "Shall I hide from Abraham what I am about to do? Because Abraham is certainly going to become a great and mighty nation, and all the nations of the earth shall bless themselves through him; and I know him intimately, that he will command his children and his household after him so that they shall observe and keep God's ways, doing righteousness and justice, so that God should bring to Abraham that which God said regarding him."

There ensues a set piece in which Abraham negotiates with God to try to save the cities, confronting God by saying (18:23–25), "Would You stamp out the righteous together with the wicked?... It's sacrilege on Your part to do such a thing!... Is it possible that the Judge of all the earth should not act justly?"

In the Noah story, we were told (6:6–7), "And God regretted having made humans upon the earth, and God was sad at heart, and God said, 'I will erase the humans I have created from off the face of the earth.'" We humans naturally think in terms of reward and punishment, so of course we read the Flood as a massive instance of collective punishment. "Why is this happening to me?" is the most natural response to tragedy, to pain. But as they say: pain is inevitable, suffering is a choice. The Torah suggests that suffering is a shortcoming of perception; it is the all too human propensity for seeing everything that happens from our own perspective. From the Torah's perspective, it is more accurate to say that God chooses to destroy the world – or humans, or Sodom – because things are not going according to plan.

Twice over now, the Torah has shown us God the Destroyer. And we shall see that aspect forced upon Abraham before this section comes to a close. It is only later that we shall also see God's own grief over the destruction of God's creations.

We saw in last week's reading that the Torah obliges us to look out for one another. Now Abraham introduces a personal, moral value distinction. God says (18:20–21), "The outcry of Sodom and Gomorrah has grown great, and their sin has been very grave; I will go down and see for Myself, and if their behavior is as terrible as the outcry that I have heard, then I will put an end to them; and if not, then I will know." God sees the city as a single entity – a meaningful lesson. We are all individually responsible for the society in which we live. As moral actors, we either contribute to the world, or we unjustly exploit it. But as nothing we do is morally neutral, we can't merely stand aside. Not ever. Neither on the personal level nor on the societal level. Those who sport the bumper sticker, *"Don't blame me – I voted for the other guy,"* refuse to accept the consequences and obligations of citizenship. Their refusal is a refutation of the values of a free society.

Abraham makes the distinction between the private and the public, between the individual and the collective. This is a very human perspective, and one God has yet to internalize. God is about to destroy Sodom and Gomorrah because they are wicked; Abraham counters that perhaps not each individual within the cities is wicked. Remember that this was God's own argument in favor of creating humans. God says,

"Let us make man" (1:26), inviting a dialogue with the angels. The angels cite all the terrible things humans will do. God argues that they will not *all* be wicked, *all* the time. But now the divine tables are turned, and Abraham uses God's own argument against God.

Buried in the text so far are hints that, even while dispensing divine justice, God is not immune to human suffering. God has the power to create, but – and this is so important – it doesn't mean God doesn't suffer when things don't work out. It is a small thing for God to create something out of nothing, yet it is a tragedy of eternal, cosmic proportions for God to have to destroy God's own creation. And if we pray – especially during moments of pain, tragedy, or suffering – what we are actually doing is trying to connect to God's compassion, to God's own deep suffering.

"You complain about Me all day," says God. "Does no one think about how *I* feel?" This is the God who regretted creating humanity, who in profound sadness chose to destroy all living beings. Not for the last time, God gives in to despair.

And so God requires Abraham to share in this burden.

## The binding of Isaac

The binding of Isaac (22:1–19) is a difficult passage. It has elicited a wealth of commentary, ranging from the most literal reading of Abraham's faith being put to the ultimate test, to the wide-ranging philosophical musings of Kierkegaard in his classic *Fear and Trembling*, to a range of counter-interpretations that condemn Abraham for failing to put his son's life above the irrational demand of an arbitrary and hostile God. Many readers say that in passing God's test, Abraham also fails one of humanity's fundamental requirements. But how to combine and reconcile his duty to his son – which is also a duty to keep alive God's promise of a future – with his duty of obedience to God? The Torah reminds us over and over that life so often doesn't seem to make sense.

"And it was after these things that God tested Abraham" (22:1) introduces the binding of Isaac. Although Isaac is the one who is nearly slaughtered, rabbinic tradition sees this unambiguously as Abraham's test. In the context of the narrative, it is clear that God is testing Abraham to determine whether, after all they have been through together, Abraham is truly fit to be a full partner with God.

We opened our discussion of Genesis with the rabbinic interpretation of "image of God": Like God, we have free choice, we have a moral sense, and we are creators who work to change and control our environment. Perhaps the rabbis hesitated to mention one of God's most important attributes – and one in which we also resemble our Creator: God as the Destroyer. Throughout the Torah, being close to God is fraught with danger, and many a righteous person perishes through accidentally coming too close. God is unpredictable. In the Noah chapters, God destroys the world because of wickedness. With regard to Sodom, it seems God is too impatient to save a city in order to preserve the righteous ones who might dwell there.

As with our gut reaction to the expulsion from Eden – which we saw was inaccurate – we read the Flood as punishment. But the wholesale destruction of all life doesn't fit with our concept of punishment to correct behavior or to serve as a warning. Neither does the blotting out of the cities of Sodom and Gomorrah. The power of the righteous was not sufficient to prevent the wickedness of the generation of the Flood, to prevent the evils perpetrated in Sodom and Gomorrah. If the righteous are not effective, what use are they? If they are not strong enough to change society, if they can't do the job that God requires of them, why should they not perish along with the wicked? The righteous of the generation, both of the Flood and of Sodom and Gomorrah, are too few and too feeble. They are not up to the task of being God's partners. It's a wake-up call.

God tells Abraham: You wanted to prevent Me from destroying the cities of the plain. Do you not believe that I wanted nothing more than *not* to destroy them? Let's see how *you* fare with this, Abraham. You are the great champion of the good; how will you react when forced to confront your own darker side – your propensity for evil? I command you to kill your son. You will have to face this test but once, while I must face it every hour of every day. "You rushed to defend the wicked city of Sodom," God seems to be saying. "Now, Abraham, let's see how you react when the sandal is on the other foot."

The world is full of evil, and it is so easy to fall into utter despair. So easy, and so tempting. And truly, despair is the greatest sin of all. Despair comes to us in a gentle guise, as a reasonable way out. "Give up on humanity," despair whispers in our ear. "After all, God has given up on you more than once." And with all that God must witness in the course of each day, why wouldn't God despair of humans?

Abraham passes the test, for he is willing to carry out God's command and slay his son. Abraham's greatness is that, unlike God, he refuses to despair. Whatever the outcome of his test – whether Isaac dies or lives – Abraham has made his covenant with God, and he remains true to it. Abraham remains truer to his faith in God than God does to God's faith in us. Abraham has no way of knowing that God will prevent him from killing Isaac, no more than the Israelites know they will not drown in the Sea of Reeds; no more than Moses knows that God will call him back up the mountain after the episode of the Golden Calf. Faith can only ever be in the moment. More important, *faith is about us, not about God*. Not, "Why did God..." "Why does God..." "I hope God will...". No. Faith means that I struggle at each moment to connect to God. And when God seems to be absent the most, that connection becomes more important than ever. Faith means that I take upon myself the full responsibility for the relationship, whether God is there or not.

If God will not step in to put right what is wrong, when God appears to have wandered off and forgotten all about us, the only thing that holds the world together is the steadfastness of those who continue to act as though God were right here, right now, immanent. And if God will not always give us the outcome we ask for, and if, tragically, God will not always prevent the misfortunes we fear, then why do we pray? I often do not know. But one thing I do know is that if ever we would cease to pray, then the world would be truly, truly lost.

May we be equal to our every trial. The world depends on it.

# 5

# The Death of Sarah, the Trials of Isaac

*Life can only be understood backwards, but it must be lived forwards.*

– Kierkegaard

This week's Torah reading begins with the death of Sarah and ends with the deaths of Abraham and his son Ishmael, clearing the stage for the next generations where the blessing of Abraham is curated by Isaac, stress-tested by Jacob, and finally sent forth into the broad world through Jacob's twelve sons and their descendants.

"And the life of Sarah was one hundred years, and twenty years, and seven years: the years of Sarah's life. And Sarah died in Kiryat-Arba; this is Hebron in the land of Canaan" (Gen. 23:1–2). Sarah is, as far as I know, the only woman in the Torah whose age at death is mentioned. This is a critical textual marker. The passages of the "begats," in Genesis 5 and 11 list male offspring together with the lifespans of their fathers. For example (11:10ff): "These are the descendants of Shem: Shem was one hundred years old when he fathered Arpachshad, two years after the Flood. And Shem lived after he begot Arpachshad for five hundred years, and he fathered sons and daughters." (Shem, from whose name we get "Semite," is Abraham's direct ancestor.) The father's age marks the birth of the designated heir. The other children are an afterthought.

We read (21:5) that "Abraham was one hundred years old when his son Isaac was born." As with the previous generations, the text records Abraham's age at Isaac's birth. Now it records Sarah's age at her passing. By stating her age, the text makes Sarah Abraham's equal in the genealogy.

Uniquely in this narrative, both parents are tied to the birth of Isaac. Sarah is as important as Abraham to the transmission of the covenant and its blessings. This is hinted at when Isaac "married Rebecca and she became his wife and he loved her, and Isaac was consoled regarding his mother" (24:67). Isaac grew up with a distant, fanatical father – characteristics he, too, will embody, though for very different reasons. But his mother, Sarah, was fiercely protective of him, setting everything aside for her son. It was likely Sarah's love that sustained Isaac at the moment his own father held the knife to his throat.

It takes two to tango. And it especially takes two to reproduce. Yet the mere act of procreation is not enough. Abraham has a covenantal relationship with God, but the covenant and its attendant blessings can be sustained only by being passed on to future generations. And that means Abraham must have children, and the children must be educated, must be formed morally and spiritually. The text recognizes Sarah as the matriarch; Abraham didn't do all this on his own. Yet now the text indicates that Abraham and Sarah are living separately. Abraham is in Beersheba (22:19) and Sarah in Hebron (23:2). How did they become estranged?

It's easy to lose sight of other people: not *even* those closest to us; *especially* those closest to us. It is often the people we most rely on in our lives whom we most overlook. Like the furniture in our home, because they are always there, it's easy to forget them. We don't like to think of ourselves as ignoring our loved ones. But it's a short step from coming to rely on someone to taking them for granted.

This kind of forgetting travels upward. It is difficult for parents to put their children out of their minds. Even when our children are grown, we long to speak with them, to see them. We think of our children when they are far away, and we wish them well. But with regard to those on whom we rely, often those to whom we owe a significant measure of our own achievements – our parents, our spouses – it is easy for us to forget the contribution they have made to our success.

We often congratulate ourselves and discount what others have done for us. What God has done for us. (Paradoxically, it is in this world, where the soul is placed into our hands for safekeeping, that we are frequently the most unaware of God.)

The relationship between Sarah and Abraham also symbolizes the relationship of the body (Sarah) to the soul (Abraham). Hasidic teachings emphasize that the body is, in one key respect, more important, because without it the soul can never attain its purpose. We are sent into this world for a reason; God's purpose for us is *here*. In our brief time in this world, we are expected to accomplish something unique that only we can accomplish. There is some once-in-cosmic-history achievement waiting to be brought about during the soul's brief sojourn in the human body. It's a great challenge – but what a blessing, to know that God entrusted each one of us with a unique task.

Since our lives happen in this world, looking for an ultimate reward is a dangerous distraction. We keep our "eyes on the prize" at the expense of paying attention to the task at hand. There's a fine line between vision and illusion. The immortal soul is not imprisoned in the temporary body. Rather, through living in this world, the soul is refined. Our job is to participate knowingly, consciously, actively, in educating the soul entrusted to our care.

As the body houses the soul, so our relationships house us. Like a pattern of fractals, our life radiates out in ever-widening circles. We must tend to the parts closest in. Only then can we effectively face the wide world into which we are cast. By the same token, we must fully bond with the people with whom we share our lives. It is only in a fully realized outside/inside partnership that we can complete God's assignment.

After the creation of Eve, we read (2:24), "Therefore a man shall leave his father and his mother and shall cleave to his wife, and they shall become one flesh." Becoming "one flesh" doesn't refer only to reproduction. All animals reproduce. Beyond the purely biological function, what is unique to humans is our ability to forge a union of souls, a relationship in which both partners draw so close together that they are no longer distinguishable as separate entities. In an ideal marriage – indeed, in any properly functioning relationship – we do not surrender our identity; we offer it up in service of a third, new and greater entity, which is the relationship itself, and all that it can accomplish.

Sarah was Abraham's kindred soul. And yet Abraham forgot, because he was so busy with his task in the world. We all face the challenge of balancing our work with the people in our lives. In a true loving relationship, each party must want for the other that thing which the other most wants. *That,* and not some vision of the future, is the prize on which we must focus. Or rather, we should focus on both. On the work, and on those for whom we work – and who truly want our happiness and success, even if they cannot find it in themselves to express it. True teammates focus on winning the game, not on who gets to score. Business partners focus on advancing the firm's interest, not on How big is my bonus. Marriage partners support one another's ambitions.

For all his greatness, there is a missing piece in Abraham. He is able to sustain the covenant with God, yet he fails his own wife. We so often see this in public figures who are devoted to changing the world, but their family life suffers. It doesn't have to be so. As with so much else in life, it begins with awareness.

It is a rare and profound blessing to find a true soul mate, someone who will enthusiastically embrace and support and share our dreams and ambitions, someone whom we respect deeply, and whose ambitions inspire us as well. For those of us who have yet to find our soul mate, we should take on the challenge of drawing closer to those already in our lives. We can work on our relationships with family, friends, and business associates. With all the people to whom we are tied – and with whom we experience unavoidable conflict. The Torah demonstrates that God contemplates the outcome of each decision, reacting with approval – even with joy – when humans behave according to

Creation's plan. And, strikingly, expressing sorrow and regret over a past that cannot be changed. Even God struggles with the consequences of what God has done. How much more necessary must it be for each of us to go through the same exercise?

None of this is easy. Yet know that the harder you work, the more will come to you.

# 6

# Isaac and the Search for the Father

*[God] visits the iniquity of fathers upon children and the children's children unto the third and fourth generation.*

– Exodus 34:7

*The fathers shall not be put to death for the sins of the children, neither shall the children be put to death for the sins of the fathers.*

– Deuteronomy 24:16

This week's reading contains some of the best-known scenes in the Torah: Esau sells his birthright to Jacob for a mess of pottage (25:27–33); Jacob covers himself with a sheep's pelt (ch. 27), tricks Isaac, his blind father, into believing he is Esau, and steals the blessing of the firstborn. Framing these episodes, the text also raises deep questions about the fraught legacy of sons and their fathers. For good or for ill, a man's identification with his father is inescapable. And it lasts a lifetime.

As men, we must recognize that our fathers reside at the core of our identity, whether we like it or not. For those of us who grew up with a strong father, that can mean adopting positive attributes and coping effectively with negative situations. For those of us who grew up with a weak or abusive father, it can mean a life mired in self-loathing and negativity, driving us to destroy others before finally destroying ourselves – though if we are blessed with the right mother, teachers, and friends, it can mean identifying negative influences and resolving never to allow such behavior, such uncontrollable urges, rages, or passions, to rule our lives.

For men who grow up without a father, the quest for identity is stymied by having no tangible point of departure, and many men spend their lives in a painful and frustrating search for a foothold. Moreover, the image of the absent father is in many ways more powerful than the presence of an actual father could ever be, haunting a son's life, sometimes ruining it. Indeed, for most men, how we relate to the image of our fathers determines the quality of all our relationships. As successful and independent as we may become, we constantly return to the quest for our origins, whether inspired by the desire to live up to the example set by our fathers, or plagued by the fear that we may repeat their worst sins.

## Isaac, the true son of Abraham

"And these are the generations of Isaac, the son of Abraham; Abraham begot Isaac" (25:19). The Midrash says Isaac looked exactly like his father so that people recognized Isaac was unmistakably Abraham's son and inheritor. But what did Isaac think? Was he pleased by the comparison? Ashamed? Devastated?

God repeatedly reassures Isaac by referring to Abraham. God blesses Isaac "...because Abraham heeded and obeyed My voice, and he kept My observances and My commandments and My statutes and My laws" (26:5). Likewise, "I am the God of Abraham, your father. Do not be afraid, because I am with you, and I shall bless you, and I shall multiply your seed for the sake of Abraham My servant" (26:24).

This is the same Abraham who held a knife to Isaac's throat. If I am Isaac, I might question God on this point: "You say You will bless me for the sake of my father. But *I* was the one who laid my head on the altar; *I* was the one who stretched my neck to reveal my throat, making a clear path for the knife in my own father's hand. It is no thanks to my father that I am still alive. Don't I get any credit at all?" Isaac is a protagonist only briefly; the spotlight swings to his twin sons, Esau and Jacob – a replay of Cain and Abel. (Indeed, there is a Cain/Abel theme underlying the binding of Isaac itself, in the murderous tension between father and son.)

What does it mean to inherit a legacy? And why does God invoke Abraham instead of blessing Isaac on his own merit?

While the rest of the world acknowledges Isaac as Abraham's successor, perhaps – as with God's seemingly harsh message to Cain – God is telling Isaac, "You're not ready yet." The rest of this portion deals with Isaac's coming to terms with his relationship with the ghost of his father.

## Digging the wells of the past

When famine breaks out, God tells Isaac not to go to Egypt, as his father had done (12:10ff) – and as his son and grandsons will do (26:1–3) as well. During the time of famine, Isaac is blessed with "flocks of sheep and goats, and herds of cattle, and many servants; and the Philistines were jealous of him" (26:14).

Reflecting the hostile relationship between those destined to share the land, the Torah tells us, "All the wells that his father's servants had dug in Abraham's time, the Philistines stopped them up and filled them in with earth" (26:15). Three verses later, Isaac digs anew the wells dug by his father, giving them the same names his father called them. Isaac's servants continue digging where Abraham dug. When they find water, fights break out between them and the locals. Finally, Isaac relocates and digs a new well – his own, not one that his father had dug previously (26:22). There, Isaac is able to establish himself. He names the well Rehoboth, meaning "open spaces," and encamps there. He has dug through his past, through all the dirt left behind by his father, blocking him from getting on with his life. Now Isaac is ready to move on and tap into his own source of water. Rehoboth – open spaces. He has freed himself from his past by confronting it head-on.

So much happens to Isaac in the time he spends on the stage. He is nearly murdered by his own father (and you thought *you* had problems...), tricked by his son – with the encouragement and connivance of his beloved wife. And yet he seems at peace. Why?

The answer is that Isaac courageously undertakes the therapeutic process of examining the past to see what it is made of. The process of digging anew the old wells dug by his father is a metaphor for introspection; for coming to an understanding of his past, in order to be free to move forward. Digging through the dirt: in modern terms, psychoanalysis. Note how this starts: "Isaac returned, and he dug up the wells that they had dug in the days of Abraham" (26:18). Unlike the surrounding verses, Isaac himself does the digging, not his servants. Isaac takes shovel in hand and courageously digs right into the mess that his father left him. The outcome is not guaranteed, but without forcing the confrontation, he will never advance in life.

We shall never be grown-up until we step out of our father's shadow. When we live in another's shadow, we can never cast our own, can never impose our imprint on the world. The fundamental definition of success is being in control of our environment and especially of how we interact with forces beyond our control. Our lives are dominated by images of our parents. But we are not they, and so we need to get out into the sunlight. We need to dig through our past, however difficult. Only then can we pitch our tent, only then can we establish our own identity. Thus, Isaac finally frees himself from his past by the only means available: he confronts it head-on. It will never go away, but now it no longer binds him. He carries it not as an open wound, but as a scar.

Our job in life is not to expel our fathers – whether memories of our actual father or the ghost of an "absent presence." Our fathers are immutably part of who we are. Our job is rather to learn to live independently. To build around that core like reinforced concrete, making it a framework for the structure of our lives. Those of us who never come to terms with our fathers are like so many rickety, half-finished buildings: uninhabitable, with rusted, broken rods jutting aimlessly, poisoning their surroundings with ugliness. We are our fathers' heirs. They form our core. It is up to us to build solidly around it.

I look just like my father? Isaac asks, looking at himself in the mirror. But, he says, I am *not* my father, and what my father did to me, I do not have to do to my children. What my father did to my mother, I do not have to do to my wife.

Isaac prays for his wife, Rebecca, to become pregnant (25:21). This is in contrast to Abraham, who never prays for Sarah to have children of her own, and to Jacob, who will react angrily when his beloved wife asks him to pray for her to have a child. The Hebrew word used here meaning "he prayed" comes from the root meaning to dig with a shovel. Isaac, who will refine his own life by digging wells, starts by digging deep for God's mercy and grace on behalf of the woman he loves. And he receives it in double portion.

After Isaac confronts his inner conflict with his father, God appears again, promising to protect and guard Isaac, and to make him and his descendants prosperous "for the sake of your father, Abraham" (26:24). Again? But now Isaac's response is to build an altar and worship God, because confronting the negative consequences of our fathers' influence doesn't mean they cease to exist. We often wish we could obliterate the past. But those who succeed in life are the ones who come to terms with their past. Who unearth the painful parts and continually work through them. Our past makes us who we are; through bravely delving into our past, we have the God-given power to make of ourselves who and what we shall become.

As Isaac teaches: it's not what we inherit, but what we do with it that makes all the difference.

# 7

# Jacob and the Fear of Living

*Some are born great, some achieve greatness, and some have greatness thrust upon them.*

– Shakespeare, *Twelfth Night*

This week's Torah portion recounts Jacob's career after leaving home, until his return twenty years later. Along the way, he falls in love, marries two women, and takes two concubines. He fathers eleven sons and a daughter, and has tremendous success caring for his father-in-law's flocks. When Jacob's flocks prosper, his father-in-law turns against him in jealousy, and he flees back to Canaan.

If ever – to use Shakespeare's expression – a man had greatness thrust upon him, it is Jacob. And let's say it up front: he can't handle it.

The Jacob we met last week leads a solitary existence until his mother prods him to trick his father into giving him the blessing of the firstborn. Then all hell breaks loose. He is torn from the bosom of his family. Fleeing literally with nothing but the shirt on his back, Jacob arrives alone in an unfamiliar land whose inhabitants are not welcoming to strangers.

Jacob is beset by fears and easily intimidated. He never stands up for himself until the very end of this portion. He is filled with doubt – which can certainly be traced to the disastrous outcome of his mother's plan – and fearful that the bond between God and the prior generations has passed him by. God has direct conversations with Abraham and Isaac, but God's first-ever interaction with Jacob isn't direct. Jacob has a dream in which God promises him, "I am with you; I will protect you wherever you go and will bring you back to this land. I will not leave you until I have done what I have promised you" (Gen. 28:15).

Jacob's dream of the ladder mirrors the Tower of Babel,

which was built "with its top in the heavens" (11:4). Jacob's dream-ladder is "set upon the earth, and its top reached toward the heavens" (28:12). Despite slight differences in the Hebrew, the translation of both *top* and *heavens* is the same, and the comparison is unavoidable. At Babel, people feared "lest we be dispersed across the earth" (11:4). In his dream, Jacob is told, "Your seed shall be as the dust of the earth and you shall burst out to the west, to the east, to the north, and to the south" (28:14). The name Babel is Aramaic, meaning "the gate of God." Jacob wakes up from his dream and says, "It is none other than the house of God, and this is the gate of heaven" (28:17).

Jacob's vision is the positive fulfillment of the project that went badly wrong at Babel. Is it truly a prophecy, or is Jacob dreaming? Is this a message from God, or has Jacob fallen victim to the fantastical desires of a desperate man? Indeed, when he wakes, he "became frightened and said, 'How this place fills one with dread!'" (28:17).

There are no coincidences in the Torah. These two incidents are binary: one of them is a failure, the other promises to ultimately turn out according to God's plan. If only Jacob can trust that this *is* God's plan.

The Torah demonstrates repeatedly that there is a right way to do things. And then there are many, many wrong ways. And what's particularly problematic about those wrong ways is that so often, they look so right. It's easy for us to mislead ourselves – spiritually, psychologically, emotionally – following our own judgment, our gut reaction. Or following what we think are signs pointing us in a direction. Or doing what others tell us.

After awakening from his vision, Jacob vows, "If God will be with me and guard me as I go on this way, and give me bread to eat and clothing to wear, and if I return in safety to my father's house, then God will be the Lord for me" (28:20–22). God has just promised Jacob a blessing, and Jacob starts bargaining for specific terms. Dark themes underlie this speech.

Jacob is confused: God spoke directly to his father and grandfather, but he himself hasn't heard a word from the Creator. Now, on the cusp of a terrifying journey, God appears in a dream. Jacob wonders, is this mere magical thinking? Jacob just had a terrible experience following the guidance of his mother. He listened to the one person who truly loved him – and who was most responsible for his well-being. This led to his being forced to flee lest his brother murder him, and now it seems he may never return home again. It's no wonder that Jacob has doubts. He is unable to trust the message of his dream. As a consequence, he also doesn't trust the Messenger.

God has offered nothing material, only the promise to go with Jacob and protect him and then bring him back. Jacob fears he will lose God's protection because of his sins against his father and his brother. He asks for three specific things: bread to eat, clothing to wear, and to return safely to his father's house. What is going on?

God is the very definition of justice, and the Torah repeatedly emphasizes the message of measure for measure. What goes around, comes around. Karma. It is a fundamental principle of Jewish theology that God's justice is the very fabric of Creation, and we toy with it at our peril. Our actions have direct consequences, and justice dictates that we suffer the consequences in equal measure to our acts. In last week's reading, Jacob took food his mother cooked and stole his brother's clothing. Using them, he lied to his father, defrauded his brother, and brought exile upon himself. Jacob is begging that God forgive the sin of the food and stolen garments with which he stole the blessing, and begging for his father to take him back again. This, Jacob is saying, will be God's sign that my vision was true. That it was not a dream, but prophecy.

Jacob is struck with the enormity of his deed, with its repercussions. Please, he begs, echoing the plea of Cain, do not punish me as I deserve. For, God, if You punish me as I deserve – using the very instruments of my sin – then I will perish. If You punish me by taking away from me food and clothing – sustenance and protection from the elements – then

I am a dead man.

During the course of his life, Jacob succeeds in the everyday world, despite never losing his status as an outsider. But he fails repeatedly in the spiritual world. It is not until the end of his life, the last seventeen years that he spends with Joseph in Egypt, that Jacob is able to connect with the spiritual role for which he was born. Until that time, Jacob spends his life in impermanence. With all his material success, he fears to stand up for himself. He remains focused on the harms done to him, on the dangers that lurk within every human contact. He flinches at life. Jacob is the kind of person who asks, Why do these things happen to me? For Jacob, life is beyond his control.

The two great Jewish traditions – the scholarly, legalistic tradition of the Talmud and the kabbalistic, mystical tradition of the Zohar – both emphasize that Jacob lives his entire life in fear. Fear that at any moment God will abandon him. Fear that God will look back at Jacob's life and will find him wanting, and thus God will say, "I've changed My mind." Until the very end of his life, Jacob struggles with the fear of abandonment. He doubts God's promise.

Jacob's ancestors spoke with God directly. God comforts Abraham on more than one occasion, telling him, Don't worry, you're going to be fine. God appears to Isaac on more than one occasion, telling him, I'll take care of you, don't worry. "What about me?" Jacob seems to be crying. "When will You speak to me?" All Jacob gets is a dream, from which he awakens to uncertainty. The lifelong consequence of this absence of certainty is that he internalizes fear, he lives in fear. And his fear deprives him of faith.

The key to faith is not faith in God. It is the deep faith in oneself – a faith that Jacob does not possess. Those who lack this faith cower before the uncertain fate that awaits them. Those who live in faith move ever forward, taking hold of what happens to them and building their destiny. In the same circumstances, one person will say, "How am I ever going to survive this? I have no money, no job, and no family, and I've been sent into a foreign land where I don't know anyone!" Another will say, "A whole new country is opening up in front of me! New opportunities! I'd better get to work!"

Will you allow your life to become your fate? Or will you make of your life your own destiny? Jacob's failure is not his fear – we are fools not to fear what lies before us. It's not his doubt in God's message – faith without doubt is not faith. It is mere brainwashing, for who knows what God has planned for us?

Jacob's failure lies in his inability to recognize his own greatness. He is a man abandoned, cast out, lied to, and manipulated by those closest to him: his mother, his father-in-law, his wives, his children. Perhaps he sees that as his fate. Jacob fears his own strength, and it takes much before he finally connects with his own natural mastery. And by allowing himself to be pushed around, he encourages more of the same. Imagine how hard it must have been for his father-in-law, his wives, and, later, his sons to respect him.

When God appears to Jacob in a dream and tells him to return home, true to type, Jacob packs up his family and all his wealth and flees without telling anyone (31:17). It is not until the end of the weekly Torah portion in which this story occurs that Jacob stands up for himself. Three days after Jacob flees together with his family, Laban and his minions catch up with them. Says Laban, "It is in my power to harm you, but the God of your father spoke to me last night, saying, 'Don't you dare say even a bad word to Jacob!'" (31:29). Finally, Jacob tears into Laban, unloading twenty years of anger and resentment at the mistreatment he has received (31:36–42). Grudgingly, Laban says, "Very well, then. Let's have a peace treaty."

Jacob has had greatness thrust upon him, and it very nearly sinks him. We will watch him continue to struggle with it. For many of us, the struggle with our own greatness doesn't come to a final resolution, but our progress is often two steps forward, one step back, take a deep breath, and forge on yet again.

## The Weight of Gold

We each stand to have greatness thrust upon us. To receive it, we must see our amazing inner qualities for what they are, and learn to use them properly and well. Those who possess true inner strength do not seek confrontation, but they also never back down. Those with true wisdom don't need to convince others; they just know, and they act accordingly.

Learn from the lesson of Jacob: don't let life just happen to you; go out and happen to life!

# 8

# Jacob – The Struggle to Become

*For I acknowledge my transgressions, and my sin is ever before me.*
— Psalms 51:5

This week's Torah portion brings Jacob back into the world he fled so many years ago.

Jacob returns to Canaan at God's instruction, but then learns that his brother, Esau, is coming to meet him, "and four hundred men are with him" (Gen. 32:7). Despite God's promise of protection and God's explicit direction to return, Jacob is filled with dread. Immediately, he takes tactical measures, hoping that Esau will not wipe out his entire family.

Jacob first divides everything and everyone into *two camps* – and note that last week's portion ended with Jacob giving the name Two Camps to the place where he crosses out of Laban's territory and returns to the land of Canaan. The name Two Camps is tied to two encounters with angels: the first in the dream of the ladder as he fled Canaan, the second one as he returns home. Jacob acknowledges God's graciousness and abundance: "I am humbled by the kindness and the truth You have done for Your servant; for with only my staff I crossed this Jordan, and now I have become two camps!" (32:11).

What is the significance of this division of Jacob's assets – and of his family? The last thing Jacob heard as he fled his birth home was that Esau was bent on murdering him for the theft of the birthright and the blessing. Twenty-one years have passed, but Jacob remembers Esau as he was on the eve of Jacob's flight. When they reunite, we see that Esau has put the incident out of mind. He is genuinely pleased to see Jacob and addresses him in brotherly fashion: "Esau ran toward him and embraced him and fell on his neck and kissed him, and they wept" (33:4). Esau may have forgotten his anger, but Jacob still feels his guilt as intensely as if the incident that triggered it happened yesterday.

But we're getting ahead of ourselves, because the key incident in this portion occurs before the brothers meet. In the opening passage (32:4–24), Jacob is frightened. He sets up an elaborate sequence of expensive gifts, instructing his servants to go ahead and offer them to Esau in an attempt to appease him. Then, in the middle of the night and under cover of darkness, Jacob ferries his entire family and all his possessions across the river into Canaan.

Immediately afterward:

> Jacob was left alone, and a man wrestled with him until the coming of the dawn. And he saw that he could not overcome him, and he thrust against his hip socket, so Jacob's hip was dislocated as he wrestled with him. Then he said, "Let me go, because the dawn has broken." And he said, "I will not let you go unless you bless me." He said to him, "What is your name?" And he said, "Jacob." And he said, "Your name shall no longer be Jacob, but rather Israel, because you have struggled with God and with man, and you were equal to the task." And Jacob asked and said, "Please tell me your name," and he said, "Why this? Why do you ask my name?" and he blessed him there. (32:25–30).

(The "he" and "him" repetition is as ambiguous in the original as in this translation, but it all works out; the speakers are in their right places.)

Who is this mysterious "man"? The rabbis say it was Esau's guardian angel, suggesting that Jacob's true struggle is twofold: First, he has never confronted his own guilt over the twin crimes he committed in lying to his father and deceiving his brother. Second, and more insidious, it suggests that there is an Esau dwelling within Jacob. This Jacob spent his entire career accumulating physical wealth, living the life of a hardworking and successful businessman, a family man, a pillar of the community. And isn't that, in fact, just what Esau is? The hail-fellow-well-met who is a success in the hunt and on the playing fields, beloved of his family and attentive to his parents? Indeed, the rabbis hold out Esau as the Bible's single great paradigm of the commandment to honor one's parents, and we could easily envision him as a favorite in the local Rotary Club, perhaps the owner of a successful string of car dealerships, along the lines of many retired professional athletes.

What is it about Esau that so terrifies Jacob, if not the acknowledgment that, in stealing Esau's blessing, Jacob has perhaps *become* Esau? After all these years of exile, of privation and endless hard work, is this Jacob's fate? To be no more than, no better than – indeed, no *other* than a poor copy of his own brother? Has Jacob become, in a poetic echo, a faint Cain to Esau's powerful and self-assured Abel? Surely Jacob's fear of having failed spectacularly at his spiritual quest is part of what the rabbis perceive in this desperate struggle.

Jacob has spent his life getting stuff, yet we have not seen him doing anything to acquire wisdom. He talks his brother out of the birthright, bartering it for the mess of pottage. He steals the blessing from their father. He acquires wives and concubines who accommodate him by producing a steady stream of sons (family standing was largely based on male progeny in that society) and at least one daughter. He has a great entourage of servants and retainers, and he amasses a fortune in livestock, with endless flocks of sheep and goats as well as great herds of cattle, donkeys, and camels. Judging by the gift he sends his brother (32:14–16), he's as wealthy as a top hedge fund manager.

True to his tremendous material success, Jacob sends forth his family, his staff, and all his worldly possessions to a place where he hopes they will be safeguarded – for what is the good of acquiring mere things if we lose them? And so he leads them all across the river under cover of darkness. Then he crosses back by himself. Without his family and entourage, and without his material possessions, Jacob remains truly alone.

And being alone, he is forced to confront himself. What's going on within? When he comes face-to-face with his unexamined self, Jacob is at a loss. Who are you, and what, if anything, have you truly gained? What shall I call you? And how shall I engage with you?

In the struggle, Jacob is injured, the result of which he will limp for the rest of his life. Yet he is also blessed, and his blessing – his new name, Israel – is given not because he won, but because he hung in. Jacob's lesson is that it isn't about winning, it's about being able to hobble off the playing field on one's own, and about being able to return to the game once more.

What do we learn when, as King David says, "I acknowledge my transgressions, and my sin is ever before me"? One way to read this is: No matter what I have done to make up for bad things I have done or said, I still bear the guilt. Never mind that I have made restitution many times over for the problems I have created; I still bear the emotional wounds as though it were yesterday. At night when I lie in the dark, my gut wrenches, my neck twitches, and my shoulders quiver in shame and grief over my past actions.

Or: I have faced my shortcomings and my worst actions, difficult as it was. I have confronted the things I have done – or have failed to do – in the past. I have explored the feelings that drove me to this behavior, and my inability to see those feelings for what they were. I have examined the impact I have had on others. I have confronted my inability to deal with my feelings, the lack of self-awareness that drove me to those behaviors in the past, my knee-jerk reaction to act out my worst impulses. And just as I have faced and overcome my troubles in the past – and yes, I still have feelings of guilt, of inadequacy, of inexplicable anger, of depression, even of despair – I can revisit my previous emotional successes to draw strength and wisdom with which to face today's challenges.

My emotions are part of who I am. They will never go away. My past will never go away. Which means it's all right there in front of me, just waiting for me to dive in and learn what it's all about. If I fail to learn from my past, I shall surely never build a better future.

In Hebrew, the name Israel is from the verb meaning to struggle. In grammatical form, it looks like a future tense form of the verb, suggesting that Jacob is renamed, not The One Who Struggled, but The One Who Will Struggle. Here's the bad news: it never gets easier. Life is an ongoing continuum of challenges, and when we win, up pops another battle. Here's the other bad news: you will lose very often. And when you do win, it will be temporary.

Here's the good news: success in life is not about winning. God needs each one of us to stay in the game. Those for whom life is all about winning – about making more and more money – will fail because there will never be enough money for them to sit back and declare victory. (See Eccl. 5:9: "One who loves money will not be satisfied with money.") How many men do we know whose lives center around building wealth? Working for decades on Wall Street, I have often heard men say, "It's not about making money anymore. Money is just a way of keeping score." But they are lying; not to us, but to themselves. Money has become the repository of all that is sacred in our culture.

Jacob learns the hardest lesson of all: that the world does not need winners. It needs people who keep coming back to the playing field and putting in a full measure of effort. People who don't make material success their sole value. People who learn from their pain and use it to make themselves stronger. We have all created suffering for ourselves and others through unthinking acts. Armed with self-knowledge, our present task is to relieve suffering wherever we encounter it in the world. For ourselves, and for others.

And therefore it is good that my sin remains by my side, because it is the best teacher. When my most painful emotions rise up, I confront them. "I will not let you go until you bless me," I say. "Until you teach me." It is only when we learn to see the blessing within the most difficult parts of our lives that we begin taking our first steps on the path of wisdom.

# 9

# Joseph in Chains

*I'd put prison second to college as the best place for a man to go if he needs to do some thinking. If he's motivated, in prison he can change his life.*

– Malcolm X, *The Autobiography of Malcolm X*

This week's Torah reading introduces Joseph, the richest and most complex figure we shall meet in the Bible until King David. In this section, all the themes of Genesis come together, forming the nucleus from which Moses and the Jewish people will emerge and setting the stage for the entire Western ethos. Joseph's greatness is, at this stage, inchoate. We saw how many catalytic events were required to awaken Jacob to exercise his own power. Joseph, the inheritor of his father's greatness, requires a far more jarring sequence of events, spread over decades, to uncover his light. Joseph inherits his father's fateful struggle with dream and prophecy with a vengeance. It takes a tumultuous lifetime for him to embrace his destiny.

Jacob makes the same mistake as a parent that his parents made. Isaac favored Esau and Rebecca favored Jacob (Gen. 25:28); now Jacob takes this a terribly misguided step further, blatantly favoring Joseph not merely *above* his other children but to the *exclusion* of the others. Jacob loves Joseph, "the son of his old age," and makes him a special coat (37:3). In the original Hebrew, this coat may be an unusual and distinctive shade of green, or a mix of colors, or a special, long-sleeved garment, but it is distinctive and confers a special status. Jacob, whose life was upended by a garment (the theft of his brother's clothing to perpetrate the far greater theft of their father's blessing) now gives a garment to Joseph, an act that will change the course not only of his family's future, but of human history. In the Bible, what goes around always continues to come around, as people seem fated to repeat patterns of behavior, for good or for evil. And note, as the hasidic rebbes maintain, everything in this world *is* either good or evil. Nothing is inert, nothing is benign. Everything is exactly what we make of it.

Joseph displays no intrinsic merit. If anything, he seems less capable than his brothers. He is his father's son. Jacob, "a simple man, dwelling in tents" (25:27), emerges as a mama's boy and a stay-at-home, in contrast to his brother Esau, the outdoorsman, hunter, and jock. Joseph is his father's pet and can't even find his way through the landscape (37:15–16 describes Joseph "blundering about" in the open fields looking for his brothers), yet the special coat and the exalted status conferred by Jacob give Joseph a sense of innate superiority. Think of today's culture of "everyone gets a trophy." Joseph does nothing to earn his status, thus he believes his superiority to be comprehensive, natural, and obvious. Likewise, it is obvious to him that he doesn't need to do anything to maintain it. When he recounts his dreams, he is oblivious to his brothers' hatred for him. Joseph knows himself to be superior and assumes everyone accepts this to be the case.

Jacob deepens his fault, dispatching Joseph to spy on his brothers: "Your brothers are tending the flocks near Shechem.... Go and check on them and on the flocks and bring back word to me" (37:12–14). But his brothers have other plans, stripping him of his coat and tossing him down an empty well.

Joseph's dreams at the beginning of the portion are mirrored in the dreams of Pharaoh's wine steward and Pharaoh's royal baker at the end (ch. 40). Jacob dreamt of a ladder with angels ascending and descending. Now Joseph dreams of himself ascending and his entire family descending, or bowing before him. The brothers are symbolized by bowing sheaves of grain, while the sun, moon, and stars prostrate themselves before Joseph as well. In the prison, the royal wine steward's dream is one of ascent – he will be restored to his former office –

while the royal baker's dream has him being raised up, only to be cast down: he is brought from the dungeon and executed. (This also contains echoes of the Cain and Abel narrative, with one offering – the wine steward's – being accepted and the other rejected.)

Joseph, too, goes up and down – literally and figuratively. He rises in his father's estimation, then is brought low and cast down into a pit. He is raised from the pit, only to be sold into slavery. And still he hasn't learned his lesson. God favors Joseph, making his work in his Egyptian master's house successful. When his master's wife attempts to seduce him, he barely manages to spurn her advances – but can't help boasting to her just how big a catch he is: "My master has turned over everything in his house to me and to my control. There is no one greater in this household than me, and my master has denied me nothing except for you, since you are his wife" (39:9). In other words, "You'd be lucky to have me! I'm much more important than your husband – he doesn't even know what's going on under his own roof." And the ultimate seduction: "But you can't have me!"

And with that, whoosh! Back down we go, as Joseph is thrown back into a dungeon. When his cellmates are troubled by dreams, Joseph becomes excited. "Dreams?" he says. "I know all about dreams!" However, this time he finally tempers his enthusiasm, telling them that God is the ultimate interpreter (40:8). This is the first instance where Joseph begins to understand that he must modulate his behavior if he wants to avoid disastrous outcomes. Most of us fail to learn this lesson completely. We have moments when we follow our impulses, convinced we are taking the right actions, only to have them blow up in our face.

Look at how long it has taken Joseph, and how much he has been buffeted about by life, before the terrible and false message of his childhood finally starts to give way to reality. And even then, Joseph's embrace of the truth is equivocal. He asks the wine steward to put in a good word for him (40:14–15), saying, "I don't deserve to be here, I didn't do anything wrong!" Doesn't every convicted criminal say that?

Joseph's day will come, and he will rise to embrace his destiny. Ironically, it will be this same royal wine steward, who deliberately puts Joseph out of his mind, who will later come to his rescue. But first, Joseph must learn to use his powers. He still needs to stew in his own juices, to age in the darkness of his prison cell, not merely until he is called, but until he is ready to heed the call. To be the truly self-aware leader he is destined to become, Joseph must realize that the life he lives does not belong to him. He will learn, after half a lifetime of pain, that his fulfillment is in service to those around him. More, it is in service to the future of his family and his people.

As long as we focus on what we can get out of life, our lives will be petty and ultimately meaningless. It is only once we devote ourselves to making the world better for everyone else that we instill true meaning in our own lives. Through that outward focus, we finally unleash the full extent of our unique inner power, our unique inner purpose – the unique reason God put us here.

Joseph possesses immense powers; he is uniquely blessed by God. Yet none of this matters as long as he does not recognize who and what he is. Indeed, it is far worse to be specially gifted, specially blessed – uniquely chosen for a special destiny – if we do not recognize it.

Each one of us possesses unique qualities, gifts that are given to us alone. If we believe we are capable of any insight into God's purpose in Creation, it would seem to be that even the least thing comes into existence for a unique purpose, and that each one finds its purpose only in relation to others. Each grain of sand has a purpose, which is to populate the shore. Each fish in the sea and each leaf on the branch serve their purpose of filling the world. How much more must we ascribe to each human being a unique – and necessary – role in God's work of Creation?

For the man of faith – even when plagued by constant doubt – the fact that you woke up this morning is proof that God still needs you to complete your task in this lifetime.

All of us alive at this moment have unfinished work. Do we recognize it? Do we try to grapple with our unique task, or are we oblivious to it, as Joseph seems to be? Each one of us is at the center of our own world. The wise man will recognize that, dwelling within that center, our task is not to take what we find within reach, but to sustain everything around us.

God's lessons are simple and clear. It is we who are slow to learn. May you be blessed with a quickened mind, and may your soul know and see clearly its unique way forward in God's world.

# 10

# Joseph Unbound

*We are each our own Devil, and we make this world our Hell.*

– Oscar Wilde

In this week's Torah portion, Joseph is released from prison and becomes viceroy of Egypt. During his years underground, he has learned the lesson of setting aside his petty hurts, to embrace his mission for the sake of others. By doing so, he saves the world. No small outcome.

Joseph's interpretation of his cellmates' dreams two years before was not so much prophetic as it was clear-eyed: The general amnesty and release from prison in honor of Pharaoh's birthday were to be anticipated (see last week's reading, 40:20). Moreover, the royal wine steward and the royal baker were not mere servants; they oversaw the production of Egypt's wine and bread, and thus their dreams would hold significant meaning. When Pharaoh recounts his dreams (41:1–7), it's not that no one knew how to interpret them; the text says explicitly that no one *would* interpret them (41:8). No one wants to speak up, as their inauspicious message is obvious.

Pharaoh dreams of standing on the banks of the Nile. Egypt is wholly dependent on the Nile, thus the river is both the giver of life and the bringer of death. It embodies the archetypical eternal struggle between order and chaos. It is important to recognize that it is chaos which is itself the stuff of Creation. It is when we grapple with the chaos of our lives that we can take charge of that chaos and make of it creations and structures of profound and lasting meaning.

As to Pharaoh's dreams, everyone knows there will be bad years in which the river will withhold its bounty. Crops will fail, animals and people will starve. Historically, when bread riots break out, the official in charge of the bread production is led out in public and beheaded. It's a fair bet that the first one to step forward and explain the obvious to Pharaoh would find himself designated as the new head of Egypt's food supply, with a likely death sentence awaiting him. Why does Joseph take the job? Well, it beats a life sentence in the dungeon.

As an internal literary reference, Pharaoh's dreams also invoke Cain and Abel: the first dream features cows, the second, crops. Each dream starts out hopeful and ends in devastation as the promise of plenty is devoured by its twin. Another parallel is with the Jacob story. The seven years of plenty followed by seven years of famine echoes Jacob's happy seven years working in anticipation of marrying his beloved Rachel ("So Jacob worked seven years for Rachel, and they seemed to him as but a few days because he loved her" [29:20]) – only to be duped into marrying her sister Leah, after which he despairingly agrees to a further seven years of servitude to marry Rachel as well.

Seven fat years followed by seven lean years. Our hopes, our dreams for a bright and easy future are followed by our confrontation with reality. Perhaps we failed because we forgot to check all the boxes, but maybe there wasn't anything we could have done after all. And so we live, building our future on the ruins of our past. It's all there in black and white. The story of our lives over and over and over again…. Will we be ruled by it, ruined by it? Or will we take charge?

Joseph's life is a sequence of events for which the readiest response should be anger. Anger at his brothers who tossed him into the pit. Anger at being sold into slavery. Anger at Potiphar's wife who framed him, at the royal wine steward who forgot him. And certainly, anger at his dysfunctional father, Jacob, who created this mess.

If ever a man had cause for anger and resentment, it is Joseph. And if ever a man achieved greatness unaided, it is Joseph. God speaks to Abraham and Isaac, and ultimately even to Jacob. God will speak face-to-face with Moses. But

God says not a word to Joseph, leaving him to work things out for himself. From a purely human perspective, Joseph is the greatest biblical figure. He achieves greatness on his own, never spoken to by God, and with nothing but his own vile existence and his slowly dawning insight to guide him.

The rabbis of the Talmud say that giving in to anger is a form of idol worship. Anger is the reaction when our version of reality turns out to be mistaken. When the world refuses to cooperate with our plans, we become enraged. We reject reality. We scream at God, "How dare You upset my fantasy!" And it is striking that Joseph never expresses anger. He is manipulated and abandoned by his father, manhandled and almost murdered by his brothers, and sold into slavery. He doesn't even get to keep his status as a slave, but is stripped – both literally and figuratively – and cast into a dungeon (the Hebrew uses the word *bor*, "pit," here, just as it uses *bor* for the well his brothers cast him down into). Even when his brothers kneel at his feet in the dust of the marketplace, Joseph's response is not one of wrath. Instead, he turns away from them and weeps (42:7–24).

On the linguistic level, the Hebrew word for anger means "nose." Think of a snorting bull preparing to charge, or of a fire-breathing dragon shooting flames of ire and wrath. And it is through the nose that we receive life. God fashions the first human from dust from the ground, and then "God blew into his nostrils the breath of life" (2:7). For the kabbalists, this is not a metaphor: God imparts some actual part of God's own self into us, the divine spark which imbues us with life. When we give in to anger, we are blowing God out, spewing God out upon the world. There is no power greater than the power of God, and no force more destructive than the power of God unleashed with wanton rage. No power more destructive to those around us, nor any act more self-destructive.

Joseph has learned that, regardless of our inner turmoil, we must control our behavior. That our every action has an effect – and a consequence. We must act, not in mere reaction to flashes of rage. Not to satisfy our appetites. Each of us lives in service of something far greater than ourselves. If we live as unwitting slaves to our emotions, then our actions will be desultory at best, destructive at worst. It is only when we envision, and plan, and craft, and even schedule our personal destiny, that our actions will be fully informed by our learning and knowledge – and that our knowledge can transform into wisdom.

Joseph demonstrates that there is no such thing as "justifiable" anger, for anger is a purely destructive force. It is the assertion that "I" am more important than anything else. Joseph recognizes that to save himself, and to achieve the transformation the world so sorely needs, he must remove that "I" – that irascible, that self-justifying, that angry and wounded Self – from the equation. This new wisdom enables Joseph to succeed where others have failed.

It is a commonplace that those in high government positions – by no means exclusively in the Middle East! – abuse their position for personal gain. We have noted elsewhere that throughout human history, famine is a political phenomenon. There is always food. But those in power use food as a weapon to punish the minorities they hate, as a favor to bribe those whose backing they crave, and to enrich themselves beyond measure. At times when grain prices shoot sky-high, expect the chief of the royal granaries to be driving a Lamborghini. The Torah's detailed description of Joseph's diligent husbanding of Egypt's resources shows that he has seen through the base human craving for immediate gain. He sees it as a losing game, and understands that if he truly masters the situation, he will gain unprecedented power. Actual power, not based on the momentary granting of favors, but based on his ability to control his environment as well as on his effectiveness in the face of the incompetence of those around him. Joseph has learned to embrace the task for which God sent him into the world.

Joseph has been given ample time and solitude, and he has put them to good use. Not all of us have the misfortune to be thrown into a dungeon, yet we are all in some fashion imprisoned.

Imprisoned by our past especially: by the hurts done us by our parents, by dreams shattered, or by mere random bad luck. By the manifold unfairnesses of life. How many of us are angry at the poor outcomes when our own decisions did not work out, still carrying rage at those who could have helped us and did not? And isn't our anger so petty, compared to what people have lived through? People like Joseph, or like Mandela, or Nehru, or Vaclav Havel?

Joseph's prison was one of damp stone, of cold, dark places crawling with scorpions and snakes, yet he emerges wiser for the time spent underground. Will we be so lucky to emerge from our personal dungeons of the heart? There is no end of work to do. May God strengthen our hands.

# 11

# Joseph Revealed

*Yesterday, upon the stair, I met a man who wasn't there. He wasn't there again today. Oh how I wish he'd go away!*

– William Hughes Mearns,
*Antigonish*

In this week's Torah portion (44:18–47:27), Joseph goes from being the man who isn't there, to being The Man Who Is Very Much There. Since their arrival in Egypt's central marketplace and their unknowing first encounter with Joseph, his brothers have described him repeatedly with one word; in Hebrew, *einenu*, meaning "he is not." Starting with their first protestation of innocence (42:13), the brothers say, "We are twelve brothers, the sons of one man in the land of Canaan. And see, the youngest is today with his father; and then the one, he is not."

Once again, the Torah reveals through seemingly straightforward narrative the obscure inner workings of the human psyche. Joseph never asks his brothers about their family, yet they immediately offer up information about their father, about their youngest brother Benjamin, and about their missing brother "who is not." So confounded are they by their guilt that when Jacob later berates them, asking why they gave up so much information, the brothers reply, "The man kept asking us about ourselves and our family: 'Is your father still alive? Do you have a brother?'" (43:7). This is not true, according to the initial description of the encounter. They cap this off with, "How could we have known he would say 'Bring your brother here'?" How, indeed? It's almost as though they engineered it.

Guilt is a powerful force. It drives so much that is both the very best and the very worst in human behavior. We note King David's heartfelt, "I acknowledge my transgressions; my sin is before me always," which is both a cry of torment and a recognition that we have so much to learn from our past – from our mistakes most of all. (And as has been said, "Learn from the mistakes of others. You'll never live long enough to make them all yourself.")

When Joseph accuses his brothers of coming to Egypt as spies, and later when they recount this to their father, what is going through their minds, what are they envisioning in their mind's eye? The words, "Do you have a brother?" are *not* spoken by Joseph, yet the brothers hear it, they vividly imagine this scene which resonates so powerfully in all their minds that they recount it to their father as fact. They are like Lady Macbeth dreaming of blood on her hands, washing and wiping and wiping and washing, and still it will not go away – "Out, out, damned spot!" the sleepwalker cries in her anguish – the brothers are desperate to erase Joseph from their memory. So much so that he is the first thing that pops unbidden into their mouths: The One Who Is Not.

Joseph's brother Reuben is in agony: "Didn't I say, 'Don't sin against the boy?' But you wouldn't listen. And now his blood is being avenged!" (Gen. 42:22). Reuben, Jacob's firstborn, is the only brother who doesn't know what happened to Joseph, and we now understand Reuben's painful offer to Jacob when the brothers try to convince him to send Benjamin down to Egypt with them: "You may kill my two sons if I fail to bring Benjamin back to you" (42:37). Reuben, who was absent at the moment his brothers cast Joseph down the well, believes himself responsible for his brother's death, and so he offers his father this dreadful eye for an eye. Only Judah is able to step out from the shadow of guilt; he was the one who convinced his brothers not to murder Joseph (37:26–27). Now, with the food supply down to life-threatening levels, he alone makes a reasoned plea: I will pledge my entire responsibility for your son – my brother. The Torah makes it plain that not everything can be fixed, not everything can be guaranteed. But Judah steps up and takes responsibility, and that is the most that can be asked of anyone.

The brothers return to Egypt, bringing Benjamin, as ordered. There, they are caught in a trap and threatened with the very thing their father dreaded, the loss of their youngest brother. And now, fulfilling his pledge, Judah approaches Joseph (44:18–34) and relates their father's hardship over the supposed death of Joseph, and his deep attachment to Joseph's brother, the sole surviving son of Jacob's beloved Rachel – Rachel, who died giving birth to Benjamin.

Finally, Joseph can restrain himself no longer. "I am Joseph!" he cries; "is my father still alive?" (45:3). This verse holds the key to the ultimate transformation of Joseph into the great figure he is, that he was destined to become. How?

With profound insight into the nature of both spiritual greatness and political leadership, Rabbi Obadiah ben Jacob Sforno (Italy, 1475–1550) comments on this verse that Joseph was not speaking out of joy and relief, but that he was startled.

Judah makes a heart-wrenching plea to Joseph. Listen as he recounts Jacob's words to him: "So if you take this [son] away from me also, and if disaster should befall him, then you will have brought my grey head down in evil to the grave" (44:29). Rabbi Sforno writes that Joseph's shocked inner reaction is, "I thought *I* was my father's favorite!" Jacob is still alive? And it's not for grief over Joseph that Jacob would die, but for grief over Benjamin, Joseph's younger brother?!

Reaffirming a key biblical idea, this replays the ongoing theme of the younger brother supplanting the older. But for Joseph it is an awakening. It is, at last, Cain reacting not with rage, but with wisdom.

Imagine ourselves in Joseph's place. Wouldn't we be furious to learn that we weren't so important after all? That once we disappeared, our father got over it? That our younger brother had taken our place?

Here is where Joseph's greatness emerges. This is Joseph, who recognized and overcame the human tendency to venality and corruption; who took control of Egypt's food supply and used it both to sustain the nation and to consolidate Pharaoh's power. A brilliant political masterstroke, worthy of Napoleon in conception and execution. Now Joseph sees that, just as his being brought out of the dungeon, just as his being placed in charge of the food supply, just as his being made viceroy to Pharaoh – just as he was successful in all this precisely *because* he did not place himself first – so too, his greater destiny is not about him, but about his family and the nation that will spring from them. To achieve his destiny, Joseph must make himself into The One Who Is Not.

"It was not you who sent me here," Joseph reassures his brothers, "but God" (45:8). Joseph sees his destiny clearly. Now he reads its signs in his life's every event.

In Joseph's place, how many of us would want nothing more than to return to our father's embrace? To wear once again the special coat of The Favorite, and to go back to being the spoiled child? It takes an immense effort and hard-won maturity to acknowledge that you can't go home again. The direction of life is forward. And if we do not move forward consciously, with determination to keep up, we will be swept along until the waves of reality wash over us, wiping away any trace that we were ever here.

Those who accomplish greatness in life all share one common quality: they see all of their life as of a piece. They do not say, "I was one person then, but I am no longer that person." They do not reject their past; they build upon it.

Everything that happens in Joseph's life works together in a vast mosaic, the pieces dropping in place one by one until the clear picture of his greatness, of his destiny, emerges. And without each tile – no matter how small in size, or dull in color – Joseph's destiny would not be complete. It is not those who *ignore* the past who are condemned to repeat it; rather, those who *reject* their own history remain its prisoners forever. Only when we learn to accept who we are – and yes, memories can continue to be painful – can we move forward to our unique destiny.

It's not about me after all, Joseph recognizes. This is more than a relief. It frees Joseph to achieve his full greatness. Life is not about getting even; it's about identifying our destiny and embracing it. If our ambition in life is nothing more than to return to our childhood, to wipe away everything that happened since the last time we remember being happy, then we have rejected that unique destiny that God has prepared for us.

# 12

# The Death of Joseph and the Passing of an Era

*Emancipate yourselves from mental slavery. None but ourselves can free our minds.*

– Bob Marley,
*Redemption Song*

This week's Torah portion (47:28–50:26) ends with the death of Joseph and closes the book of Genesis. The end of Genesis is the end of the story of the family of Abraham, setting the stage for the saga of the nation of his descendants.

Rabbi David Silber, one of the teachers who has had the most profound and lasting impact on me, the man I refer to as my "rebbe," my personal Torah guide, observes: People ask why the stories in the book of Genesis are so often interrupted by genealogies, when they really just want to get on with the narrative. The whole point, says Rabbi Silber, is that the book of Genesis is a book of genealogies, illuminated and bound together by stories, thus forming a coherent narrative which is not merely instructive in itself but provides the key to what comes later; a psychological and spiritual DNA for us to understand the people and events of the Bible.

Genesis 48 opens with Jacob on his deathbed, where Joseph has been called to his side. Joseph enters, bringing his two sons Manasseh and Ephraim, and Jacob makes a dramatic admission: "When I came from Paddan, Rachel died on me in the land of Canaan, on the road…and I buried her there on the road to Ephrat, which is Bethlehem" (48:7).

The expression, "Rachel died on me," is good colloquial English; in the biblical Hebrew it is more properly read as "Rachel died, and it was on me," meaning, "it was my fault." Remember that Jacob, after years of toiling for his father-in-law, Laban, packs up his family and runs away. Laban catches up to them and takes Jacob to task. "And," he rages at Jacob, "you stole my gods!" (31:30). The gods are the *teraphim*, common household gods in the ancient Near East; they were embodied as stone tokens that also served as deeds of ownership. Unbeknownst to Jacob, Rachel had made off with them. Jacob shouts at Laban (31:32), "With whomever you find your gods, let that person not live!" Jacob unwittingly calls for the death of his beloved wife, and the curse comes true when Rachel dies giving birth to Benjamin.

Jacob unburdens himself on his deathbed, acknowledging to Joseph that he, Jacob, is to blame for the death of Joseph's mother. This may illuminate the particular bond between Jacob and his youngest son, Benjamin. In last week's Torah portion, Judah told Joseph he dared not separate Benjamin from their father, "As his soul is bound to his soul" (44:30). Jacob's love for his youngest, the son of his old age, is shot through with his guilt over Rachel's death.

Now Jacob sees Joseph's sons. "Who are these?" he asks (48:8). Jacob had just told Joseph that Joseph's sons are to be considered Jacob's own. Yet now, looking directly at the boys, Jacob can't remember who they are – a heartrending picture of the mind evanescing in old age. Joseph reminds Jacob who they are, and Jacob reaches out his hands to bless them.

Josephs positions his sons, the older, Manasseh, on his left, Ephraim on his right, thereby guiding them to Jacob's right and left hands, respectively. Joseph intends the greater blessing, that of the right hand, for his firstborn, Manasseh. But Jacob crosses his hands, placing his right hand on Ephraim's head, his left on Manasseh. Joseph objects, but Jacob "guided his hands with intelligence" (48:14). He knew what he was doing.

Joseph gave his sons names freighted with meaning (41:50–52). Manasseh is from the Hebrew root meaning forgetfulness. Says Joseph, "God has made me forget all my hardship and my father's house." Joseph names his second son Ephraim, from the root meaning fruitful, because "God has made me fruitful in the land of my suffering."

It appears that Jacob understands the names of Joseph's sons and grasps their message. Now, as Jacob acknowledges his failures as a husband and as a parent, he teaches Joseph that we cannot undo our past. God does us no favors if God helps us to forget. Forgetfulness is for those too weak to face life. For the rest of us, no matter how dreadful, how difficult, no matter that it is a task we may never fully accomplish in our lifetime, we must face our past. Continually. We can thrust our past out of our mind over and over, but like a hungry cat, it keeps coming back. It will find its way back in no matter how securely we bar the door against it.

This one, says Jacob – Ephraim, the one who knows and acknowledges that his life comprises both triumph and suffering – this one shall be first. As Judah took on the role of the leader, setting aside the firstborn Reuben, Ephraim has the capacity to lead. Manasseh still has work to do. His body was born and raised in Egypt, but his soul agonizes over fragmented memories of a land he has never seen, wallowing in a past not his own – and from which he nonetheless can never free himself.

Jacob is about to gather all his sons together and bless each of them (ch. 49). Unlike the prior generations, where the blessing and the covenant passed to one son only, each of Jacob's sons will inherit. Each one will bear the continuity of the family, of Abraham's blessing and covenant. The Torah is establishing a clear program of a social structure based not on equality but on equitableness. The Torah teaches plainly that we are not the same. But we are each essential. God creates each of us for a unique purpose. Jacob knows that some of his sons are smarter than the others, some stronger, some more prone to violence, some more devious. No matter. Each of them has a role to play. And we each play our role best when we learn to play together, supporting and assisting, correcting and criticizing, and sometimes even opposing one another. The greatest actor in the world can't play Hamlet if there is no one else on stage.

This is Jacob's final lesson to Joseph. Jacob's admission

about Rachel's death frees Joseph from the last bits of unresolved resentment over his past. Jacob's lesson about embracing our past, with all its pains and troubles, propels Joseph forward to fully accomplish his task as the leader of a family that will, in the book of Exodus, become a nation.

As we have noted, God never speaks to Joseph. God has spoken to all the male protagonists in the Torah, from Adam through Jacob; and to some of the women. Now, when the family is in danger of being dispersed, of never returning to the land of God's promise, God is out of the picture. We need to learn to do for ourselves. That was ultimately the success of Jacob – his doing for himself, even as God helped. And it is certainly the message of Joseph's whole existence.

|•|

Before we close the book of Genesis, allow me to look at what must be the single most poignant verse in the Torah.

Immediately before blessing Ephraim and Manasseh, Jacob says to Joseph, "I did not pray that I would see your face; and behold, now God has even shown me your children!" (48:11).

This is translated and interpreted to mean that Jacob had despaired of ever seeing Joseph again, that after Joseph disappeared, Jacob gave up hope. But I believe the deeper meaning – the true meaning – comes from a straight literal reading: I did not pray to see your face.

When Jacob marries Leah, she immediately goes into a frenzy of childbearing. But Jacob's beloved Rachel is having difficulty conceiving. After Leah gives birth to her fourth son, Rachel approaches Jacob and begs him, "Give me children; if not, I am dead" (30:1–3). Jacob flies into a rage. "Am I in God's place – God, who has withheld from you the fruit of your womb?!" A shocking response from the man who loved her at first sight.

This is in harsh contrast to Jacob's father. After Isaac marries Rebecca, he sees that she is having difficulty conceiving. Unasked, he prays fervently to God for his wife to conceive.

His prayer is answered, and the result is the twins Esau and Jacob (25:19–22). Jacob came into this world as the result of prayer. And yet when his beloved wife begs him to intercede on her behalf, he not only refuses to pray, he attacks and berates her. "I have four sons already!" Jacob seems to say. "If you can't have children, it's your problem!" How dramatically our feelings change when we have to deal with the pressures of day-to-day life! We marry for love, but then we have to figure out how to earn a living. We marry for romance, but then we must also deal with our spouse's deepest fears, with their all too human weaknesses.

I did not pray to see your face, Jacob admits to Joseph. I did not pray for you to be born, not as my father prayed for me. And yet you came into the world. Not only did you come, but you have sons of your own and now they stand before me! Jacob is overwhelmed by God's unwarranted generosity, by this staggering show of grace. At the end of his days, his life comes together. However brief his happiness, it is complete. Jacob is able to recognize and acknowledge and unburden himself of his guilt, and to acknowledge the abundance of God's graciousness to him personally. In so doing, he teaches Joseph how to be a man in the world.

May God grant us the wisdom not just to learn these lessons, but to feel how urgent they are. Let us not wait until our last hour. There is so much at stake.

# *Exodus*

- 13 • *Shemot*          (1:1 – 6:1)
- 14 • *Va-Eira*         (6:2 – 9:35)
- 15 • *Bo*             (10:1 – 13:16)
- 16 • *Beshallach*     (13:17 – 17:16)
- 17 • *Yitro*           (18:1 – 20:23)
- 18 • *Mishpatim*     (21:1 – 24:18)
- 19 • *Terumah*      (25:1 – 27:19)
- 20 • *Tetzaveh*       (27:20 – 30:10)
- 21 • *Ki Tisa*         (30:11 – 34:35)
- 22 • *Va-Yaqhel*      (35:1 – 38:20)
- 23 • *Pequdei*        (38:21 – 40:38)

## 13

# Enter Moses

*I wish I knew how it would feel to be free.*

– Billy Taylor

This week we embark on reading the book of Exodus. This first portion plunges us right into the action, from Pharaoh's decision to oppress the Israelites, to Moses' returning to Egypt as the appointed leader of a nation. Genesis provides an archetypal grounding for the Bible, laying out distinct personality types and their qualities. Exodus is about revelation; what happens to both an individual and a society that experiences a confrontation with the Divine.

To understand the context in which Moses emerges as a leader, let's look at the negative traits which some of the main actors in Genesis represent. This is not to denigrate the spiritual ideals or religious messages these characters, at their best, represent, but to see what we can learn by viewing them as archetypal personality types.

Abraham exemplifies what can happen when excessive good intentions go wrong. His enthusiastic embrace of God estranges him from his family. On the one hand, God favors him precisely because "he will teach his children and his household after him to keep God's way, doing charity and justice" (Gen. 18:19). On the other hand, Abraham becomes captive to his relationship with the Divine, at the expense of "his household" – a sort of spiritual Stockholm Syndrome. He backs down from holding God to absolute standards of justice, allowing God to walk away from the negotiation with regard to Sodom. And he zealously accepts God's command to sacrifice Isaac. Can it be that this moral paragon will slaughter his own son and then say, "I was just following orders"?

Isaac experiences firsthand the full horror of human

behavior at its most extreme. His father binds him, lays him on a funeral pyre, and prepares to slit his throat, looking him in the eye all the while. The text explicitly says angels call to Abraham (Gen. 22:11–18). Applying the principle that the Bible does not waste words, Isaac may not have heard the angels telling his father to stop, telling Abraham that he has withstood God's test, that his willingness to slay his son is proof of his dedication to God, and that henceforth Abraham's name will be a blessing for all humanity. Isaac returns to explore his father's legacy, digging anew the wells that Abraham's enemies had filled in. He goes on to dig his own wells, yet this "return to the scene of the crime" illustrates how difficult it is to fully reconcile or force closure with our past.

In order to grow into adulthood, we need to confront the very worst that is within us. In order to know how to deal with the evil that surrounds us, we need to see and experience and acknowledge that the same propensity for evil dwells within us. The book *Ordinary Men* by Christopher Browning follows a group of upstanding German citizens in early middle age – lawyers, pharmacists, accountants – who were drafted as policemen during World War II. Too old to be sent to the front, they were hired for the quieter tasks of walking the local beat. Within a short time, they were sent into Jewish villages and towns across Poland where they were ordered to slaughter the inhabitants at close range – often by bayonet, to save bullets. The men balked at first, but quickly came round, even as they suffered headaches and nightmares, and were showered with the spurting blood of their victims. Their commanders told them they did not have to participate, that they were free to go back to Germany. Only one or two left. Most stayed on, not because they relished the task – which they did not – and not because they believed in what they were doing – which they did not. They stayed in order not to abandon their comrades to this dirty work. We dare not think such a thing could not happen to us. Yet it is only once we acknowledge that *it very well could happen to us* that we are on the path to preventing it.

Jacob engages in more garden-variety evil, the kind we so often encounter in our daily lives. Exactly the kind which rarely strikes us as being evil, so we engage in it ourselves. We are uncomfortable at first, but we quickly get over it.

Jacob sees an opportunity to get what his older brother has. He completes the task that Abel merely stumbled into, actually securing the position of the firstborn and the birthright. He then colludes with his mother to lie to his father, and completes the task by stealing the blessing. When he returns two decades later, Jacob tricks his brother once again, saying he will meet up with him, then heading off in a different direction.

Alone among the Patriarchs, it is Jacob who finally confronts his demons in a wrestling match in the dead of night. It is only once we have grappled with our dark side – a more obvious metaphor would be hard to come by – that we can move on in life. After the fight, the mysterious man blesses Jacob, saying, "You have struggled with God and with man, and you were equal to the task" (Gen. 32:29). As we have seen, the important thing is not winning, but being able to stay in the contest. The man changes Jacob's name to Israel, meaning, "the one who will struggle." Jacob – the meaning of whose original name means "he catches at the heel," and perhaps even "he delays" – is not able to return to Canaan. Now, as Israel, he is prepared to move forward and enter the Promised Land.

Uniquely with regard to Joseph, God does not speak or appear to him at all – although Joseph routinely invokes God to outsiders. The Torah insists that what God wants is nothing less than a full partnership with humanity. Thus, humans must learn to stand on their own. Starting from full and continued dialogue with Abraham, God weaned the patriarchs off the Divine Presence bit by bit, until Joseph was left to fly solo. This imagery will find expression in the Exodus narrative, embodied for example in the symbolism relating to Moses' staff.

Moses is raised by a conspiracy of mother figures, but has no father. (His biological father is named only once, and not in the narrative of his birth.) Because of Pharaoh's decree that all male babies be drowned, Moses' mother places him in a basket and sets him afloat on the Nile. His sister runs alongside, keeping watch, and is nearby when Pharaoh's daughter fishes him from the river (Ex. 2:1–10).[1] The girl brings their own mother to serve as wet nurse, and Pharaoh's daughter raises Moses as her son (2:10).

Moses grows up and goes out into the world (2:11–20), where he sees an Egyptian beating an Israelite. Without a word, he strikes the Egyptian dead. The next day, he sees two Israelites fighting and asks, "Why are you hitting your fellow?" The Israelite responds, "Do you mean to kill me as you did the Egyptian?" Immediately afterward, "When Pharaoh heard about this matter, he tried to kill Moses" (2:15). The structure of the verses – with the additional words "this matter" – suggests that Pharaoh was angry at Moses not over killing the Egyptian, but about Moses' exchange with the Israelites. Moses learned Hebrew from his mother and he knows he is an Israelite, despite having grown up in the palace: "He went out to his brothers and he saw their burdens" (2:11).

"This matter" that enrages Pharaoh is Moses' attempt to reconcile between Israelites. Moses is seeking to instill a group identity and to institute a legalistic process, to create a sense of social cohesiveness and responsibility. The two Israelite men have greater cause to stand together than to fight one another. Moses presents exactly the threat, that of a fifth column, which Pharaoh foresaw when he ordered the Israelites enslaved: "If a war comes, [the Israelites] will join with our enemies and fight against us and rise up from within our midst" (1:8–10).

Moses flees to the land of Midian (2:15–21), where he intervenes to protect a group of sisters from the local shepherds. As pointed out by Nechama Leibowitz, one of the great Torah teachers of the twentieth century, Moses is staunchly on the side of justice. He exacts summary justice when only

---

1   Unless otherwise noted, all references in this section are to the book of Exodus.

force will succeed, he seeks to create solidarity between those who share a common plight and a common identity, and he intervenes to defend the weak against the strong. Notably, as Leibowitz observes, he intervenes whether or not the injustice involves Israelites.

Moses marries one of the Midianite sisters he protected. When their son is born (2:22), Moses names him Gershom, meaning "a stranger there," because, says Moses, "I have been a stranger in a foreign land." Jacob had to correct the names Joseph gave his sons, teaching Joseph that you can't forget where you came from. Moses gives his son a name that ties him to the experience of exile. Moses is twice an exile: born in Egypt, in exile from the ancestral home in Canaan, and now exiled even from Egypt. Despite having lived forty years in Midian, Moses remains connected to his origins – or rather, to his estrangement. He is still a stranger in a strange land.

God now decides to intervene and save the Israelites (2:23–25). It is precisely Moses' identification with the Israelite people and their destiny that provides the tool God needs to put into motion the next phase of the divine plan: the appointment of a leader. God approaches Moses at the burning bush (3:1–4:17) for an extended job interview, but Moses insists he is not up to the task. The most telling thing he says about himself is, "I am not a man of words; I have never been" (4:10). When Moses first comes on the scene, we see him as the man of action, indeed, of impetuosity, striking dead the Egyptian overseer. When he tries to reason with the two Israelites the following day, he is rebuffed. If anything, this might seem to affirm that Moses' actions speak louder than his words ever can. In Midian, again, he dives right into the fray and chases the shepherds away. Toward the end of Moses' career, we shall see this play out again, with fateful results.

Moses' impetuosity has landed him in exile, fleeing for his life from the royal household in which he was raised. What does it mean to be in exile?

The exodus from Egypt is the historical defining moment

of the Jewish people. It is referenced repeatedly in the Bible itself, and in rabbinic works down the ages. References to the Exodus feature centrally in the daily prayer services, and everyone is familiar with the holiday of Passover and the Seder, the celebratory meal commemorating the Exodus.

The biblical commentator Nachmanides (Spain and Israel, 1194–1270) says that Jewish identity is forged in exodus – not the centuries of exile after the destruction of Jerusalem in 70 CE, but the experience of the Israelites after leaving Egypt. Torn from a land where they had lived for over four hundred years, they wander the wilderness not knowing what to do with themselves. The Russian Nobel Prize-winning poet Joseph Brodsky (1940 – 1996) writes that *exile* has two opposite meanings. The first is a verb: you are thrown out of your homeland. You then pick yourself up and forge ahead, building a new identity and a new life in your new home. The second, and the fate of so many of Brodsky's countrymen, is a noun, an identity. You spend your days in a tragic holding pattern, mourning your past and wishing against any reasonable expectation to one day be permitted to return.

In addition to confronting the propensity for evil within himself, Moses must lead the Israelites away from the sense of exile, from the tragic yearning to return to a past that never was. He must teach them to unify, to embrace a new identity, and to accept reality. To stand on their own morally, to stand up for one another, to pursue justice and truth at all times, and to embrace the role God has in store for them – which is to bring God's Presence into this world which so desperately needs it.

Being chosen is a tremendous burden. But perhaps, as the Israelites are about to discover, not so much of a burden as it is to be free.

# 14

# God Enters History

*Seek the wisdom that will untie your knot. Seek the path that demands your whole being.*

– Rumi

In this week's Torah portion God launches the campaign of plagues against the Egyptians. But first, God designates Moses as the earthly leader, the man without whom the divine plan cannot be implemented. For if we are here for a purpose, the Torah teaches us, it is to be active partners in God's work. The opening passage of this portion spells out a profound difference in the way God is presented in this book, in contrast to the way God appears in Genesis.

Says God to Moses (6:2-8) "I am God [the four-letter spelling of the Divine name, represented in English by the letters Y/H/W/H]. I appeared to Abraham, Isaac and Jacob as 'El Shaddai,' but with my name Y/H/W/H, I did not make myself known to them. In addition, I established my Covenant with them, to give them the land of Canaan... In addition, I have heard the groan of the Children of Israel being enslaved by Egypt and I remember my Covenant. Therefore, I say to you, I am God (Y/H/W/H) and I shall take you out from under the burdens of Egypt..."

The introduction of the Divine Name mirrors the first two chapters of Genesis; God is called by the name Elohim in chapter one, designating the God of the world, the God of nature, and the God of judgment. Once humans are created, the world becomes a much more complicated place. The name Y/H/W/H is introduced in chapter 2. This is God's aspect of mercy and compassion. It is also the name of the God of Israel, the personal God and, as we are about to see, the God who gets directly involved in human history.

God tells Moses "I appeared to [the Patriarchs] as 'El Shaddai'..." This name represents a transition from the universal God of nature, to the personal and national God of the Hebrews. The name El is a generic Canaanite name for a deity. The name Shaddai invokes the mountains, and the mysteries of the great heights. And indeed, among the most striking features of the land of Canaan are the mountains that dominate the landscape. Upon entering Canaan, Abraham enables the revelation and transformation of the local chief deity into the one eternal God.

Historically we know that older local rituals and practices are subsumed into newer religions when they take over. Ancient springtime fertility festivals were brought forward and associated with Passover, and thence with Easter. Winter solstice observances found their way into Hanukkah and Christmas. The spread of religion comes hand in hand with political or military conquest. Alexander the Great used local religions to his advantage. He left permanent garrisons of troops in each place he conquered where they would marry and integrate into the local population, taking on the local gods – a good way to ingratiate the conqueror with the locals. The opposite approach was applied in Islam, where faith was spread at the point of the sword and local practices largely discouraged.

The Biblical narrative advocates a third way.

God interacted with Abraham, Isaac and Jacob in the outward form of the powerful local deity, El. This was true of the time and place in which the Patriarchs lived. The notion of monotheism was too great a challenge to the established order. But within their view of the world, it made sense to the locals that Abraham's God could become "top god," not to be messed with. There is also an historical argument which says that monotheism creates a particularly sharp form of intolerance. This theory says the notion that there is only one God means that everyone else is wrong, a frightening development that gives to religion an unprecedented destructive power.

For those who complain that, if only religion did not exist, there wouldn't be war – this is too simplistic. It is but another way of giving overly much power to the Deity. Wars erupt because people aggregate into groups; rivalries grow up, and tribalism takes hold, setting groups against each other. Organized religion is a pillar of tribalism. It is inseparable from conflict – but not its cause. Necessary, but not sufficient.

One of the great modern rabbinic thinkers and leaders was Rav Abraham Isaac HaCohen Kook (pronounced "cook," born 1865 in the Latvian region of the Russian empire; died 1935 in Jerusalem), the first Ashkenazic chief rabbi of Palestine under the British mandate. A visionary who saw the world with intense clarity, Kook explains that the individual quest for spiritual realization lies at the core of organized religion. But on no account should we believe that the *purpose* of organized religion is for us to realize our spiritual quest. Indeed, it is only once we accept the dual role of religion – its primary function as a social adhesive, and its secondary role to promote the growth of the individual as a contributing member of the community – that we can tend to our own spiritual needs without resenting religion's demands on us, treating us as part of the herd, while often seeming indifferent to us as individuals.

God says to Moses, when I appeared to the Patriarchs, my purpose was to form a personal bond with each of them; as El was the god of Canaan, I became for each of them their unique God whose place was wherever they were. (As God said to Moses last week, "I shall be," implying, "I shall be what and where I am needed..." Indeed, the four-letter name Y/H/W/H is an amalgam of the verb "to be" comprising past, present, and future tenses in a single appellation.) But now, says God, I come to you as both the God of Creation, and the God of a nation. God of the world, as well as a personal God to each of you. The rabbis tell us that the unique concept of personal divine providence is born with this relationship, binding forever the fate of the individual to the destiny of the nation.

God has taken great pains to craft a relationship with each

of the Patriarchs. God speaks to their weaknesses: God tests Abraham, whose core quality is loving-kindness, by making him give far in excess of anything that might be required of any human being. In passing God's test, Abraham also fails humanity's requirement. But how to combine and reconcile his duty to his son – which is also a duty to literally keep alive God's promise of a future – with his duty of obedience to God?

The Torah introduces us over and over to the human reality that life doesn't make sense. God is irrational, arbitrary and harsh with Isaac. The Kabbalists assign to Isaac the attribute of Judgment and Limitation. Isaac limits Abraham's excess of kindness. In doing so, he also suffers, for when we withhold from others, we deny ourselves interaction with the world, that contact with others which is the touchstone of our humanity. God is remote with Jacob; present in promise, though not always palpably so, and at critical moments Jacob loses his nerve. Jacob's greatness is that, despite feeling cut off from God, he nonetheless forges ahead. In Kabbalistic terms Jacob symbolizes balance, synthesis. He reconciles the excessive generosity of Abraham with the iron limitation of Isaac. Finally, Jacob begins to be able to live in the world.

Joseph is a transitional figure, left on his own, notably without any communication from God. And he succeeds. Just as the Covenant passes from personal to familial, now in Exodus, it will pass from familial and tribal, to a national identity.

Moses' task is to create that national identity. Says God – I never showed myself in the fullness of my own Self. Now I come to you, just as I did when I placed Adam in the Garden. Humans are problematic, and so I needed to temper my own aspect of Truth, which is Judgment, with my softer aspect of Compassion and Mercy.

I had to delve deep within myself, says God, in order to complete the task I set myself, that of creating a world. I had to learn to relate to the world I created. To bring out the Patriarchs' inner qualities without disturbing the balance.

To shake them up without tearing them to pieces. I needed to probe deeply into their unique essence, for each person's unique strongest point is also where they are vulnerable. It is where they will be most sorely tested. We never grow until we push ourselves beyond where we believe we can go.

Moses must learn this about himself – and what better guide than God? What better role model? Moses must learn to delve within himself, to learn and understand and develop each of his unique inner abilities and strengths, to understand his weaknesses too, and to know his true limitations. Not those limits he fears to go beyond; Moses needs to know that he actually can go farther than he ever believed. And he needs to know what will happen when he does.

A true leader touches that which is unique in others and is capable of bringing out each person's strengths. As we shall see, Moses' greatness as a leader emerges in moments when he believes in us, even when we have given up hope. Indeed, Moses will believe in us, even when God has given up on us completely.

The truest role of a leader – of a captain, of a teacher, of a spiritual guide – is to help their teammate, or pupil, or friend to identify what is greatest within themselves, and to bring that selflessly to fruition.

May God bless and sustain the work of our hands.

# 15

# Hard-Hearted Pharaoh

*Things fall apart; the centre cannot hold;
Mere anarchy is loosed upon the world.*

– Yeats, *The Second Coming*

This week's Torah reading opens with a grammatical anomaly, the use of the pronoun "I" (10:1). Since in the Hebrew language verbs define the person, number, and gender of the one performing the action, God does not need to say "*I* have made his heart heavy." The action, "I have made heavy," is expressed in a single word; the pronoun *I* is subsumed within it. God's use of the pronoun *I* will be echoed later in the portion (11:4–5) when God announces the slaying of Egypt's firstborn: "*I* shall go out into the midst of Egypt, and every firstborn male in the land of Egypt shall die." God is telling us here that, unlike the previous times when Pharaoh hardened his own heart, now God has taken direct control. "I," says God, "and *I alone*, have made Pharaoh's heart heavy."

The story of God hardening Pharaoh's heart is one the most terrifying sequences in the Torah, because God directly intervenes to deny a person the freedom to choose.

At the moment of Creation, God introduces humans "in our image and our likeness." This "image and likeness" mirrors God's creative aspect, and is bound up with free choice. The one decision upon which our individual humanity rests is the way we choose to relate to the world. Now God removes Pharaoh's free choice, making Pharaoh mistreat the Israelites, and making him and his people pay with their lives as punishment.

In their first encounter at the bush, God tells Moses, "I know that the king of Egypt will not allow you to go out except by a strong hand" (3:19). Subsequently, as Moses is on the road back to Egypt, God adds, "And I shall strengthen [Pharaoh's] heart and he shall not send the people. And you shall tell Pharaoh, Thus says God: Israel is My firstborn son. And I am telling you, send My son so he shall serve Me, and you refuse to send him; behold, I shall kill your firstborn son" (4:21–23). Notice that God's plan is laid out in two parts: there is a prediction – Pharaoh will not let the people go; followed by a dire judgment – then I shall harden Pharaoh's heart so that he cannot let the people go even if he wants to.

Up until the first plague, that of blood, Pharaoh repeatedly refuses Moses' plea to liberate the Israelites. Immediately before this plague, we read, "And Pharaoh's heart was strong, and he paid them no heed, just as God had said" (7:13). The difference now is the revelation that God has stepped in. For the first time, God announces, "I have done this." Until now, Pharaoh did not need any assistance in hardening his own heart.

Pharaoh carries on his escalating stubbornness from the plague of blood through the seventh plague, that of boils. He has not only rejected Moses countless times, but he and his people have experienced myriad signs and wonders as well as seven plagues. Now, at the beginning of this Torah portion (10:1), God informs Moses that God has "made heavy" Pharaoh's heart.

In the Egyptian religion, the Pharaoh goes through a test after death, in which his heart is weighed against a feather. Purity of the heart was the key to the Pharaoh's entrance to the eternal afterlife. If his heart was heavier than a feather, the afterlife was closed to him for all eternity. In the Exodus story, God makes this Pharaoh's heart heavy. Through divine intervention, Pharaoh loses not merely his kingdom in this world, but his royal access to the afterlife as well.

The first time death is mentioned in the sequence of plagues is when Pharaoh reacts to the eighth plague, that of locusts (10:12–20). It is also the first time he appears ready to repent: "Pharaoh summoned Moses and Aaron and said, 'I have sinned against God and against you. Now please forgive my sin this once and entreat God, that God may remove from me this death.' But God reinforced Pharaoh's resolve, and he did not send forth the Israelites" (10:16–17).

Pharaoh approaches Moses with the language of repentance, whereupon God leaps into action to ensure that Pharaoh does not repent, forcing the Egyptian leader to prolong his cruelty against Israel. By closing off freedom of choice, the one characteristic which makes Pharaoh human is denied him. Why?

Clearly, Pharaoh is to be made an example of. At the end of last week's reading, Pharaoh acknowledged his guilt (9:27–28) and conceded the fight. "I have sinned this time: The Lord is the righteous one, and I and my people are the evil ones. Pray to God...and I shall send you out and you will no longer stand here." This is the trigger. Up until the seventh plague, Pharaoh remained steadfast. Now, though, he has broken down. In order for God's plan to be completed, God must take the reins. "Come to Pharaoh," says God (10:1), "because *I* have hardened his heart and the hearts of his servants." And once more, after the plague of locusts, Pharaoh tries to repent (10:16–17): "And now please forgive my sin," he pleads with Moses. But Pharaoh's plea and his repentance are cut short by God's heavy hand.

The rabbis consider the power of repentance among the greatest forces in Creation, crucial to keeping the world in existence. The midrashic literature says that repentance had to come into existence before the creation of the world, because God realized that our free choice would lead us to make wrong decisions, to sin unwittingly. Thus, in order not to have to destroy the world, as an expression of God's utter perfection, God had to imbue the fabric of Creation with repentance. And God also had to be a willing receptacle for that repentance. It is not sufficient for humans to repent; God must also be willing to accept our repentance. God must be able to forgive.

Thus, we face a dilemma: we must believe that, even for

so great a villain as Pharaoh, God's natural aspect of mercy cannot be shut off. God would need to set aside the divine qualities of compassion and forgiveness, or God would have to rip from one human being the ability to repent. Either way, God must effect a fundamental change in the fabric of the very universe God has created, either by undoing the nature of one human being or setting aside the nature of God. The latter is a terrifying alternative.

Starting with Eve and Adam, there are many passages where God expresses rage, anger, sadness, or displeasure over humanity's inability to stick to the modes of behavior God has commanded. But not once does God say, "I wish to become other than how and what I am." Indeed, God's answer to Moses, "I am what I am," asserts God's fundamental aspect of eternal unchangeableness. As unpredictable and daunting as this world is, the one thing we humans are told to rely on is that God never changes.

From a human perspective, we deal with a world that is constantly changing, unpredictable, and frequently terrifying. But amidst the unpredictability, there is a dreadful and yet somehow comforting predictability to even the most tragic aspects of life. Death. Disease. Pain arising from other people's wrong decisions, or from our own. All these are unavoidable. The inevitability of tragedy does not prepare us to deal with it, or even to accept it. But it can push us to appreciate the good things we have, to cherish them while they are ours, and perhaps to relinquish them gracefully when the time comes for us to lose them. Whatever pain we experience, we ultimately can never say we did not expect it.

There is much suffering in life, much pain that is unavoidable. Pharaoh starts out as a strong leader. His determination to hold on to power is understandable. Perhaps his determination to stand firm for his nation is admirable. At a certain point, though, he goes too far. The punishments are being meted out not against him personally, but against his entire nation. A leader who sacrifices his people for power, for revenge, in anger, is not fit to lead a nation. Such leaders bring disaster, no matter how loudly they proclaim they are acting for their country. Throughout history, we have seen leaders who come to power doing their all for their nation, and end by making their nation suffer merely for them.

Now God performs the most dreadful act of all by uncreating God's own greatest creation – a human being. In the biblical context, its purpose is plain, which is to force the liberation of Israel and to make it an eternal emblem of God's might exercised on behalf of the Israelites.

None of us is immune to hubris, to carrying our program to destructive extremes. The notion of prayer rests on the axiom that God helps us along the way, propels us along the path we choose. Thus, it is critical that we choose the right path. While we may never know for certain, we at least have the ability to watch ourselves, to see the results of our actions, the impact of our behavior. The message of God's withdrawing Pharaoh's free will is likewise: I will help you along the path. In every course of action you embrace with passion, I will propel you forward. Therefore, choose wisely, for a cause once set in motion is difficult to reign in.

Put the simplest way I know: It is easier to make a mess than it is to clean it up.

# 16

# Seeing Is Believing

*There are no proofs for the existence of the God of Abraham. There are only witnesses.*

– Abraham Joshua Heschel
*The Prophets*

This week's Torah reading contains one of the Bible's most cinematic scenes: the splitting of the Sea of Reeds and the escape of the Israelites, followed by the drowning of Pharaoh and his armies. Amidst the majestic imagery and the grandeur of the narrative lie two verses which at first glance are a rousing affirmation of God's love for Israel, yet on closer examination they are troubling: "On that day the Lord saved Israel from the hand of Egypt and Israel saw Egypt dead upon the shore; and they saw the great hand which the Lord used on Egypt, and the people feared the Lord, and they believed in the Lord and in Moses, the Lord's servant" (Ex. 14:30–31).

Rabbi Kalonymus Kalman Shapira (1889–1943) was the hasidic rebbe of the Polish town of Piaseczno (pronounced *pia-SETZ-no*) until he was deported to the Warsaw Ghetto and murdered by the Nazis. Rabbi Shapira was a brilliant educator. Like all the great hasidic rebbes, he had a profound understanding of human psychology. Speaking of intellectual argument, he says people who trot out proofs for the existence of God are actually desperately trying to overcome their own lack of faith.

In that context, we need to recognize that, by definition, seeing is *not* believing. Seeing is, in fact, the very opposite of believing. When we see something, we do not believe it. We experience it. And all experience is subjective and transitory. We lose our way because we believe our own experience – our seeing – to be objectively true. Then we lose our footing, because what we experienced yesterday is not the same as what we experience today. We live in a world of constant flux, which we experience as being inherently self-contradictory, and thus impose structures on it. Like little children stopping up their ears and squeezing their eyes closed, we shut out the chaotic real world and rebuke anyone who refuses to share our hermetically sealed environment.

Perhaps the most common manifestation of this is the supposed conflict between science and religion. The falseness of this conflict becomes obvious when we acknowledge that they both arise in the human mind; indeed, both from the same point within the mind: the need for meaning. Our minds are structured to tell stories. Evolutionary scientists say this is how we get better and better at surviving; religious teachers say this is how we discover the existence of God. Both agree that we have the capacity for understanding truths about the world that are not obvious, but which require deep contemplation to arrive at.

The simplest way to cut through the apparent contradiction is to recognize that science teaches us what the elements of existence are and how they interact, while religion tells us what we are to do regarding these elements and interactions. Most powerfully, religion places moral value on the objects of existence and their interactions, something science is incapable of doing. For all the advances in psychology, sociology, and brain science, morality remains the domain of the spirit. The closest brain science comes to a moral conclusion is the determination that humans are hardwired to make certain choices, which we call moral decisions. These discoveries are critically important, but they do not change the reality that morality is the province of the spiritual side of the mind.

Science and religion belong together. Like the soul, which dwells in the human body, they are closer than two sides of a coin. The Jewish mystics describe the mind grappling with the teachings of the Torah. The Torah, in the mystical realm, is seen as God's mind. Thus, when we engage in deep study (religion), we are enwrapping our mind within the mind of God. But because God gives us a mind capable of comprehending the world (science), our mind also wraps itself around God's mind.

Those capable of entering into this relationship can experience moments when the physical world reveals itself as profoundly mystical; at the same time, the mysteries of the invisible cosmos become concrete, graspable.

This process is hard work. More, it encourages individual spiritual exploration, which inevitably leads people to question the canned statements emanating from religious authorities. No wonder the religious reject science! Much as this process of yielding the intellect to God is a powerful engine for personal growth, it undermines that lowest common denominator so critical for maintaining organized religion in place.

Thus, the two aspects of our mind are held apart, rather than joined in partnership as they naturally should be. To Karl Marx's adage about religion being the opiate of the masses, Irish poet William Butler Yeats retorts that science is "the opiate of the suburbs," and everyone flees to their own simplistic view of the world.

What the spiritual quest calls for is a mechanistic view of the invisible coupled with the divine aspect of the material. For those committed to the Religion versus Science view, our ability to interact scientifically with the world looks increasingly suspect as we learn more about how chimpanzees, birds, octopuses, and smaller organisms make and use tools. The increasing similarities across all life forms risk making humans ever less unique. Ever less the crown of Creation. Yet if it is the rational understanding of the world that makes us *Homo sapiens*, only the spiritual quest for moral perfection can make us fully human.

The quest for God isn't supposed to cut us off from society. Maimonides cautions against extreme spiritual practices. When we see a truly pious person fasting, or living on a mountaintop, or wearing sackcloth, we are tempted to say, I will fast. I will withdraw from society. I will wear sackcloth. Says Maimonides, the real challenge, and the proper way to live, is to follow a balanced existence, specifically including a balanced intellectual and spiritual practice. Maimonides goes so far as to call this balance the way of nature, recognizing that the natural world exists only through its exquisite equipoise. More remarkable than the hermit, and far more difficult to sustain, is the spiritual seeker who goes through daily life in outwardly unremarkable fashion, yet whose inner focus is alive with an awareness of the Presence of God. Just because someone fasts and sits on a mountaintop doesn't mean they're a saint, and just because someone goes to an office every day and does people's tax returns doesn't mean they aren't.

Let's get back to the Torah's problematic take on our sense of sight. In Hebrew, there is a unique verb for *create*, as in "God created the heavens and the earth." This verb – *bara* – built on the root meaning "to see," is used only for acts of creation performed by God. The text continues this leitmotif when, after each day of Creation, we are told that God "saw…that it was good." Creation begins with sight and continues with sight.

Genesis 1:4 is traditionally translated, "God saw the light, that it was good." But it can also be translated "God saw the light, *because* it was good." Does God "see" only things which are good? Could this be why God does not see Adam after the sin (Gen. 3:9)? God calls out to Adam, "Where are you?" God asks Cain, "Where is Abel, your brother?" Faced with evil, the text may be suggesting that God's vision becomes clouded. What will it take for God to be able to see evil?

Eve appropriates seeing: "And the woman saw that it was good, the tree, for eating" (Gen 3:6); precisely God's language of Creation. This first use of seeing by humans completely upends God's plan of Creation. Eve *sees*, she analyzes, and she takes. The first instance of science without religion – and the world is forever changed.

The ink is not dry on the Creation story when the very act of seeing becomes contaminated: "And God saw that the wickedness of humans was great" (Gen 6:5). God sees "that it was" the opposite of good. The Creation formula itself is contorted. "And God saw that it was…*very bad*!" How is seeing to be restored to "good"? How can we redeem the world?

Throughout the Exodus, we *see* proof of God's existence: the signs, the plagues, the miracles, and now the splitting of the sea. Yet it is problematic. Even Pharaoh, king of the country with the greatest base of scientific knowledge in its time, refuses the evidence of his own eyes, rejecting the first signs and plagues, even before God actively intervenes to harden his heart.

The Abraham narrative makes use of the human ability – or inability – to see as a demonstration of people's spiritual level. Cast out into the desert, Hagar is standing beside a well, yet she tells the angel that her son will die of thirst. It requires divine intervention for her to see the water that was there all along (Gen. 21:19). Abraham, on the other hand, is uniquely clear-sighted. When commanded to sacrifice his son, Abraham doesn't need angelic guidance; he lifts up his eyes and sees. He sees the mountain, he sees the ram. Abraham sees clearly what God expects him to do.

"Seeing is believing"? If you need to see it, by definition you will never believe it. And as numerous psychology experiments demonstrate, if you don't believe something, you literally will not see it; your mind will not process the images transmitted by the eyes! Like infants who have not yet developed object permanence, the Israelites in the wilderness must see constant manifestations of God. Otherwise, they believe God has abandoned them.

And after we have seen all the miracles, then what? Spiritual practice is not an end in itself. Its purpose is to enable us to return to the world of nature with new tools, with a new awareness. To heighten our connection to God in the everyday, strengthening us to work to bring holiness and justice into the world. The downside of spiritual practice is that we cling to experiences. We wish desperately to repeat them. We withdraw from the natural world, trying to repeat the circumstances and actions that led to our moment of awakening. Instead of identifying places within ourselves that require fixing, we embrace practices to recapture a feeling. In this way, our meditation, our chanting and prayer – indeed, our whole service of God – risks becoming just another way of satisfying our appetites. Like Eve, our service of God is nothing more than a sweet piece of fruit for us to enjoy. Like Hagar at the well, we become so wrapped up in our own experience that we fail to see the world before our eyes. Whether it is family, community, or nation – or especially our self, we cannot engage with what we do not perceive. Our very quest for spirituality risks robbing us of our humanity.

You want to *see* God? If you need to see God, then even seeing God will not be sufficient. The craving for spiritual experience works like a drug. And we build up a tolerance. First, I want to recapture the feeling I had in prayer this morning. Then I want to meditate. Then I need to get away to meditate and "connect," to abandon my job, my family, my culture.... If God actually came to stand before us, fully visible, we would say, "Okay, what *else* can you do to keep me interested?"

God took a great risk in creating us, putting us here with freedom of choice and an endless capacity to do both good and evil. What was God thinking? If God is willing to take such a great risk for the sake of this relationship, imagine how important each human being is. Not just ourselves, but each person made in God's image. If we follow our superficial tastes and appetites, we will be traveling our path, not God's. Not learning to do God's work, but abandoning God for our own enjoyment.

As much as we desire to connect with God, God wants to connect with us. Like any relationship, this works only when both parties come to it independently, wholeheartedly, fearlessly accepting the consequences. God has a unique task set aside for each of us. We can follow the path of our appetites, our urges, and our passions. Or we can strive to know ourselves deeply, then harness our passions, urges, and appetites to fulfill our mission on this earth. By our acts they shall know us.

# 17

# Ten Words

*The Bible is very easy to understand. We pretend to be unable to understand it because we know that the moment we understand, we are obliged to act accordingly.*

– Kierkegaard

In this week's Torah reading, Moses ascends Mount Sinai to receive the Ten Commandments. In the Hebrew they are called "the Ten Sayings." There is a Hebrew word for commandment, which is actually not used here. It would be more precise to call these "the ten principles." The specific rules, laws, and observances commanded in the Torah are not meant to be exhaustive; they are expressions of God's will, principles that God wants us to apply in our behavior. These fall generally into the categories of our relationship with God, our relationships with one another, and our relationship with ourselves, introducing principles governing, respectively, ritual practice, societal behavior, and personal ethics and spiritual growth.

The Ten Commandments is not a unique event. The principles enunciated at Sinai comprise all of God's message for humanity: how to relate to God, how to build a just society, how to care for others, and how to work to realize our personal potential. These principles are eternal. Far beyond being merely words spoken by God in a particular setting, they are definitional to who God is.

The weekly Torah portions are generally named by the first key word of the portion. Thus, the first three readings in the book of Genesis are "In the Beginning," "Noah," and "Go." This week's portion is named "Jethro," after Moses' father-in-law. God's law is given at Mount Sinai in a reading that bears the name of an outsider, a non-Israelite. Jethro was the priest of Midian and is not destined to become part of the Jewish people. He was an idolater. The rabbinic tradition tells that Jethro recognized the power and greatness of God because he had worshiped every other god and thus was able to recognize God as authentic. Of course, this is still tainted by the fact that Jethro accepts God as true because of the miracles: the exodus from Egypt and the splitting of the sea. In short, seeing is believing for Israelite and non-Israelite alike. At this point in the Torah's narrative, humans still need concrete experience as the touchstone for religious faith.

Even after affirming the greatness of the God of Israel, Jethro will return to his homeland and, presumably, to his position of leadership, with all the priestly duties that entails. Far from criticizing him for not following Moses into the wilderness, the rabbis give Jethro great honor, naming this portion after him. During his brief stay in the camp of the Israelites, the people benefit from Jethro's involvement. Jethro demonstrates practical wisdom beyond that of his son-in-law and explains why Moses needs to radically change his mode of leadership. Without Jethro, Moses' teachings will not outlive this generation. Without Jethro, the Torah will disappear from history.

Acting in his role as judge and lawgiver, Moses stands from morning to night as the Israelites line up to present their questions (18:13–23). Consistent with the Torah's overarching message of creating and maintaining a just society, the rabbis tell us that people came to Moses not to charge one another with wrongdoing, but to ask whether they themselves had behaved properly, and if not, how to remedy the situation.

Observing his son-in-law, Jethro tells Moses, "You will surely wither away, you and also this people who are with you" (18:18). This is understood to mean: This judging is too much for one person to take on. You need to share the burden. However, the Hebrew word translated as "wither away" means a dead body, specifically an animal who dies of natural causes. Jethro is not merely saying, Moses, you work too hard. He is saying, This system of government, this Torah, will die with you unless you take steps now to create a structure. You must not merely choose a leader to fill your sandals, you must design a robust system of governance that will retain its integrity down through the ages. Jethro tells Moses to create a society.

Jethro, who acknowledges all God's miracles, says, This generation experienced the miracles. They stand before you today in humility, afraid to take one penny that doesn't belong to them. But after you are gone and after they die out, future generations will argue bitterly over what the Torah means. If the plain law is not clear to these people who actually experienced God's Presence and miracles, how will people react after a generation, a century, a millennium?

Nothing disrupts a society like money. Today they stand in line to ask whether they are entitled to keep their own money. Tomorrow they will kill each other over pennies. And it will all come down to leadership.

At the end of the reading, God says, "You shall not make with Me gods of silver, nor shall you make for yourselves gods of gold" (20:19–20). The rabbis say that the gold and silver vessels and ornaments that will be made for ritual use in the Tabernacle are not to be worshiped. Even the gold cherubim atop the Ark of the Covenant are not holy in themselves. Rather, they enable holiness to be practiced.

On the societal level, money has the power to rip the fabric of the social system. Says God, I expect you to create justice on the ground. Do not invoke My Name to take from others. In today's world, where the marketplace is enshrined as the ultimate deity, it is no wonder people are ignorant of these verses.

God says, Don't think I will be flattered by your money. When you lie and cheat and steal and take unfair advantage of the weak – or even if you are one of those fundamentally decent people who blithely benefits from the injustices that have crept into the fabric of society – do not think I will be appeased if you put your name on a $100 million university research facility or library. People speak about "giving back." But no one questions how they got it in the first place. When we "give back," we need to acknowledge that we took. Otherwise, it is just "giving," and not "giving back." We must be infinitely mindful of each thing that comes to our hand. So little of what we possess is truly ours.

Before you take silver and gold, says God, examine carefully how you came to receive it. Specifically with regard to business and money matters, go out of your way to ask, to be careful. The way to create and maintain harmony in society is to be careful of the property of others in the first instance. Giving back what was taken away restores the arithmetic, but not the moral balance. Think of the man jailed for a crime he did not commit. Freed after a year – or four decades – he will say, I am glad that justice was finally done. But then, the abstract notion of justice is all he has. No court on earth can restore his lost life, his lost years, his lost mental health and dignity, or the family whose lives have been wrecked.

What does this have to do with the giving of the Torah? Everything. It has to do with examining the inner nature of righteousness. That right and wrong are not defined by what I like, but depend on objective standards, especially with regard to protecting the weak, the minority, the disenfranchised. We dare not assume that we are in the right. Through ceaseless contemplation and self-observation, through constantly challenging our own assumptions, and through bottomless compassion for the rights of others, we must apply justice in every aspect of our lives.

It's tempting to get hung up on the letter of the law, because that doesn't require us to think about the world from anyone else's perspective. This is true whether discussing the Torah, the New Testament, the Qur'an, or the United States Constitution. But in every case, the foundational document is just that: a foundation, and we are responsible for building and maintaining a structure based on it.

The Talmud says Jerusalem was destroyed because the people became obsessed with the letter of the law and forgot that the letter is but the starting point. God requires us to go *beyond* the letter. To apply the underlying principles, rigorously, and with compassion and mercy. Therein lies the difference between law and justice. Let us continue to apply the lessons.

# 18

# We Will Do, and We Will Learn

*If it be now, 'tis not to come; if it be not to come, it will be now; if it be not now, yet it will come. The readiness is all.*

— Shakespeare, *Hamlet*

This week's Torah reading presents a long list of laws, after which Moses ascends Mount Sinai where he receives the entire Torah over the course of forty days and nights. The Torah is a cosmic fractal pattern wherein each component both embodies and reflects the whole. Approach any verse of the Torah and the commentaries will lead you to another, and to another and another in an eternal hyperlink. The entire Torah will emerge from any starting point. The Ten Sayings are categories of behavior God wants us to internalize. The meta-message of this week's reading is that individual laws are themselves categories of principles.

Before receiving the Torah, the Israelites loudly exclaim, "Everything that God commands we shall do and we shall hear!" (24:7). The word *hear* in Hebrew here means "pay attention to," "obey," "understand." This is universally interpreted to mean the Israelites were eager to assume their obligations under God's covenant and agreed in advance to observe all the rules, even the ones they didn't yet know about – which at that time was nearly all of them. This is a clear and straightforward statement of what is expected of adherents of any religion: to observe all the practices, even – or especially – the ones you don't understand.

This is a useful misinterpretation. Maintaining a society's identity rests upon a history of those who unquestioningly embraced the core message in the past. Like a nation's war dead, our having ancestors who clung to a belief system stokes the flames of empathy and identity in our breasts. How can we turn our backs on them? And weren't they somehow superior in their simple faith to us in the shiny modernity of our skepticism? Do we really believe that being better educated makes us superior to their unquestioning acceptance?

The challenge is to bring that faith forward into the realm of modernity, a task at which religious educators often fail because they are charged with maintaining homogeneity and exhorting their charges to embrace the core values of their closed religious community. Thus, religion comes to be represented by its lowest common denominator.

While there is much to criticize in organized religion, many of those who challenge religion seem to do so out of peevishness. They don't like being told what to do, and they believe a purely secular society provides utter freedom to the individual. But living organisms thrive in relational structures. We are only individuals insofar as we have a group within which to differentiate ourselves; from which we can distance ourselves or against which we can rebel.

If you reject existing structures, you must come up with a structure to replace them. Many people vociferously reject religion, yet are not capable of articulating on what their Goodness rests and often define it in vague and general terms: I don't kill; I don't lie; I don't cheat. This level is the moral equivalent of a society of three-year-olds; they participate correctly in group games because they mimic the older children with whom they play. But they can't explain what the rules are. They are members of the group, but they will never lead until they mature and examine the rules for themselves. We will never build anything of lasting value as long as our relationship with the world remains unexamined, as long as our identity of self goes unchallenged.

The purpose of applying the Torah's laws is to constantly learn their underlying principles. Religious observance should be an iterative process. Torah observance is not *only* the performance of ritual acts and specific commandments; the action must be paired with the lessons derived therefrom. Our job is not to serve God in a vacuum; it is to teach others to serve, to create a society based on charity and justice, to ensure a world in which God will be fully at home.

It's much easier to cling to the externals. And therein lies the danger, because people tend to subvert ideology to their own ends. Our finest institutions are misused to create human suffering for the benefit of the powerful, and no institution, no religion, no system of government, and no social philosophy is immune.

Those who reject organized religion – and there is good reason to do so – should be encouraged to come up with a robust alternative and not rely merely on being "good people." This one-sided morality is an abdication of responsibility that permits the worst excesses to take control of society. The market has become our religion, and "business" is our creed. Warren Buffet is the "prophet of Omaha." The dollar bill trumpets "In God We Trust." Under Socialism, the state owns the means of production. Under the latest avatar of capitalism, the means of production own the state. I lift up mine eyes unto Mammon. From whence cometh my salvation, if not from a bull market?

The message emanating from the Ten Sayings on Mount Sinai is that moral leadership requires clarity of vision. And make no mistake: the Torah demands moral leadership, not naked power and force of arms. It is not sufficient to know what is right; we also must know how to implement what is right within our sphere of influence. In our personal lives, within the family. In our work life, among our peers and counterparts. In the broader society and in the world. The Torah insists that there are, in fact, objective moral standards. This week's portion ends with a striking image of how difficult it is to bring them into practice.

Moses ascends Mount Sinai to God (24:13), while Joshua remains partway downhill. He and Moses call to one another, but Joshua can't see God. Further down still stand Aaron and the Elders, and below them are gathered the Israelites at the foot of the mountain. The imagery is powerful: every person and group stands in their designated spot within the hierarchy, yet none of them can see or fully interact with the others. If "seeing is believing," then what is the message of disembodied voices and indistinct sounds echoing up and down the mountainside in the mist and the dark clouds?

Joshua stands alone. He knows Moses is above, but he can't see what is going on. He hears sounds from the camp at the foot of the mountain, but cannot discern their meaning. Neither Moses, nor Aaron, nor the Elders will enter the Promised Land. Joshua, unprepared as he is, will be called upon to lead the next generation.

How will he lead them? What will he teach them? Joshua stands in a fog on the mountainside, perceiving only bits and pieces from above and below. This is the image of leadership: how to cut through the fog and learn the true core of the message; and how to cut through the confusion and communicate that message to the community. The process of continually learning the Torah's lessons provides the foundation for a just society. The danger is that people and their leaders cling to the outer framework and do not do the challenging work of delving to the heart of God's message. There, they risk finding out that they are wrong, that they are not as important as they thought. Remember that this was Joseph's greatness: he realized that his story was but a small piece of a vast narrative. And once he embraced his role, his true greatness emerged. How many of us are capable of such clarity of vision? Of such self-abnegation in service of a higher cause?

Joshua will not be ready when Moses hands over the mantle of leadership, just as Moses was not ready at the burning bush. The only figure in the Torah who was ready when God called was Abraham. God said, "Go," and he went immediately. Will we be ready when our moment of destiny calls? When the world needs us to stand up and act? And when will that moment come? Or has it come already and we weren't prepared?

As the Israelites said, we will do. And in that doing, we will also study and learn. We will learn the Torah's principles,

## The Weight of Gold

and we will learn to apply them more and more, and we will learn yet again from our doing. We must constantly work to derive the eternal principles from the Revelation at Sinai, we must stay attuned to God's message in every aspect of our daily lives. Destiny takes us by surprise. Let us nonetheless do everything we can to not be completely unprepared.

# 19

# Generous of Heart

*Let it be known there is a fountain
That was not made by the hands of men.*

– The Grateful Dead, *Ripple*

This week's Torah reading launches the grand project of building God's sacred dwelling place, a tent in the wilderness to house the sacred space which is the core of God's relationship with the people of Israel. Thus, God tells Moses to instruct the Israelites to bring contributions: "From each person whose heart makes them generous, you shall take My contribution" (25:2). These contributions – gold, silver, and copper; precious and semi-precious stones; spices, dyes, oil, animal skins, and wool – shall be used for the furnishings and fittings of the Tabernacle. Thus begins the project of creating God's sacred dwelling within the sacred space of the wilderness, a sacred emptiness surrounding Israel's relationship to God.

It was into the emptiness of the wilderness that God led the Israelites from Egypt. In this emptiness, God gave the manna and the Sabbath, and here God descended to give the Torah on Mount Sinai. (Note the Hebrew word, *ba-midbar*, meaning "in the wilderness," can also be read as *b'medaber*, "by means of speaking," or even, "while in the act of speaking." It is in the emptiness, the wilderness, that God speaks the words of the Torah.) Now God ordains that a structure, an address for God, shall be erected: "They shall make a sanctuary for Me, and I shall dwell in their midst" (25:8). The Torah connects us to the reality of living in the physical world – the world of space, time, and motion. Yet at the heart of the Tabernacle will reside a sacred emptiness. And it is there, in the emptiness at the core of the Tabernacle, that God will communicate with us.

Why "each person whose heart makes them generous"? Shouldn't everyone pay taxes? Those who have gold should bring gold, those who have only wool should bring wool, but everyone should bring something. Why does God specifically ask that contributions for God's earthly dwelling be taken only from those who are moved to generosity? Isn't the construction of the Tabernacle precisely the teachable setting in which all members of society should be encouraged to give according to their means?

The construction of the Tabernacle is a metaphor for the Creation. We are put on Earth to be God's partners, and though we are both spirit and body, we have an innate awareness that what is important is our spiritual part. Because we don't experience God physically, we believe our God-like part is the intangible. Thus, we strive to hold proper attitudes, we seek justice, we give charity and help the widow, the orphan, the sick, the poor, the stranger. But often we forget to sanctify our physical world, what the Bible refers to in various places as "the work of our hands." The Tabernacle teaches us that God's work proceeds not purely from the spiritual, but that we contribute our share to this joint project by transforming the physical world.

Creation is not a onetime event. The deistic concept of a God who made the universe, then walked away and let it run on its own, is foreign to the Torah. God's act of Creation is not in the past tense. It's not that God *did* create the universe; God *does* create the universe. God creates perpetually. At every instant, all of Creation is forever new. The flow of God's creative aspect is ceaseless and constantly renews Creation. The Torah instructs us, as God's partners, to create, too; to leave nothing out, from the lowest physical level to the highest spiritual plane.

The Tabernacle is also clearly a paradigm for a functioning society. God requires contributions of gold, silver, and copper, as well as wool (25:3). (To the modern–Western mind, this evokes the social classes in Plato's *Republic*, which are represented by gold, silver, bronze, and iron.) The Torah requires not a rigidly stratified society – although there are designated groups with unique access to parts of the community and unique permission to perform certain parts of the divine service – but a society in which each individual is encouraged to identify their specific gift and to realize their unique potential, to contribute their unique ability to the greater good. This is something an individual can accomplish only if they are aware of who they are, if they are motivated to dig within and then make a gift of what they have mined from their soul. This is generosity of heart.

At the very heart of the Tabernacle will stand the Ark of the Covenant. Atop the Ark, two gold statues of cherubim stand in a precisely described stance: their bodies turned away from each other, their faces turned back to look at one another, and their wings arched back over their heads. This creates an empty oval or round space bracketed by the Ark and the gold statues. And it is here that God will speak to Moses (25:22). God does not speak from the gold or the silver, nor from the wool or the precious stones; rather, God speaks from the emptiness framed by the wings of the cherubim. Though we live in the physical world, it is in the emptiness that we must seek God. In the spaces between our giving and our taking, our earning and our spending. The Torah is telling us that the physical world in which we live is itself the framework within which we shall seek the Divine. We cannot abandon the physical in search of the spiritual – rather, we must imbue the physical with the spiritual.

The generosity of heart God seeks is not merely a willingness to part with a bit of gold jewelry or a bag of silver coins – nor, for the poor, their gifts of wool. However significant the material gift, what the Torah seeks is the ongoing commitment of each human being to work to find their true inner self, to work ceaselessly to express that unique self, making it the very best it can be, and to apply the unique capacities of that inner self for the ongoing betterment of the world and society. True generosity resides not in the giving, but in the realization of the outcome for which the gift is designated. Otherwise we risk "making with Me gods of silver, gods of gold" (20:20).

We said last week that merely obeying God's negative commandments – thou shalt not steal, thou shalt not murder, and the 365 categories of negative commandments codified by the rabbis – does not make us good people. In general, it merely makes us not actively bad people. But from the hasidic perspective, there is also an active way to observe negative commandments, which is to identify our own inner appetites and desires.

I have never truly wanted to kill another human being. Thus, I must not compare myself to the murderer and gloat over my ability to control my urges. Rather, which are the urges I can't control? Those for sex, perhaps, or for alcohol, for cigarettes, for money. And what about my tendency to overeat? I must seek my own inner demons, however paltry they may seem in comparison to, say, Cain's slaughtering of his brother. In exploring my own uncontrollable urges, I will finally identify with people who commit horrible acts. If I fail the test of self-examination, self-honesty, then I can be of no use to others.

It comes as a shock the first time we realize that, if we had been part of the majority at any of the most horrific periods in history, we would have behaved the same as the others. We would have sent our friends and family to the concentration camps, to the Gulag. We would have fingered our next-door neighbors as being of the wrong ethnic group; we would have chopped them to death ourselves. Why do I say this? Because the overwhelming majority of humans – in all societies, and at every point in recorded history – have done the same. How dare I believe that I alone am different?

We are all a product of our environment. We intellectually subscribe to certain values today, but why should we believe we would live by those same values if born in a different place and time – and in the face of the opposition of the entire society? Why would we think for a moment that we, and we alone, would be the ones to stand up to the great evils of history? People who tell you they would have behaved differently from the majority have never truly looked into themselves.

By exploring what is darkest within ourselves, we activate tremendous power for good. If I know how badly I want to take what is not mine, to abuse other people physically or sexually or financially, to subjugate them for my own lust for power, then my restraint becomes a positive act full of spiritual force. With fearless insight into the dark complexities of our own soul we strive to purify our inner darkness in the service of God.

This is the deep reading of the famous verse from Ecclesiastes (2:13) translated as, "I realized that there is an advantage of wisdom over folly, like the advantage of light over darkness." The superficial reading is certainly true: light has advantages over darkness, and wisdom has advantages over folly. But in Hebrew, the preposition of comparison is the word *from*. Thus, the deeper reading is, "I saw that there is an advantage of wisdom *coming from* folly, like the advantage of light *coming from* darkness." Suddenly, a new world opens before us: the truest form of wisdom is that which comes from a fearless examination of our own folly. When we believe we know who we are, that is precisely the time to pause and look deep within. We are right to fear what we may find, but we should be much more fearful if we refuse to take that plunge. For why did God put us here if not to perfect ourselves? Put differently: we think we're unique – who are we kidding?

How do I make my heart generous? When the gold I give becomes part of the Tabernacle, I will never get it back. It will be melted down and no longer recognizable. It will neither return to me nor commemorate my giving. Through my desire to serve God, my contribution becomes eternally part of God's dwelling place. With my self-awareness and my openness to others, my drive to reach out and do the right thing, I become forever a driving part of the society in which I live.

From the willingness to give up the things I have, I make of myself the greatest gift of all.

# 20

# Of Leaders and Locusts

*Nearly all men can stand adversity, but if you want to test a man's character, give him power.*

– Abraham Lincoln

Here's the mock-profound question: "Why is there something instead of absolute nothingness?" Here's the real question: Why is there more than one thing? If God desired to create something, whether as an act of will, love, compassion, or loneliness, it would suffice to create just one thing. The great mystery of the universe is its diversification. Is the infinite diversity of Creation necessary?

In the Neo-Platonic world of Jewish thought, diversity proves the perfection of Creation; there is nothing that the universe does not contain. This week's Torah portion presents a microcosm of Creation, laying out ways for us to make our unique contribution to God's world. It does this through the elaborate preparation of the priestly clan to serve in the Tabernacle, and by portraying Moses as having the greatest leadership quality of all: that of knowing when to step aside.

This portion is voiced in future tense, beginning with the words, "And you will command." God is not merely commanding, but also describing the actions that Moses will take at the dedication of the Tabernacle – as well as reassuring Moses that he will, in fact, perform the rituals surrounding the consecration of the Tabernacle. Moreover, the use of the future tense anticipates next week's portion, where the sin of the Golden Calf threatens to derail God's enterprise. Despite this portion being a sequence of instructions to Moses, the formulaic verse, "And God spoke to Moses, saying," which appears repeatedly throughout the Torah, is absent. In fact, this is the only portion from the beginning of Exodus to the end of the Torah in which Moses' name does not appear at all. Aaron's name, however, appears seven times.

Maimonides says the importance of the opening words of the portion is the word *you*: do not delegate to another. Moses' name is missing from this portion because he must stand aside and relinquish all claim to the priestly title, yet he must personally ensure that the priestly role is perfectly executed.

## Dividing the leadership

Throughout the Exodus narrative, God works to transfer power and authority to humans. At first, Moses is the absolute, political and religious leader of the nation. He exercises the power God has urged on him. It is Moses who raises his staff and his hand at the splitting of the sea, causing the waters to flow back and drown the pursuing Egyptians. It is Moses who ascends Mount Sinai, who sits face-to-face with God, and who returns bearing the Tablets of the Law. Not long afterward, Moses' father-in-law, Jethro, teaches him that differentiation of authority is critical to a functioning society, whereupon Moses turns over political authority to a leadership structure. Later, he will further differentiate authority by turning over the religious leadership to his older brother, Aaron.

The rabbinic understanding is that Moses was supposed to be both king and priest, but he is disqualified from the post of High Priest on two grounds. First, he hesitated at the Burning Bush: when God called him, he was not ready to serve. Second, Moses killed the Egyptian, and one who has blood on his hands is not permitted to serve in the Temple. This theme finds its apotheosis in the narrative of King David, who consecrates the ground on which the Temple will be built, yet who will not live to see the building itself. Instead, his son Solomon will build the Temple – and though the Temple will stand, Solomon will subsequently fall through his own shortcomings.

Moses transfers his religious authority to Aaron through the act of clothing him. Although born the rightful bearer of the priesthood, Moses must transfer it of his own free will. If he does not give it over, then the priestly function, and with it the ability of the nation to seek closeness with God, will die with him. God instructs him to invest Aaron and his sons with their priestly office, describing their garments in detail. ("Investment:" literally, to be clothed in a garment.) Aaron remains in place as the religious figurehead and communicator. Moses announces and enacts the law, while Aaron tends to the ritual and spiritual needs of the nation. In this partnership, science and religion find their balance. Aaron is not a pretender, not a substitute; he steps into his brother's sandals and fully assumes the priesthood. This is a radical restructuring of society.

The Talmud says the priests had to be properly clad in their ritual garments, otherwise the Temple service was not valid: at the time that their priestly garments are upon them, their priesthood is upon them. Without being properly clothed, the sons of Aaron are only potential priests, not empowered to perform the divine service. Outside the Tabernacle, they remain bound by the prohibitions of their clan, but are not permitted access to God except under rigid rules of time, place, dress, and preparatory rituals. Even when not performing their official ritual duties, they are to behave with the dignity required of their roles as the representatives of the nation in the service of God.

Moses' embrace of God's instruction to give over the priesthood is the key to Moses' greatness. We saw this with Joseph, who reaches the fullness of his powers once he is freed from the need to be at the center of his family's narrative. So too, it is only when Moses emerges from the shadow of his birthright that he becomes free to achieve his own greatness. We are what we are born, yes. But may we not become more than that? To the extent we fall back on our birth identity, we deny ourselves the world and all that we can become. By contrast, the greatness we craft for ourselves is immeasurably superior to anything we are born with.

## Of locusts and mobs

Recall the plague of locusts. Locusts move in great clouds like a giant, evil spirit. Observing their behavior at close range, the rabbis of old pronounced that locusts have no king. Though they come and go together in tight formation, when they alight it is every locust for itself. They are a mob, not a society. If you have ever experienced a swarm of locusts, you will sympathize with Pharaoh. So terrifying was the plague of locusts that it is the only time Pharaoh expresses fear: "Pharaoh hurried to call Moses and Aaron and said, 'I have sinned against the Lord your God, and against you. Now please remove my sin also this time and entreat the Lord your God that He should remove from me this death!'" The locust swarm is terrifying in itself. It is also a frightening metaphor for human behavior. The identity of the raging mob is humanity's bottom-line birthright.

Before Sinai, the Israelites are a mob. They move together, but they look out only for themselves, driven to survive. Jethro instructs Moses in structuring a hierarchy, enabling orderly human expression within the infinite differentiation of God's Creation. Once we relinquish our mob identity, we can become aware of our unique place in the world, embrace our unique gifts. Once we become aware of our uniqueness, we can appreciate the uniqueness of others. We can band together in a community. Only once we embrace our own – and each other's – unique place in God's infinitely differentiated world are we ready to receive the Torah. True spiritual practice comes not from withdrawing from society, but through embracing our role as a contributing member of society. It is neither challenging nor spiritually defensible to be a moral person when you are alone on a mountaintop eating carob fruit and drinking from a stream.

Moses accepted Jethro's advice and radically changed his approach with regard to political leadership. The establishment of hierarchy tamed the mob and pushed people to embrace their unique roles in society. So too with the priesthood. Like society itself, religion is also a team sport. Our yearning for spiritual fulfillment stands in service to organized religion, and not the other way around. One should never make the mistake of believing otherwise. Organized religion arises of its own in human society. Like the locust, it seeks neither good nor evil, but merely to thrive. And like every other organism in nature, it will consume everything in its path.

Secular political structure, wherein power is based on earthly principles, is subject to challenge. Not so the authority of religion. Kings are bad enough, but so are priests. History reveals again and again the terrible destruction that follows when the two combine. Religion has been the too-willing handmaid to war, the government the too-eager enforcer of the church's agenda for the state's illegitimate gain.

Here, right where it all begins, God makes the determination to separate church and state. And it is precisely because of Moses' greatness in stepping down from the priesthood that the Torah can teach this eternal lesson. He lost part of his birthright, only to forge ahead and create greatness in the way he lived his life.

The greatness of Aaron and his sons lies in their acceptance of their place within society. Priests must be clothed: their role must be made visible. They are not inherently close to God, but have the ability to approach God when properly prepared. The rest of the time, their uniqueness rests not in closeness to God, but in guarding against behavior that would prevent their coming close when called upon.

Throughout history, church and state naturally arise as twin pillars. They are both the critical foundation and the necessary evils of human society. States collapse into corruption and decay, we as individuals allow our appetites, our urges, and especially our anger to rule our actions. Just as a functioning society requires each member to do their part, we can achieve our own destiny only when all that is within us works in harmony.

# 21

# Erase Me!

*Like anybody, I would like to live a long life – longevity has its place. But I'm not concerned about that now.*

– Martin Luther King, Jr.

If the purpose of a religious text is to cement its dogma in the hearts of its adherents and to strengthen their commitment with a straightforward depiction of the acceptable versus the unacceptable, this week's Torah portion so powerfully transmits its message of organized religion that it risks leaving us incapable of seeing its inherent dangers.

At the core of the portion is the sin of the Golden Calf. If the book of Genesis is a list of genealogies strung together by a narrative, the book of Exodus is concerned with the consequences of the Revelation at Sinai and the process of giving over the law. For all their drama, stories are generally not the point of the Torah. They serve to illustrate underlying concepts, and also emphasize the unpredictability of God's supreme creation, the human being. But stories also appear to signal that God has not communicated clearly, or that we have not heard well.

If the book of Exodus were only about God conveying the law, it would be very short indeed, ending the moment Moses receives the two tablets of stone "inscribed by the finger of God" (31:18). But just as the book of Genesis is about the family of Abraham coming to terms with the consequences of God's covenant with their ancestor, the book of Exodus is awash in the disarray of a fledgling nation struggling to come to terms with a new form of covenant, one which embraces both the individual and the communal, the particular and the universal.

While Moses is on the mountaintop with God, the Israelites

below are seized by panic. Like infants who shriek when their mother walks out of the room, the people assume that Moses will never come back. Desperate for a leadership figurehead, they create an idol, and the rest of the portion (chs. 32–34) is taken up with the Golden Calf and its aftermath.

But again, this portion is not "about" the Golden Calf; it is still part of the main narrative about the significant event of Moses' receiving the Written Torah and learning its interpretation from the mouth of the Creator: what is known as the Oral Torah. Like Eve and Adam with the fruit, the episode of the Golden Calf is not what the Torah is about; it is what humans are about. It is about what happens when we are not keeping our eye on the core principles by which we say we live.

"Hurry up!" the Israelites cry. "Let's make gods to lead us, because this man Moses who brought us out of Egypt, we don't know what has become of him!" (32:1). A group used to being told what to do, they panic when there is no longer anyone to tell them. Yet recall the sage advice Jethro gave to Moses and ask, Where were the leaders? Where were the Elders, and where were the designated Heads of Tens and Heads of Hundreds? Without the support of the hierarchy, the best Aaron can do is to give in to the demands of the mob. Under pressure, and without Moses at their head, the entire structure crumbles in an instant.

A word to those who exercise leadership, or who would: the power of the leader can quickly become absolute. People willingly abdicate their own responsibility and judgment when there is a strong leader – or even a weak one. The leader must be aware of his or her own capacity, either to cause the group to do good or to bring about tremendous harm through not being aware of the ramifications of leadership or by believing that things can somehow run themselves. Leaders do not get vacations. They walk away, even briefly, at the peril of the enterprise.

The immediate and dizzying descent into idol worship and chaos is not an exaggerated parable. People really do behave this way the moment the strictures are off. Societies need structure, and a leadership void unleashes a terrifying blend of anarchy, mingled with the search for an autocrat. Napoleon understood this fully in 1795 when he saved the Revolution, putting down the royalist revolt. Within four years, he had undermined that same Revolution. He became the ruler of France and, by 1804, the revolutionaries who did away with the king overwhelmingly elected him emperor.

The replacement of God by a golden god is nothing new. It's tempting to blame the chaos on the institution of religion itself, but we should remind ourselves that the three greatest human disasters of the twentieth century were under the antireligious movements of Lenin and Stalin, Hitler, and Mao. Wars are never purely about religion, though religion is a handmaid to mass violence.

Organized religion serves an important, unifying role in society, and it can work to the good under wise leadership. Left to their own devices, people search out ways to express the instinct to tribalism. In our panic to align with people most like ourselves, we seek the lowest common denominator, and we viciously shut out anyone who fails to conform to the most simplistic bottom line. The more unsophisticated the basis for unity, the more likely that challenges to this identity will be met with anger and violence. When we fail to examine the basis for our own identity, the natural response to outsiders is primal rage.

Did Moses go up the mountain too soon in the history of Israel's wanderings? Was that his fault? Was it God's fault? Should Moses have waited, perhaps ascended the mountain a month later? Or a year? No matter when Moses went up the mountain, and for no matter how brief an absence, the sense of a vacuum would remain. Someone would become anxious. Someone would attempt to step in and take over. Perhaps, then, it was best that the Israelites got this out of their system early. If the scene had taken place a year later, with more of a group identity and more of a leadership structure in place, perhaps there would have been not mass religious hysteria but a bloody coup that would have left a people with a political identity – but without a Torah.

If leadership requires constant attention to the community, it also calls for tireless advocacy on the latter's behalf, and Moses comes back in stunning form when God makes him the ultimate offer: "I will wipe them out and I will make you into a great nation" (32:7–10). Moses will continue to lead, and his own descendants will be God's chosen.

Here ensues a striking bit of language in a heated exchange between God and Moses. Moses acknowledges the magnitude of the sin of the Golden Calf when he uses the Hebrew term "to lift up," which in the context of the following oddly structured verse can mean forgiveness: "And now, if You would only forgive their sin; and if not, then erase me from the book You have written!" (32:32). But "lift up" is also the term God uses earlier to tell Moses to take a census: "When you lift up the heads of the Israelites…" (30:12). Using the same term in the same sense in the later verse, the text invites a stronger translation: "But now," says Moses, "if You're going to count up their sins, then erase me from the book."

Moses tells God that we humans are imperfect. That by our nature, we will make mistakes – even the gravest of errors. Moses presses the point home. If God is so willing to throw away the Israelite people, then why did God make such a fuss at the burning bush? When Moses said it wouldn't work, why didn't God reply, "Yeah, I guess you're right. Bad idea"? Because God made a promise to Abraham, and the Israelite nation is the fulfillment of that promise, regardless of how many obstacles they themselves throw in the way. God sought a partner in this world and found Abraham. Now, God is stuck with the promise, the covenant God made. Be careful what you wish for, someone might have told God.

Partners in a committed relationship are often on different wavelengths. Couples who do not communicate openly about their feelings experience these as periods of stress. If not addressed, these pressures can wreck a relationship. It is frightening to open up to another person, frightening to acknowledge that I may feel less connected to you right now than you need me to be. Each partner in a relationship must be willing to hear the other's distress, the other's sense of alienation, without reacting with anger or resentment. This is a tremendous challenge. But it is liberating, and immensely strengthening to a relationship, to be allowed to discuss these emotional discontinuities without fear that it will destroy what the partners have built. What they continue to work toward.

Relationships are both past-based and forward-looking. In the moment, every emotion feels eternal, and the brain is structurally incapable of differentiating between emotion and objective fact. Thus, it is scary to face those moments when we feel out of sync with our partners. At such moments, we feel our relationship will die. We fear that Moses will never return from the mountain.

And so Moses says to God, This is what You asked for. This is the basis on which I agreed to this task. Says Moses, We're in this together. It is the ultimate expression of Moses' leadership. At a time when the Israelites have lost faith in themselves, when even God has lost faith in them, Moses believes in them.

Believe in yourself, and remember that your every act has consequences. We are obligated to work to build the good, to remedy the bad. The time is short, and the task is great, and it falls to each of us to do our part.

## 22

# The Consequences of Creation

*I have finally found a place to live*
*Just like I never could before*
*And I know I don't have much to give,*
*But soon I'll open any door*

– Eric Clapton (Blind Faith),
*The Presence of the Lord*

This week's portion opens with the laws of the Sabbath, then shifts to a detailed description of the making of the Tabernacle's elements and furnishings. The Sabbath is the crowning moment of Creation; it is reflected in the Tabernacle, the fulcrum that brings humans into partnership with God. God makes time, which we sanctify by observing the Sabbath. God also makes the world of space and motion, where we now build a physical Tabernacle that will be sanctified by God's Presence. The Tabernacle's parts are listed in this portion, and they will be fastened together and the final structure erected in the next Torah portion. Thus, the Tabernacle reenacts Creation as the concrete enactment of our partnership with God.

The Tabernacle differs from the Creation in Genesis. There, the consequences of Creation play out as the world of space, time, and motion starts behaving differently from the way it is intended to behave. This is every creator's experience – and that of every parent. We envision a perfect design; which, however, never quite translates into execution. Disorder is an unavoidable concomitant of every creative act, and of God's Creation no less than ours.

This may not always be obvious to us in the natural world, but it emerges once humans enter the picture. The natural world's constraints of space, time, and motion – of sequence – force us into the thorn bush of free choice, where to choose one thing is necessarily to forsake another. We cannot both stand still and move at the same time; we cannot be both asleep and awake; we cannot both slay and protect, cannot both speak and be silent. This interplay of desire paired with loss, of success tinged by eternal disappointment – longing for what can never be – lies at the heart of the human condition.

The primary consequence of every human act of creation is that the created thing is going to be different from the envisioned image and plan. This same tension plagues God's Creation, with the highest level of misunderstanding, of disobedience and error, reserved for humans. Unlike God's act of Creation, which it reflects, the Tabernacle will be perfect in every dimension, unerringly balanced and exquisitely executed. Paradoxically, the Torah uses this state of perfect equilibrium to underscore the superiority of God's perfect Creation: balance equals stagnation; a perfectly balanced Creation is the result of artifice. God *creates,* while humans merely *make.* We take finished bits of God's creation and fashion them into an immovable piece. The very exactness with which the Tabernacle is executed announces its inferiority. God's creative force flows eternally through all things; the creative work of building the Tabernacle takes place once, during the lifetimes of its builders. They die, and the structure remains because, in a cosmic sense, it too is dead.

The Tabernacle is the focal activity by which the Israelites bind themselves to God in the wilderness. By reenacting God's work of Creation, we both embrace and enact our eagerness to take on what the rabbis call the yoke of Torah, our acceptance of our obligations as God's servants.

The Sabbath is the focus of Creation, perhaps even its ultimate goal, and it is the core defining practice of Judaism. The Sabbath was given to Israel in the wilderness before the revelation and the giving of the Torah on Mount Sinai. One of the major liturgical poems sung at the inauguration of the Sabbath every Friday evening states this explicitly with the verse, "Last in realization, first in conceptualization." The Sabbath imbues human time with sanctity. In Hebrew, the names of the days of the week reflect that all time emanates from the Sabbath: first day, second day, third day (Sunday, Monday and Tuesday), and so on up to sixth day, the eve of the Sabbath.

The Sabbath is the touchstone for human acts of creation as well. While creative work is prohibited on the Sabbath itself, proper observance of the Sabbath requires us to work for six days, and only then to rest on the seventh. Like God at the Creation, our Sabbath comes only after a week filled with labor. Mystics tell us that human activity on earth causes activity in heaven. Just as heaven reaches down to sanctify the Sabbath, our actions on the Sabbath touch heaven itself. This relationship of the Tabernacle to the Sabbath, and to God's act of Creation, is more than metaphorical. The Sabbath is the day on which we return the world to God's keeping.

The commandment to "rest" on the Sabbath entails desisting from a range of activities derived from the work of making the Tabernacle and its furnishings, and it remains the basis for Sabbath observance today. Thus, prohibited "work" on the Sabbath includes such activities as farming, because animals were shorn and skinned, and their wool and hides fashioned into curtains and coverings within the Tabernacle; wheat was harvested to bake bread that was offered in the Tabernacle; and plants were grown, their fibers used for weaving and their colors for dyes. Kindling and maintaining a fire are prohibited, because the priests maintained a constant flame on the altar, and because the eternal light burned in the Menorah. Cooking is prohibited because it requires the use of flame, and breads were baked and animal offerings burned in the Tabernacle.

Underlying all this is a fundamental restraint from intervening to change God's world. On the Sabbath, the mechanism of running the world – and all choices and decisions – reverts to God. For a night and a day, we suspend human striving and dwell as recipients of God's graciousness, grateful and humble, meditative and prayerful.

Now Moses commands, "Let all whose hearts are *generous* bring it, a donation for God.... And every *wisehearted* one among you, let them come and make what God has commanded: the Tabernacle and its tent and its cover" (35:5, 10). We have emphasized the words *generous* and *wise* to bring out the Torah's message: generosity provides the raw materials, a bounty of gold, silver, and copper, of animal skins and dyed wool, of wood – rare in the desert – and spices, oils, and pigments. Tempering generosity, wisdom provides the work of turning these raw materials into the Tabernacle and its furnishings. Every proper act of creation balances giving and holding back, excess and restraint.

Every act of creation is fundamentally an act of generosity, the ability – or the compelling urge – to share what is most precious to us, to give it over to someone else. In God's case, before the act of Creation, there was no one else. Some hasidic masters describe Creation as a pure expression of God's generosity, the only one of God's infinite aspects that does not completely fulfill itself, as by definition it requires an Other to give to. God's Creation is the ultimate act of generosity, creating both what is shared and those with whom to share it:

> And all the congregation of Israel departed from before Moses. And everyone whose heart inspired them came; everyone whose spirit moved them to generosity brought a contribution for God for the work of the tent of meeting and its service, and for the holy garments. And the men came as well as the women, everyone of generous heart brought bracelets and nose-rings, and rings, and body-ornaments, all ornaments of gold, everyone who lifted up an offering of gold to God. (35:20–22).

Not every Israelite returns with gifts, though many do, contributing so much that there is an imbalance of overflowing generosity. The words "generous" and "bring" resound in these verses. Biblical scholar Richard Elliott Friedman notes a foreshadowing of the book of Leviticus, where overwhelming generosity will collide with God's restrictive specifications and result in the death of Aaron's two sons. The verse (35:29), "Every man and woman whose heart moved them to bring for all the work…," twice juxtaposes the Hebrew words *nediv*, "generous"; and *heviu*, "they brought." These Hebrew roots echo the names of Aaron's oldest sons, Nadab and Abihu, who will feature in the central episode of the book of Leviticus – what I will argue is, in fact, the central episode of the entire Torah.

As we said at the beginning of this piece, after restating the laws of the Sabbath, Moses lists the items to be brought for the Tabernacle. Then he pauses to go up the mountain and receive the first set of tablets, as if to say, Be wise, don't act without thinking through the consequences of your actions; then take action. Measure twice, cut once. He instructs the people, Bring out of generosity tempered with wisdom. Bring prudently. Be not like the one who loved not wisely, but too well, for that way lies tragedy.

Moses already took God's Torah and destroyed it once, then rewrote it as a book to live by. Now Moses takes the essence of God's command – that we give our all for God and for Torah – and frames a legalistic concept of restraint. Our noble sentiments, sparked by the experience of spiritual loftiness as we carry out God's command, express themselves in generosity. But generosity must be kept within proper bounds, lest it become excess. This theme of unthinking kindness becoming a destructive force plays out repeatedly throughout the Torah.

Which is perhaps the answer to the question: Why do "all the congregation of Israel" depart from before Moses, but only some, "whose heart inspired them," return? Perhaps some Israelites remember the last time they were bidden to bring precious things: they threw their gold earrings into a molten mass from which arose the Golden Calf. Those earrings, representing the very ears that heard God at Sinai, now became the instruments of abandoning God. Yet here, many people do return, bringing all manner of gold jewelry. Indeed, this is what they were about to be commanded when interrupted by the episode of the Golden Calf (ch. 33.).

Now the process unfolds according to the program. The components of the Tabernacle are made, each precisely according to instruction. By the end of next week's portion, which closes the book of Exodus, the Tabernacle will stand and the Presence of God will fill it.

The purpose of the Tabernacle is to bring atonement for Israel's sins, both for wrongs done to another human being and for departures from God's ritual requirements. It is itself an acknowledgment of the overwhelming imperfection that runs through Creation. Yet its components fit together precisely as intended. Each serves perfectly its designated role and the Tabernacle will rise exactly as planned. Exactly as commanded. From the human perspective, God's Creation appears flawed, while our own creation is perfect.

It is far easier to make a perfect tent than to build a perfect society, far easier to make sure that pieces of cloth are all the same size than to ensure that all people receive equal treatment before the law. The Tabernacle is a metaphor for human perfection – it is critical for the fulfillment of God's ritual commandments, but in the human sphere it is only a metaphor. The test will be, not how closely does the Tabernacle correspond to the Torah's written plan, but how closely will our actions correspond to the Torah's expectations.

## 23

# A Full Accounting

*If most of us remain ignorant of ourselves it is because self-knowledge is painful and we prefer the pleasures of illusion.*

– Aldous Huxley

This week, we come to the final reading in the book of Exodus. The Tabernacle, so much spoken of, is raised for the first time (40:17). The closing verses of Exodus provide a literary full stop: Moses completes the work of erecting the Tabernacle, whereupon God's Presence and glory – concretized in a cloud – cover and fill the structure so that even Moses cannot enter. Perfection, it would seem. Or is it?

If, as the rabbis say, the Tabernacle is a replay of the Creation, where does Israel stand now that they have recreated Creation? The portion opens with, and takes its title from, the most multifaceted word in the Hebrew Bible – *paqad*. This root gives rise to a range of words, all revolving around relationships between unequal parties: one party either takes responsibility for the other, or demands something of the other; one party bestows on the other something of great value, or requires that the other bear some obligation.

"And God *remembered* Sarah..." (Gen. 21:1). "And the head executioner *appointed* Joseph..." (Gen. 40:4). "God will surely *remember* you..." (Gen. 50:25), says Joseph to his brothers. "I have surely *remembered* you..." (Ex. 50:25), God instructs Moses and Aaron to reassure the Israelites in Egypt, to tell them that the time of redemption has come.

In all these passages, the italicized words are from the same *paqad* root. Other meanings associated with this root include: to examine or inspect; to have a marital connection with someone; to decree upon; to command; to give or deposit something as security; to charge someone with a duty; to count, as in a census; and – notably – to provide an accounting.

"These are the *accounts* of the Tabernacle," opens the portion (38:21), "... *tabulated* according to Moses' instruction."

This closing reading of Exodus could indeed have been written by an accountant. It presents a detailed inventory of the elements of the Tabernacle and its furnishings: the garments and regalia prepared for Aaron and his sons, the Ark of the Covenant, the altars and table for bringing offerings – all these, and more. The details are emphasized and listed: the tent pegs, rings, and hooks; the sockets, ropes, and poles; the boards and pillars; and the coverings of animal skins and wool. The accounting of the priestly garments includes the shoulder straps; the chains to hold the breastplate, as well as its carved stones – each by name; the materials and colors of robes, tunics, and headgear. The altars are recorded, together with their appurtenances of lattice-work, copper laving bowls, utensils for bringing offerings, and the incense and salves used in the Tabernacle service. True to its opening words, with the completion of the work, everything is accounted for.

In its dry and detailed listing of each element of the Tabernacle, this portion foresees the didacticism of the book of Leviticus, which is an instruction manual for the priestly service. We have told so many stories, the text seems to be saying. We listed everywhere we went and everyone we encountered; now let us also mention everything we carried with us, all that we put to use to execute the design of God's earthly dwelling.

After the splitting of the sea, when God's miracles are once again hidden, the people accuse Moses of bringing them into the desert to perish. When Moses ascends Mount Sinai to receive the Torah, they turn to a god of gold – precisely the practice that God has explicitly forbidden in the Decalogue.

While the Tabernacle has taken up much of the book of Exodus, it is receiving the Torah and God's revelation at Mount Sinai which constitute Israel's greatest moment in the wilderness. A major function of the Tabernacle – and later, of the Temple at Jerusalem – is to atone for the sins of

Israel. Thus it is worth emphasizing that the commandments regarding the Tabernacle are given to Moses at the moment of the sin of the Golden Calf. In the aftermath of the Golden Calf, the construction of the Tabernacle brings order emerging from chaos.

If the Tabernacle is the corrective for a people who are forever breaking faith with their God and with their leaders, then what message does this extensive inventory convey?

The Hebrew word for Tabernacle is *Mishkan*, from the verb "to dwell." This root first appears when God stations cherubim at the gates of Eden, to keep Adam and Eve out (Gen. 3:24): "And [God] *positioned* to the east of the Garden of Eden the cherubim and the fiery sword turning this way and that way to guard the path to the Tree of Life." The cherubim now return to dwell at the heart of the Tabernacle, where they become the gate providing access to God.

The two cherubim stand atop the Ark of the Covenant. Their arching wings – hovering close, yet never touching – form an emptiness from which God addresses Moses, and through him, the entire nation of Israel. Unlike the cherubs placed at the gates of Eden to keep humanity out, these cherubim invite us into intimate dialogue with God. The Tablets of the Law, residing within the Ark, are given not only to Moses; all humanity participates in the divine conversation. Finally, we have turned around the narrative of rejecting God's authority. The Tabernacle brings us back to that most intimate of relationships, the face-to-face encounter with God. Eve and Adam ate the fruit, and they were banned from God's Presence. Now Israel, who worshiped the calf of gold, are invited back into God's Presence – indeed, God has taken the first step, instructing that a physical dwelling be erected.

At Mount Sinai, God's revelation was overpowering. The Israelites cowered in fear and told Moses to go forward on his own. Now the Ark of the Covenant rests at the center of the Tabernacle, the Tablets of the Law resting within. Unlike much of the unsuccessful communication in Genesis, God has decided to limit God's own Presence to a tiny space at the heart

*Exodus*

of the complex structure of the Tabernacle. God has chosen a new way of speaking with us; perhaps by communicating one word at a time, God hopes we may be able to assimilate it. Now we must meet God's message by revealing our own inner essence. Word by word, we must make a full and honest spiritual accounting: Who am I, really? What unique gifts set me apart from all humanity, and how can I best use them in the service of my destiny? What shortcomings limit my ability to move toward that destiny, and how can I guard against them? What does God expect from me – now, and at every moment?

We are told that this world is broken. Yet we each hold one small tool, and when we know how to work in harmony, we can make progress toward repairing it. We, who could not withstand the voice of God at Mount Sinai – can it be that we are sent to save the rest of humanity? The answer is Yes. Beginning with ourselves. Yes, the world is broken. But so are we. And it is precisely in the awareness of our own brokenness that we open ourselves to God's wisdom. God has invited us back into Eden. In order to enter, we must give a full accounting of ourselves. For surely, God will call us to account.

# *Leviticus*

24 • *Va-Yikra*       (1:1 – 5:26)
25 • *Tzav*           (6:1 – 8:36)
26 • *Shemini*        (9:1 – 11:47)
27 • *Tazria*         (12:1 – 13:59)
28 • *Metzora*        (14:1 – 15:33)
29 • *Acharei Mot*    (16:1 – 18:30)
30 • *Kedoshim*       (19:1 – 20:27)
31 • *Emor*           (21:1 – 24:23)
32 • *Be-Har*         (25:1 – 26:2)
33 • *Be-Huqqotai*    (26:3 – 27:34)

# 24

# Render unto God

*If it weren't for the sins the holy book would've been / smaller.*
— Mahmoud Darwish, *A State of Siege*

*The one lamb you shall offer in the morning, and the other lamb you shall offer at twilight.*
— Exodus 29:39

This week we begin the book of Leviticus. Storytelling, as we have seen, both conveys and interrupts the Torah's flow of lawgiving. Conveys, because our human consciousness is based on narrative – we make sense of the world by means of our stories. Interrupts, because the transmission of the laws is repeatedly thrown off course by human actions, forcing the text – and God – to switch course. Eve and Adam eat the fruit, capsizing the project of Creation. Cain kills Abel, leaving God in shock. Yet only after Noah emerges from the Ark does God explicitly prohibit murder. Abraham challenges God to be merciful at Sodom; God reverses the positions later, as though asking Abraham, "How does it feel to hold the knife at your own son's throat?" After the sin of the Golden Calf, God instructs Moses to build the Tabernacle, turning what was meant to be God's dwelling into the means of atonement.

The stories also provide broad frames of reference – a "Torah's-eye view" of history. Genesis lays out the fundamental nature of the characters whose descendants populate the Bible; a biological human family that will become the nations of the world, arising from a core of infinite possibility – Adam – and fragmenting into a multiplicity of identities. As readers, we experience these identities as fundamental character types. More than mythic archetypes, real people embody ways of seeing, as well as behaving in the world, and the differences between them give rise to the very human conflicts and – fewer – triumphs that fill the Bible's pages.

Exodus introduces the problems of revelation. Humans need an intellectual experience of the world, as well as an emotional and imaginative one. We need both fact and faith; the head as well as the heart. Science, to describe the world; faith, to teach us how to act in the world. When God stands revealed at Sinai, the faith part of the brain is confounded: God is no longer "religious," but "scientific." No longer believed in, but tangible. As much as the direct experience of the miraculous ratifies our faith, it undermines it, too, because of the impossibility of replicating spiritual experiences. How are we to bring together fact and faith? How are we to serve God in the physical world?

We come now to the central book of the five books of the Torah. Here we find compact lists of highly specific instructions for the priestly rituals in the Tabernacle. The name Leviticus signifies that this book pertains to the tribe of Levi. Specifically, it relates the laws of the Kohanim – the priestly Levite clan of Aaron and his descendants. Here the Torah retreats from the flow of storytelling and marches resolutely into listing and commenting on the ritual laws.

It may be that ritual laws need to be seen purely in technical terms. Illustrative stories about offerings of incense and slaughtered bulls and goats ultimately come down to images of God enjoying food, drink, and pleasurable smells, and the rabbis fight long and hard against the anthropomorphic view of God. Perhaps by now the reader understands that the Torah is a book of laws and doesn't need as much storytelling to stay engaged, and it may feel less challenging to take in this flow of ritual laws in this prescriptive telling. The moral quandary of Adam – who truthfully says, "God, you gave me the woman, and the woman gave me the fruit…" or of Cain, who says, "I didn't know that I am my brother's keeper" – these do not plague us as we slog through lists of livestock and the details of the sacrifices.

There are, in fact, two stories later in Leviticus, one of

which is a shocking depiction of the Torah's world. But for the most part, the book breezes by without incident. As an (almost) uninterrupted recital of rules, Leviticus is arguably the most "Torah-like" of the five books.

Still, humans need more than rules. We need reasons. And we do not understand reasons from explanations; rather, we internalize them through observing behavior, and through narrative. Leviticus is just short enough to hold our attention and manages to end before we lose interest entirely. Yet because it focuses on ritual, the book goes to the core of our relationship with God. If organized religion is a dangerous behemoth – as we saw in the latter portions of Exodus – it is also a unique vehicle for individuals to craft a personal relationship with the Divine. Within the Tabernacle, we meet God in the most intimate of terms, as a pure voice floating in the void of the Sacred Space. Finally, God is invisible once again, and perhaps that is enough for the mystery to return.

It is to this aspect of religion that Leviticus speaks. It opens with a highly detailed list of sacrifices and offerings, and begs the question of why we engage in such practices at all. It is to this fundamental question that we now turn: If we can begin to formulate an understanding of the sacrificial offerings, we will find within them the key that unlocks the door to a direct intimacy with God. Who knew organized religion could provide such a thing? Obviously, the Torah knows, and it is bursting with the desire to teach us.

The sacrificial offerings detailed in Leviticus are the human key to our intimate relationship with God, a relationship predicated on giving.

The human need to share lies at the basis of relationships, of society and its institutions. It lies at the heart of art and invention – and certainly at the heart of organized religion. This need is by no means the only component of these social structures, but it is an indispensable driving force in all of them. The Talmud says the most important verse in the Torah is, "The one lamb you shall offer in the morning, and the second lamb you shall offer at twilight" (Ex. 29:39, also

Num. 28:4). This elevates the repeated daily ritual of giving to God to the status of a be-all of Jewish practice. (Similarly, the giving of *tzedaka*, charity, is frequently referred to as the single most all-encompassing religious commandment.)

What purpose do the sacrifices serve? Benjamin Franklin wrote that whenever he came to a new place, he would seek out the most important and influential man in the community and ask him for a favor. Franklin understood the profound and counterintuitive psychological truth that people would rather give to others than take from them; would rather have others in their debt than be in debt to others. The moment we contemplate giving a gift or providing assistance, our emotional engines kick in. We begin formulating an emotional attachment to the person – even a complete stranger, building a positive opinion of them, such that we actually *want* to do the favor, give the gift, offer the charity, such that we feel good about it afterward.

The Hebrew word for love – *ahava* – comes from the verb "to give," and numerous commentators have observed that more than the love encourages the giving, the act of giving generates the love. We are bound in love to those who depend on us; the more helpless, the stronger our emotional bond. We dissolve with aching love at the tears of our newborn child, we melt with poignant delight as we fondle a kitten or puppy. The more we give to others, the more we draw close to them. The ultimate closeness, teaches the Torah, the ultimate intimacy, is with God. If the act of giving generates love, how much must God love us, having given us our very lives, this whole world? And the Torah, to teach us our place in it?

Yet offerings to God look like the ultimate example of, "What do you give to the man who has everything?" The answer is that our offerings are not for God. They are our training in gratitude, in opening ourselves to the relationship that our own soul desires. A visible God is spiritually problematic, but our own need to give remains a mystery, enabling us to ground our spiritual work in the exercise of freely giving. In our own practice of compassion and generosity, we find the source of our own gratitude, our personal connection to the Eternal. Today, the rituals of the Tabernacle and the Temple are replaced by daily prayer, by the daily giving of charity, by the weekly observance of the Sabbath, and by the seasonal and annual round of the holidays. And, not least, by the annual cycle of reading the Torah. Through joining together in ritual, and through selflessly giving to the stranger, we devote our time, our energy, and our money to our relationship with God, thereby creating within ourselves a sense of attachment. It is a way of opening our own hearts.

Just as a world-class athlete must train each day, a spiritual practitioner must engage in daily observances. This is why it is called religious *practice*. The Talmud teaches that, over time, through constantly performing religious observances even by rote, one internalizes the values and the message, and ultimately comes to observe the practices for their own sake. We connect to our own unique relationship to God.

The book of Leviticus is an instruction manual. If the Torah is the user's manual for the human soul, Leviticus is the guide to installation and maintenance. In our daily search for spiritual connection, we need all the help we can get, and ritual, well applied, is an important tool. Each action taken in isolation seems weary and stale. Flat and unprofitable. But taken together and repeated over time, our constant offering of ourselves to God strengthens the soul within us, teaching us to discover new depths within and enabling us to reach out to support others and to fully contribute to the world.

Leviticus exhorts us to make of ourselves an offering. Every day. Each morning and each evening. Constantly.

# 25

# Sacrifices of Love

*I don't know how to love him...*

– *Jesus Christ, Superstar,*
by Webber & Rice

This week's Torah portion is a straightforward accounting, a long list of offerings and sacrifices to be brought by the priests. While the types of offerings are specified, the underlying reasons are left for other passages. This portion lists, among others, the burnt offering, the meal offering, the inaugural offering brought by new priests, the sin offering, the thanksgiving offering, and other aspects of the priestly ritual.

These are the offerings "which God commanded Moses on Mount Sinai on the day God commanded the children of Israel to bring near their offerings to God in the wilderness of Sinai" (Lev. 7:37–38).[1] The Hebrew word most commonly used to designate sacrifices or offerings to God is *korban*, from the root meaning "to draw near." Offerings are ways in which we seek to draw near to God. This is exemplified by the very first offerings in human history. The first is Cain's gift. There, the Hebrew word used is *mincha*, meaning a gift given freely. This is copied immediately by Abel. When God contemplates this, the first human invention, God decides that Cain's concept is acceptable, but Abel's execution is superior.

The next offering in the Torah is Noah's, which is again spontaneous. Noah has been saved from death; his response is to slaughter animals as a sign of gratitude – the very animals he just saved from the Flood. This foreshadows rabbinic interpretations of the sacrifices as stand-ins for us:

---

[1] Unless otherwise noted, all references in this section are to the book of Leviticus.

we transgressed, and we deserve punishment. Rather than be killed ourselves, we buy an animal and slit its throat, offering its life – and our expensive asset – to God in our stead.

God smells the pleasant odor of Noah's burnt offerings, yet God's reaction is not one of mercy and compassion so much as of resignation, perhaps even disgust: "The imaginings of man's heart evil even from his youngest days" (Gen. 8:21). Humans are incorrigible, God reflects. They will never learn. God, it seems, has destroyed the world for naught.

Each weekly Torah reading is followed by a reading from the prophetic books, in Hebrew called the *haftara*. The prophetic reading associated with this week's reading is made up of two dismal passages from the book of Jeremiah (7:21–8:3, 9:22–23), in which God despises the people for their sacrifices. "I did not command your forefathers to bring burnt offerings," says God. "Only this did I command them: 'Heed My voice, so that I will be your God and you will be My people; thus you will go in all the ways that I shall command you, so that it should be well with you."

God asks only for a relationship. But the Israelites, coming out of four hundred years of Egyptian culture – and anyone else too, bound as we humans are within the world of space, time, motion, and our own flesh – cannot express their relationship to God without concrete manifestations. We live in the material world; how are we to relate to a transcendent God? The Revelation at Sinai paradoxically undoes the mystery on which transcendent faith is based. This is a problem created by God. Since that revelation, humanity keeps searching for ways to concretize our relationship to the Divine. Still, despite humanity's bottomless well of creativity, we must wonder at the complexity of religious observance.

Is there a historical context for the rituals in Leviticus? Maimonides presents the sacrificial rites as something the Israelites learned during their sojourn in Egypt. They were exposed to a highly structured, religious-based society in Egypt, and they clung to the practices and trappings of idol worship as a template for making sense of the world. Once

## Leviticus

out in the wilderness, they meet God face-to-face. "Come," says God, "let's have a relationship!"

"This is familiar," say the Israelites. "You want a priestly class, and a temple, and a set of rituals. You must want songs and prayers – and we assume You certainly will want sacrifices!"

This is hardly the first time the Torah has had to temper its message in response to human actions, and the Israelites' reaction gives rise to an extensive list of ritual behaviors. We humans need a framework for our relationships. If we are left on our own, most of the time we will not communicate clearly, even (or especially) with those on whom we are on the most intimate terms. So much is assumed within relationships, often to the detriment of the relationship itself. We are often cautioned about the power to do harm that our words have. We should also be mindful of the terrible harm that can be caused by what is left unsaid.

It is not sufficient to love someone. Love is a private, even a selfish emotion. At the very least, we must say to our loved ones, "I love you." And we must listen very carefully to their response. Underlying our beloved's often unspoken requests lie themes of, "If you loved me, you would..." or perhaps, "Since you love me, will you...?" This is not to suggest that love is nothing more than a sequence of market exchanges. Yet it remains true that in order for love to take root and truly flourish, it must be constantly nurtured by concrete acts. They may be simple acts – between people it can be flowers, going out for a meal, or even a gesture as simple as a caress, a smile – but just as infants will thrive only if held and cuddled, love between people cannot thrive without ongoing physical expression.

The Israelites need to make their relationship with God real, if it is to last. Thus, God lends it a physical and temporal aspect, including highly explicit instructions. The Torah offers a uniquely Jewish structure of organized religion, as though to say, "You will have your own practices. To an outsider, they will look like everyone else's practices: you will have priests, and prayer services, and special clothing and songs. You will have offerings and sacrifices, and holidays and celebrations. You will do all these common human things," God says, "but you shall do them the specifically Jewish way. In the way identified by the Torah. In this way, you shall maintain your unique relationship with Me."

God is also teaching a meta-lesson: In order to have an intimate relationship, both partners must clearly express their needs and desires. They must be open – indeed, eager – to hearing each other's needs. How can we meet the needs of those we love if we do not know what they are? How can we learn what they are if our definition of "love" is limited to our own feelings?

While the Hebrew word for love is *ahava*, from the verb "give," our immediate emotional craving is to take from those we say we love. The Torah teaches us that love is a set of behaviors, not a feeling; a set of behaviors that constantly evolves as we learn more about those we love – and more about ourselves. Love resides in the act of giving. It has been said by the rabbis that we do not give to our children because we love them; we love our children because of how much we give to them. Think deeply on this statement and you will see the truth of it.

In the previous portion, we spoke about the psychological mechanism whereby the act of giving ties us to those to whom we give. If that works so well on a stranger, how much more potent will it be when the object of our giving is someone to whom we long to be tied forever? Someone without whom our lives will be empty of meaning? Someone – God – for whose love and blessings we yearn, and whom we struggle to love?

May we all spend our lives learning and the studying the practice of love.

# 26

# The Still, Small Voice

*And Aaron was silent.*

– Leviticus 10:3

Leviticus continues its pedantic tone, drily listing laws and observances even as tragedy unfolds in the midst of rejoicing. We might try to imagine what the Torah would be like if we had only Leviticus, because it seems that may have been what God intended before we humans came on the scene with our freedom to choose, to act, to think for ourselves, and to disobey.

This week's Torah portion marks the literal center of the Written Torah, a point emphasized by the rabbis. In Leviticus 10:16, two forms of the Hebrew word for "inquire" appear one right after the other, straddling the exact midpoint of the *word* count of the Five Books. "Inquire," says the Torah as it ends the first half, and "inquire," opening the second half. Moses urgently *inquires* of Aaron's sons and learns they did not eat the sacrifices which they were explicitly commanded to eat as part of the inauguration of the Tabernacle.

The midpoint of the Torah's *letter* count comes in the list of animals prohibited for consumption (11:42) in an unusual word meaning "belly" – the same word used to curse the serpent (Gen. 3:14). Here at its center, the Torah reminds us that we were thrown out of Eden because we ate prohibited fruit. The Torah's stories always hark back to the earliest pages of Creation.

Historically, there are three competing Jewish understandings of Creation. The first, probably the earliest historically, is now rejected as being "wrong" (in the twenty-first century, we no longer call ideas "heretical"). This is the notion of an eternal God coexisting with eternal, formless matter. Genesis shows God taking control over this primeval matter and forming the cosmos. Time and motion arise when undifferentiated matter takes form. Distinct forms occupy space and move toward or away from one another, and time measures the relationship of objects in motion.

The second trope is Creation *ex nihilo* – something out of nothing. It appears that this concept was first worked up into its most robust dogmatic form by the early fathers of the Christian church, then migrated (or returned) into Jewish thought. It is quite a striking idea: God creates the cosmos and all of us out of nothing. Without God's creative act, we would have never come to be.

The third idea is that God is the only thing that actually exists, and that all Creation is part of God – in fact, *is* God – emanated through attenuating processes or "contractions" described by the kabbalists and embraced notably by the influential Chabad school of Hasidism.

Each Creation story implies a theory of evil. If God takes hold of primal matter and forms order out of chaos, then evil is chaos reasserting itself. If God creates the world from naught, then each created thing has its own independent existence; evil arises when the fundamental nature – the trajectory of needs, appetites, and free choice – of different elements of Creation come into conflict and seek to fulfill their own drives and desires, rather than hewing to the path laid out for them by God.

But if God creates everything out of God's own self, then evil, too, arises organically from God's own nature. Indeed, both good and evil co-inhabit the entire fabric of Creation. This kabbalistic approach speaks directly to the Torah's fundamental paradox, which strikes us like a blow in the midst of this week's reading: we are called to worship a God who creates both life and death. In a polytheistic system, one worships the gods who bring life, while appeasing or fleeing those who bring sickness, suffering, and death. But how are we to reconcile our religious devotion, our worship, and our gratitude with the knowledge that the same God who brings us to life will also kill us?

In Isaiah 45, the prophet addresses the Persian monarch Cyrus (c. 600 – 530 BCE), whom God has designated as the instrument in human history through whom the Jews will return from the Babylonian captivity and rebuild Jerusalem. God tells Cyrus, "I have proclaimed you by name and knighted you, though you did not know Me.... I will gird you, though you did not know Me...I am God; there is no other. Who forms light and creates darkness, Who makes peace and creates evil; I, God, do all this."

This text is so important that the rabbis of old incorporated it into the daily morning prayer, which opens with a slightly altered version: "Blessed are you, Lord our God, King of the universe, who forms light and creates darkness; who makes peace and creates *everything*." The rabbis hesitated to emphasize God's role as creator of evil, but it is blatantly there. Isaiah contrasts the God of the Old Testament with the Zoroastrian religion of ancient Persia, which believed in one god who is wholly good, and who bestrides the universe as the battleground against the forces of an opposing god who is all evil. Isaiah puts before Cyrus the notion that one God, and one God only, creates everything. The implications were staggering in their time. They are no less so today.

As we strive to take our lead in life from the Bible, we receive a jolt in this week's portion when, at the height of the inauguration ceremony in the Tabernacle, Aaron's two older sons, Nadab and Abihu, are consumed by fire (Lev. 10:1–2).

Aaron has just completed the initial sacrifices under Moses' guidance when Nadab and Abihu spontaneously take their firepans – ritual incense burners – and offer "a foreign fire [one outside the prescribed parameters of the sacred practice] which God had not commanded them. Then a fire went out from before God and consumed them, and they died in the Presence of God. Moses said to Aaron: This is that which God spoke of, saying 'I will be sanctified by means of those close to Me, and I shall be honored before the entire people.' And Aaron was silent" (10:1–3).

## The Weight of Gold

Aaron and his remaining sons must still officiate in the Tabernacle. They do not have the leisure to mourn, and contact with death will render them ritually impure. Moses rushes them through their steps, making sure they complete the ritual (10:12–20). The next chapter then seamlessly launches into detailed lists of animals, birds, fish, and insects: those permitted for human consumption and those prohibited; and laws of ritual purity and impurity. This is jarring, though consistent with Leviticus as lawgiving over narrative. Moses' abrupt dismissal of Aaron's family tragedy mirrors the Torah's own urgency to get on with the matter at hand. In a striking sense, this episode is precisely what the Torah is about: God is giving us laws. Occasionally, people do things they should not, whether out of ignorance or malice, or even out of spiritual elatedness, but ultimately God needs to get the message out. We deviate from God's instructions at our peril – and we must carry on regardless.

What are we to make of God's seeming wantonness, Moses' impatience and urgency to get the job done, and Aaron's acceptance of it all? How can we worship and serve a God who kills us? And yet we do. The Torah's Creation narrative blames the serpent, and Eve and Adam – like a master magician, the Torah's misdirection lets God off the hook for the fact that we die. It is not until this week's portion that the Torah admits that death also comes from God.

This Torah portion begs the existential question: Why do we yearn to have a relationship with a God who is so predictably unpredictable? So harsh and so arbitrary? Who gives us life, only to kill us off?

Is it fair for me to leave you with nothing but a question? With no "happy ending"? In a world ruled by death, religion – with all its problems – offers the hope of meaning. How pathetic must we humans be to cling to that promise. This is the most existentially challenging passage in the Bible, yet the rabbis mainly deal with this by following the example of Moses and Aaron: the show must go on.

The hasidic rebbes make the radical suggestion that Nadab

and Abihu knew what they were doing. That they desired the death of the body in order to release their spirits to return to eternal communion with God. But this is the wrong approach to serving God; our job is in this world. It is to serve God through serving others. To bond with our community, to create a just society, and to relieve suffering.

The Torah comes clean in this reading: Yes, there is death in the world, and yes, God created it. Look not to your end, says the Torah, except insofar as it makes your life more urgent. Make the most of everything that comes before death. And consider that we do not mourn the eons elapsed before our birth. We care about death only because we are alive. And who ever hinted that life should last forever? Rather than dwelling on the certainty of death, we should dive with full enthusiasm into the challenge of being alive. God gives us life for free. God doesn't *owe* us life. God doesn't owe us anything.

We are put on this earth for a brief moment, each of us possessing infinite capacity. Our lives are measured by how much of our potential we realize, how much we help others to realize their own potential, by the compassion and the love and service we provide to others using our unique talents.

A man once said to me, "I don't know much, but I do know that I will spend a lot more time dead than I will alive." Nothing is more certain. Nothing is more true.

## 27

# Social Distancing

*Satan had his companions, fellow-devils, to admire and encourage him; but I am solitary and abhorred.*

– Mary Shelley, *Frankenstein*

In the midst of the Tabernacle's bringing order to the world, we are forced to confront death and disorder. Tragedy erupts amidst rejoicing as Aaron's sons perish in divine immolation, which sharply underscores the harshness with which we experience the randomness of life and the desperation of our struggle against chaos. We crave continuity, and we cannot find it. Not from day to day, nor even from moment to moment. God provides a shaky foundation at best. When we most need them to act boldly, our leaders frequently provide only vague murmurings that "God runs the world." Is this all there is to the Torah's theology, here at this critical inflection point?

It is folly to take a person at their word; rather, we see a person's fundamental beliefs in their actions. God's apologists – our religious leaders – tell us over and over again of God's eternal love for all humanity. But Creation is shot through with fatal design flaws, for which the Torah blames us: humanity's overriding activity at all times, in all places and in all conditions, is to wipe one another out with extreme violence. It is natural to question this: How can I believe in a God who allows my loved ones to die? How can I believe in a God who permits slavery and war? How can I believe in a God who allowed the Holocaust? The standard answer is: The problem lies not with God, but with the imperfections and evil of humans. This answer is not satisfactory, and our leaders fail us when they do not address it.

The Tabernacle narrative embodies the incomplete nature

of the relationship between God and humanity. God expects created beings to conform to the original design concept. But the project stumbles in the fluid world of space, time, and motion. The serpent challenges God's rule, Eve and Adam eat from the forbidden tree, and Cain kills Abel. God saves Noah from the Flood, only to realize that human nature is eternally flawed. Later, Abraham takes God to task, charging that divine justice is nothing more than collective punishment and mere wanton cruelty.

By explaining how humanity will interpret God's black-and-white definition of justice, Abraham is telling God that God does not know how to communicate with us. There the confrontation has an unsatisfactory outcome, for humanity at least. The Midrash takes Abraham to task, saying he should have insisted that God back down entirely. And would God have listened? We shall never know, but it's fair to speculate that God has an aspect of divine stubbornness. Perhaps Abraham sensed this, and feared to press too forcefully. Perhaps, after the Flood, Abraham felt he should settle for the lesser victory.

We perceive the death of Nadab and Abihu as a punishment; it is our unavoidable habit of mind. Perhaps it is better to say, as the rabbis do, that once the elements and energies of Creation are unleashed into the world, God chooses not to control either natural or divine processes. It appears that, from God's perspective, the flow of energy must run its course in this world. Nadab and Abihu place themselves in the way; it wasn't that they did what they were commanded *not* to do, but that they did what they were *not* commanded. They die, which we experience as God abandoning us. The Torah rushes to reassert linear order: these are the foods you shall share with Me, says God, these are the times when you shall approach Me.

The restrictions imposed by the Torah establish a hierarchy of who is allowed to approach God, placing Aaron and the priestly clan in charge of overseeing all interactions. These restrictions also create a baseline of shared expectations, a shared routine with God. No less than we, God desires a world with no surprises, with laws designed to create predictable cycles. The consuming fire on the altar, the unleashing of fire and brimstone on Sodom, the Flood, the Revelation at Sinai – these are unbearable and terrifying moments when God is fully revealed in the world.

This same phenomenon plays out in microcosm in our relationships: our interactions are forever colored by our first encounter with another. Only once we establish a shared routine – when we are not overwhelmed by the strangeness of their presence – can we build a relationship with another person. We are not comfortable with people who are unpredictable. We may enjoy their energy, we may be excited and amused by them. But we crave stability. If we cannot find it with God, at least we can seek it in our relationships with one another.

Last week's reading ends with the laws of ritual impurity transmitted by animal carcasses and an exhortation to Israel to remain pure – to remain obedient and not fall into the messiness of an unbridled nature. Now that the Torah has introduced the concept of impurity in terms of permitted and prohibited animals and birds, this week's reading lists a range of human cases of ritual impurity – all of which require people to separate from the community for a period, and to go through ritual cleansing before being permitted back into the encampment and to engage in the sacred rituals of the Tabernacle.

The Torah then leaps into laws of ritual impurity relating to childbirth: after the inexplicable death of Aaron's sons, the creation of life; the means and signature whereby we give meaning to life. The miracle of birth, every bit as astonishing as the harsh mystery of death, and every bit as laden with social taboos.

Ritual impurity is transmissible, and the ritually impure stay away from others for fear of contaminating them. A woman who gives birth dwells apart for a time, then brings a sacrificial offering of an animal, with poorer women permitted to bring doves, the least expensive living being. When Abel offered an animal, it resulted in the first death in history. The act of giving birth, every bit as chaotic as death, requires the offering of Abel to bring the mother back into the camp, to make society whole.

Next, the Torah describes a person afflicted with one of the skin conditions lumped under the Hebrew term *tzara'at* (frequently mistranslated as "leprosy") who is required to live outside the main encampment. He is visibly distinguished by torn garments and wild-grown hair. He covers his mouth with his garment and calls out in a loud voice, "Unclean! Unclean!" And he must live outside the camp until his affliction passes (13:45–46). The parallel to isolation of those bearing infectious diseases is unavoidable, even down to the covering of the face with the garment. Here, though, it is *only* the lips – the mouth, which attests to its own guilt – that are visible, for in the rabbinic understanding, blemishes that cause uncleanliness are the result of evil speech.

But if he lives outside the camp during the term of his affliction, to whom does he address his cry of "Unclean!"? The only other people who do leave the camp do so only to dispose of remnants of sacrifices – which likewise render the one who bears them temporarily impure – or to dispose of noxious trash. The image is of a bleak society of wanderers, prohibited from all human contact, cast out of society until the priest once more declares them healed of their uncleanliness. Until then they wander, keeping their distance from society and even from one another – the repeated cries of "Unclean!" drive away any who approach.

This is the punishment of Cain, who is sent forth to the east and caused to wander all his days, who bears an indelible mark for all to see in order to keep others from approaching too close – and who tells God, "My iniquity is too great to bear!" (Gen. 4:13). Cain's sin lies forever in his heart. It accompanies him throughout his wanderings.

Cain was sent east of Eden to the land of *Nod* – from the Hebrew root "to wander." Furthermore, God says, "You shall be a vagrant and wanderer [*nod*] in the world" (Gen. 4:12).

The Hebrew word for the ritual impurity of a woman who gives birth (Lev. 12:2) is *nidda*, from the same root meaning to wander; she, too, is sent out of the camp. This parallel to childbirth is embedded in the text.

Ritual impurity arises from nature, affecting our physical selves and surroundings. It arises from forces forever beyond our control. It is partly a response to natural squeamishness about bodily functions; but whereas one person can leave a room if they become uncomfortable, a society *is* the room, and what on a personal level might be mere discomfort becomes harsh disgust at the societal level and quickly morphs into hatred. Societies respond to this anxiety by expelling their members, and by enforcing clearly defined, acceptable behaviors meant to cover up natural tendencies for those who cannot control them. And which society does not impose this type of rigid order, this expectation of sameness? Again and again, it is the weaker members of the community who are made weaker still by harsh judgment. Again and again, societies seek to protect themselves by punishing people for their weakness, for doing what in many cases is unavoidable – menstruating, carrying on homosexual relations, or falling in love with someone deemed inappropriate – rather than embracing them, rather than offering them strength.

The fact that these restrictions arise in all societies makes it that much more urgent that we should challenge them. Societies rush to eliminate people who seem different, to shut out ideas and practices they don't understand. Yet they continue to creep in, because reality is messy. The more people a society deems "unclean," the weaker the social fabric. The more ideas a society bans as "dangerous," the weaker the foundations of the social order. Those societies that insist on the greatest degree of conformity are the weakest of all.

Rather than impose restrictions on us, the Torah goes to the heart of human behavior. You desire a structured way of religious worship? I give you the priests, the Tabernacle, and the sacrifices. You desire a societal hierarchy? I give you Moses and the Elders as chiefs of groups of tens and hundreds and thousands. You recoil from fear of death – or from the ability to bring forth life? I give you the laws of ritual purity.

The Torah gives us boundaries for containing our worst tendencies, while exhorting us to confront them. We believe God wants us to be partners in an ongoing act of Creation, but the Torah doesn't assume that we know how to do that. God gives us the basic ingredients; it remains our challenge to apply our unique talents to perfect the world. We do this by sorting out our own fears, our false assumptions. Our urges, appetites, and inclinations. By examining our inner selves to see where justice truly lies. Only through fearless introspection can we realize our own potential, and only by ceaselessly working on ourselves can we help others. Underlying it all is our obligation to relieve suffering in the world, because it is difficult to reach for an exalted prize when one is in pain.

We should not be too full of ourselves. While God invites us to be partners in Creation, it is not we, but God who brings forth both death and its opposite. *I* determine life and death, says God. If you challenge My decision to create death, so much the worse for you. Do not believe, says God, that death is the most terrible thing in My world. And do not believe that merely because life emerges from your bodies, you have made life. The rabbis say, "Against your will you are formed; against your will you are born; against your will you live; against your will you die" (*Ethics of the Fathers* 4:22).

In times of greatest challenge, there are those who fall back on a theology of submission: God runs the world; let us bow to the will of the Creator. But why would we not demand answers to the hardest questions of all? We should demand them from our leaders. We should even – or particularly – ask them of God.

This tragedy of human suffering – is it the doing of humans, despite the desire of the Creator? Or is this the will of God? I, for one, cannot answer the question. Yet I insist that it be asked. Again and again.

# 28

# The Freedom to Choose

*We must believe in free will, we have no choice.*

– Isaac Bashevis Singer

This week's text continues the Torah's treatment of ritual impurity, describing the purification of people and objects afflicted with *tzara'at*, which, as we learned above, is often (mis)translated into English as "leprosy." Once the condition passes, the person who suffered it must undergo a ritual of purification before reentering society.

We are far from finished with the issues raised in these central passages of the Torah. What kind of God does the Torah command us to serve? And how do we survive when God has planted us in a hostile world? Can we reconcile our obligation to worship God with the horrors with which God burdens us – horrors which emanate from the very nature of Creation itself? Which appear to lie at the heart of the divine plan? It is critical to address these questions. Not to answer them; for when we arrive at an answer for any fundamental question, we can be certain that it is, at best, only partially correct. Such answers must be viewed out of the corner of the eye. If we look directly at them, they evaporate, leaving behind a derisive, laughing ghost. But it is increasingly urgent to acknowledge these questions now, as the Torah transitions from the exposition of Genesis and Exodus, through the cataloging of commandments, into the political turmoil of Numbers – fraught with power struggles, bursting with avoidable disasters; and the book of Deuteronomy – Moses' personal account of the Israelite nation, his brilliant and poetic, peevish and majestic, farewell to his flock as he chastises them, then blesses them, for being merely human.

Leviticus is a fulcrum between two very different sets of

narratives, serving both as the coda to the first two books of Torah and the overture to the last two. Now, right now, we need to figure out who God is.

Ritual impurity arises when we focus too much on ourselves. We find ourselves facing a God who is not so much unforgiving as impenetrable. We cannot refrain from asking why: Why can we not serve God after having touched a corpse, or giving birth? Why did Nadab and Abihu die? The very structure of our mind screams for meaning; we cannot relinquish the thought that God killed them on purpose. We cannot let go of the very human notion that God punished them. And for what?

God seems not so much distant as disconnected. God keeps saying, This is how I expect things to be, this is how I expect you to behave. And we, for our part, say to God: Please pay attention, try to see things our way. This was the crux of Abraham's conversation with God before the destruction of Sodom. It is a history of God and us forever talking past one another. We are never certain how it is that God speaks to us, but we do know how we attempt to speak to God, which is through prayer. Does God hear? And if so, of what does that hearing consist? In what does it ever result?

We *need* God to hear us. We humans are hardwired for two unshakeable habits of mind. The first is that everything has meaning. The second is that we are important – and thus, that everything has meaning *for us*. These phenomena of brain activity can distract us endlessly from the task at hand, which is to live our lives in a meaningful way. Meaningful is as meaningful *does*, not as meaningful merely contemplates.

The Torah never tells us why God created the world. It tells us how the world works and, most important, it tells us what we need to do about it. It is a set of instructions for the human soul and a guide to creating a society that is just and righteous in our generation, and where justice will be renewed perpetually, creating a sustainable and repeatable process for maintaining a just society. The book of Leviticus will close with precisely this, bringing together the three main purposes of religion: the individual and communal relationship with God; maintaining a balance of stewardship with the natural world we inhabit, and for which we are responsible; and creating a society based on justice, and in which justice self-renews from generation to generation.

This week's reading leaves the door open to the Torah's message of the importance of our own decisions – to act, not to act – the exercise of our free choice. Look at this: "God spoke to Moses and to Aaron to say, 'When you arrive in the land of Canaan which I am giving you as an inheritance, and I inflict a house of the land of your inheritance with the affliction of leprosy...'" (14:33–34). The Talmud quotes an opinion that this affliction – leprosy of houses – never happened, and never will. Rather, the Torah mentions it so that we can study God's word, because both the spiritual growth and the merit derived from knowing God's laws override their practical application.

But the discussion recorded in the Talmud points to something much deeper, because neither Moses nor Aaron will enter the land of Canaan. Does the notion of God's omniscience make the statement, "*When* you arrive in the land of Canaan," a black-and-white contradiction? Is God saying something which God knows not to be true? What might be the purpose in God stating a falsehood? In human terms, we lie to manipulate, to obtain an outcome. This raises the uncomfortable possibility that God is misleading Moses and Aaron so that they will not despair, so that they will continue to throw their energies into leading the people. But if God is going to lie in order to manipulate the Israelites, why doesn't God intervene at the episode of the spies (Num. 13–15) which results in the Israelites' wandering forty years in the wilderness? Wouldn't it be in the best interest of God's plan to fool us into changing that outcome?

This is the Torah's message of our freedom to choose, of our responsibility in shaping our future. God has not yet barred Moses and Aaron from entering the Land of Israel. At this point in the narrative, both men have the ability to direct their future behavior in such a way as to ensure that they *will* enter the Promised Land. Consider also that the Torah from which we are reading is the text written by Moses, who took dictation from God on Mount Sinai. Moses already knows his own fate, and *still* God implicitly tells him, you can choose a different future. It is difficult for us to contemplate the immensity of our own power to change the world.

However we express it – through the Buddhist notion of Karma; through the Torah's notion of measure for measure; through the Christian admonition, As ye sow, so shall ye reap; or through the Muslim concept of reward and punishment – all wisdom traditions recognize an inexorable link between our present actions and our future condition. By our actions today, we create our own future world. Never mind the world God created; what kind of world are we making for ourselves?

When we pray, instead of asking God to change the future, we should be asking for the insight to change our own behavior to bring about a better future for ourselves and for those around us. Are there matters beyond our control? Of course. Should we then ask God to alter the course of nature on our behalf? Rather, to quote the Serenity Prayer, let us ask for the wisdom to know the difference between what we can change, and what we shall never be able to change. And let us then change those things we can. God, it seems, at least gives us that much. Let's take advantage of that.

# 29

# The Goat for Azazel

*Wear your best for your execution and stand dignified. Your last recourse against randomness is how you act – if you can't control outcomes, you can control the elegance of your behaviour. You will always have the last word.*

– Nassim Nicholas Taleb

After describing the deaths of Nadab and Abihu, last week's portion ended with an admonition to separate the ritually clean from the unclean, "so they should not die as a result of their contamination, if they contaminate My Tabernacle" (15:31). Moreover, in the book of Numbers, the families of the Levites are assigned to carry specific components of the Tabernacle when the Israelites break camp and move on to their next destination, and touching a part designated for a different family is dangerous. Unauthorized contact with holiness causes death. At its midpoint, after all the tales of heroism and magic, the Torah acknowledges that closeness to the Divine is fraught with danger. Indeed, it can be fatal.

The danger associated with closeness to God is articulated at the beginning of this portion: "And God spoke to Moses after the death of the two sons of Aaron, when they brought their offerings before God and they died" (16:1). God then instructs Moses to warn Aaron not to enter the inner sanctuary of the Tabernacle casually, lest *he* die (16:2). Immediately afterward, the text segues into a detailed enumeration of the highly structured Yom Kippur service (16:3ff).

This juxtaposition between the death of Aaron's sons and the listing of the priestly duties is reminiscent of the speed with which Moses rushed past their actual moment of death to finalize the list of commandments of the dedication service. Staying true to the theme of Leviticus, our portion underscores the need to complete every aspect of the required service. Not to exceed, as we saw in the extreme case of the death of Aaron's sons, but also not to think that spiritual good intent or heightened spiritual experience is a substitute for the physical rituals commanded by God.

"With *this* shall Aaron come to the Sanctuary" (16:3). "*This*," say the rabbis, refers to an extensive list of commandments including the Sabbath, circumcision, the giving of tithes, animal sacrifices, commandments specific to the priestly family plus those unique to Aaron in his role as High Priest, and particularly, to the complex ritual performed by the High Priest on the Day of Atonement. Bearing all "*this*," Aaron may safely enter the holy precincts. Bearing all "*this*," and at "*this*" specified time of Yom Kippur, and wearing "*this*" set of High Priestly garments, and enacting "*this*" ritual whereby all Israel atones, both individually and as a nation – with all *this*, Aaron may safely enter.

The Yom Kippur service includes the commandment of the scapegoat (16:8–22). Aaron brings two goats to the entrance of the Tabernacle and draws lots. One goat is designated by lot for God, the other for Azazel. Aaron sacrifices God's goat on the altar, together with a bull and a ram. This is all part of the service in the Tabernacle – later in the Temple in Jerusalem. The goat for Azazel, the scapegoat, bears the sins of the entire nation: "Aaron shall lean his two hands on the head of the live goat and shall confess upon it all the iniquities of the children of Israel and all their rebellious transgressions and all their sins; and he shall put them onto the head of the goat and he shall send it by a designated man to the wilderness. And the goat shall bear upon itself all their iniquities to the designated place, and he shall send the goat into the wilderness" (16:21–22).

One designated man takes the goat for Azazel and leads it out to the uninhabited wilderness, where he shoves it forcefully over a cliff edge. The goat tumbles down the sheer slope, unable to gain a foothold. He smashes against jagged outcrops and tumbles over sharp stones and is ripped to death long before he comes to rest at the bottom of the treacherous slope.

One randomly selected goat is sacrificed with pomp and ceremony, its throat cut by the High Priest in the holy confines of the Temple; the other is tossed from a high cliff edge and meets its end in a desolate wasteland, with none but its killer as witness. Thus does the Torah place the utter randomness of life before us. Whether in high ceremony, among singing Levites and the swirling incense of the Temple, or in the cracked horror of the empty desert – we shall all surely die. We think we can judge a good death versus a bad one. But no one really knows.

The rabbis downplay the designation "for Azazel" because of its overtones of superstition. Azazel is not identified in the Torah; the name is left a mystery. Azazel is described in later Jewish literature as a fallen angel. Some Islamic sources identify him as the devil. Whatever he – or it – is, Azazel seems to embody evil, or perhaps the hopelessness of the barren desert, as opposed to the order and formality of the camp with the perfect structure of the Tabernacle at its center. Azazel is the random emptiness of life, terrifying to contemplate, against which we fortify ourselves by hiding in our encampment, behind our walls, surrounded by the paltry comforts of priests with their singing and their headgear and their rituals. Priests who, like all of us, will also die one day.

The great rabbinic sage Nachmanides addresses this head-on. He says the Torah explicitly instructs us to send one goat as an offering to the forces of darkness. These forces, he says, are real. They are not mere superstition. The forces of evil are nowhere near as mighty as God's aspect of compassion, but they easily prevail in this world. It is as though God sits patiently awaiting our call, while the forces of darkness are filled with boundless energy. And remember that this is the God of whom the prophet Isaiah wrote (Is. 45:7), "I make light and I create darkness; I make peace and I create evil."

People sometimes ask, How can a God who is all good (which is axiomatic for so many people, though not clearly stated in the text of the Torah) permit the existence of evil? Says Nachmanides, if we remove evil from God's hands, we make God into a puny and powerless being, a bug to smash underfoot. Can there be anything in existence which God did not create? Anything that God does not at every moment sustain in existence? The fight against evil is not God's task, but our own.

Nachmanides brings us back to the here and now. The randomness of life is very real; we experience it every moment. As noted both by the rabbis of old and by Nassim Taleb, above, if we had more complete information, then what we perceive as randomness would resolve itself. The problem, of course, is that each level of clarity only leads us to a higher level of randomness in an endless spiral.

This is the world in which we live. We bring both goats before God in order to sanctify all aspects of our lives. We are not "bribing the forces of darkness"; we are balancing our offerings, corresponding to the balance of good and evil in the world. Acknowledging concretely that both light and darkness are created by God.

Our lives are a constant battle against randomness. We build structures: calendars and schedules; nations and communities; cities and households; religions, conventions of behavior, societal norms. And still, from time to time, all this blows up in our faces. The only thing we can do is to consciously be at our best under all conditions. As Taleb says, to dress in our finest suit as we are marched out to the firing squad.

We do not understand the universe. To quote Taleb again, "We cannot truly plan, because we do not understand the future." To push back against the frightening randomness of life, we must "transform fear into prudence, pain into transformation, mistakes into initiation, and desire into undertaking."

We must plan, taking into account our limitations; taking into account that all our plans are but the faint dew of our wishes. When the sun of reality rises upon our dreams, all that we hoped for and strove to accomplish will evaporate in a mist.

Still, we must build. We must plan and continue to forge a structure in the world, to hold at bay the forces of randomness, of confusion. Ultimately, of chaos.

Says Taleb, "It just takes guts." Indeed.

# 30

# You Shall Be Holy

*The future is unwritten.*

– Joe Strummer

This week's reading opens with the overarching principle: "You shall be holy because I, the Lord your God, am holy" (19:2), a bewildering statement in the shadow of the death of Aaron's sons. Now God exhorts us to be like God, "holy." What are we to make of this? And if the calamity we have just witnessed is characteristic of God's behavior, what shall we choose as our model?

Last week's reading ended with an admonition not to follow the "abominable practices" of the inhabitants of the land of Canaan, enumerating particularly a list of forbidden sexual practices. Now, preparatory to the Israelites' imminent possession of the land, we are commanded to be holy. And how do we separate the nice moral messages of this portion from the fact that the "holy" God now addressing us is the same God who slaughtered Nadab and Abihu when they sought to serve God in their own way?

In the context of the book of Leviticus, we are being challenged to look squarely at the terrors and randomness of reality – expressed in last week's description of the scapegoat. This week's portion shows that passive goodness does not suffice. After last week's list of prohibitions, notably sexual prohibitions which articulate the sanctioned relationships within society, the Torah now proceeds to a list of commands in furtherance of the goal of becoming a just society, culminating in what the Talmud calls "*the* great principle in the Torah": "You shall love your neighbor as yourself – I am God" (19:18).

The text spills over with moral teachings required for a well-functioning society: Leave a corner of your field unharvested so the poor can take for themselves, don't steal, don't lie, don't swear false oaths. Don't cheat, don't rob, don't withhold your workers' wages. Don't make fun of people behind their backs. Don't permit perversion of justice, neither over-favoring the poor nor honoring the rich and the important. Don't stand by while your neighbor's blood is being shed. Talk out your differences; don't bear a grudge or seek revenge. Love your neighbor as yourself. Signed, God (19:11–18).

The juxtaposition of this portion's list of commands with the Canaanite abominations at the close of last week's reading conveys the Torah's true moral message: it is not sufficient to not do evil; we must actively do good. We must, in fact, *become holy*, the mechanism for which is the observance of God's commandments – both the moral and the ritual – and constant mindfulness as we seek to internalize God's vision for the world. Repeated throughout this portion is, "I am God," "I am the Lord your God," sealing the commandments over and over.

Like the sacrificial goats who prance out into the teeth of uncertainty, we are sent to bring God's teaching into the world wherever we find ourselves, and under all circumstances. Fundamental to this is our everyday behavior: we are commanded to behave in God-like fashion, to behave as a holy people.

The Torah requires that we see God's face in the face of the other, creating an imperative both to treat others well and to not harm them. Beyond this, the morality of the Torah challenges me to see God's face in my own. To care for the world as though it were my own creation. To see myself as God sees me: a precious and necessary partner in Creation, one who actively makes the world a better place.

Ritual is one key that opens a door to this challenge. By binding us to the physical reality of our day-to-day existence, ritual emphasizes our obligation to imbue everything with holiness, and Jewish observance makes much of handling objects which, while not sacred in themselves, become sanctified when used in rituals: tying fringes on the corners of the prayer shawl, taking up the citrus fruit and the palm branch on the holiday of Sukkot, blowing the ram's horn on Rosh Hashana. If we learn to sanctify the mute physical objects in the world, how much more sensitive will we be toward our own sanctity? How much more will we be aware of the sanctity of others?

God creates the physical world, and we dare not turn away from the physical in search of the spiritual. Our body is the receptacle for our soul, and this physical world is the receptacle for God's holiness. Ritual is spiritual training, a springboard for giving charity, caring for the destitute, protecting the weak, feeding the hungry, creating a just society – and on a purely spiritual plane, for introspection and self-improvement. The ultimate spiritual encounter is to be found in this world, in this life.

### Love your neighbor as yourself

What does it mean to love one's neighbor as oneself? And how does rebuke overcome the passion for revenge or bearing a grudge?

We always justify our own behavior. When others are angry, we say they are being unreasonable. But when we are angry, it is with good reason, and the other is at fault. Our anger is justified, other people's anger is not.

If we look into our own hearts, we might at last come to understand human behavior. When we look at ourselves honestly, we regret behavior that does not live up to our own standards, and we acknowledge that we erred in permitting our emotions to dominate our behavior. We try to be aware of this, and to not permit it to happen again. We rebuke ourselves gently, with an understanding born of honest self-acceptance, with compassion for the hurt child within, and with the understanding that we must go through this process of fearless self-evaluation again and again. This is the core of the process of repentance and, crucially, of forgiveness.

Are others so different from ourselves? The frightened child cowering within my heart cowers and trembles equally in yours, in everyone's. If we can learn to pause before lashing out in anger – to feel the deep hurt and fear emanating from the other – to learn to rebuke one another as gently as we rebuke ourselves, then we will truly be working to make the world a better place.

We can even catch a glimpse into God's heart. In midrashic and talmudic literature, God is frequently depicted as sad, weeping over the pain God inflicts on God's own children. The rabbis say God created the world with its own set of rules – we call them "nature" – and God agrees to play by those same rules. Because we have freedom of choice, God does not intervene to prevent us from behaving foolishly, from doing evil. From destroying others or ourselves. Here we watch as God weeps, we hear God's anguished cries at the fate of humanity. No less than the sacrificial goats – one for God, one for Azazel – God's anguish expresses the existential terror that runs through human existence, the agony of the fatal choices that face us each day.

The portion ends with a list of punishments, and it may be that they, too, point to the existential paradox of life: that for all the world's beauty, we must also experience its harshness. God, having established the rules by which the universe operates, does not step in to interfere. When we drop a brick off a rooftop, it will fall whether we intended it or not. If a person is standing below and the brick hits them on the head, they will be killed whether we intended it or not; all our repentance will not alter physical reality. It is not God's intention – and certainly not God's wish – to punish. God told Adam and Eve there was a consequence to their act; the Torah now reminds us that all our actions have consequences as well. We must act; it is our mission to make this world a better place, to relieve suffering – and yet, we shall make mistakes.

We will make mistakes for which we, and others, will pay the price. But mistakes are not the purpose of life. We will all die. But death, too, is not the purpose of life. We must find and embrace the purpose of our lives – that is last week's simple message as both goats perish. One dies all but painlessly; its throat slit. It is brought on the altar amidst incense and song. The other is cast down a ragged cliff face. Israel's atonement cannot be partially bought. Both goats go to their fate.

Who were the holy ones: Aaron and Moses, with their painstaking adherence to God's instructions? Or Nadab and Abihu, with their spontaneous desire to go above and beyond? Our job, the Torah teaches, is to set ourselves apart for the work at hand. It requires restraint, with regard to both our negative responses toward others and our enthusiasm for our own spiritual fulfillment. Spiritual practice is ongoing. We shall never attain perfection, yet we dare not cease striving.

Says God, You were personally designated for a specific role, and Creation will not be complete until you attain self-realization. Strive to be holy, says God. Strive to be like Me – for whom mindfulness of My task is My eternal, unceasing activity. Do not cease until you find the path for which you were chosen. Once upon that path, do not cease. Do not cease at all.

# 31

# Whose Responsibility?

*The society in which each man lives is at once the basis for, and the nemesis of, that fullness of life which each man seeks.*

– Reinhold Niebuhr

Leviticus won't let go. This central book of the Torah keeps driving home the message of religious ritual, the "organized" part of organized religion. In this week's reading, God commands Moses to transmit to Aaron and his sons the ritual laws relating to the Tabernacle service (21:1–6). Moses gives over the instruction, and the section ends with, "Moses spoke to Aaron and to his sons, and to all the Israelites" (21:24). We have come to expect this cadenced phrase, so it takes an extra measure of attentiveness to ask, what's it doing here? These laws are explicitly for the priestly clan, for Aaron and his male descendants who will minister in the Tabernacle. Why do all Israel need to hear?

While these behaviors and qualifications are incumbent on the priestly clan, it is the responsibility of the entire society to be aware of them in order to enforce them and to support the Kohanim in their role as representatives of the nation. The Kohanim's focus is service within the Tabernacle, but the Tabernacle and its service are properly the responsibility of the nation.

Harking back to the seminal episode of Nadab and Abihu, this week's portion (chs. 21–24) opens by prohibiting Aaron and his sons from contact with the dead. At the root of this prohibition lies a paradox which the hasidic rebbes, with their profound grasp of human psychology, understood only too well. The natural human response to death is despair, fear, and anger. When we behold the death of another, we are reminded of our own mortality – a shadowy figure looming at the end of a narrow corridor. We rarely look back to the eternity before we were born, yet we behold with dread the eternity that stretches beyond our last mortal hour. This descent into despair, this anger against God for creating a world that ends in death, is not the proper state of mind in which to serve God on behalf of others.

The Torah opens by, in effect, relieving God of the blame for our mortality. Genesis never states explicitly that humans were mortal at their creation; the actions of Eve and Adam are said to have brought death into the world. For most orthodox thought, both Jewish and Christian, the notion that death is God's doing feels mildly heretical: God being wholly good, how can God be the cause of death? Yet religious people respond to the death of loved ones by saying, "God took her," or "It was God's will." It is difficult to reconcile "God is all good, and does only good" with the reality of death, and the common response: "God's ways are mysterious," comes across as a dodge.

The apologist approach skirts a paradox which even the teacher – even the rabbi, even the priest – knows to be irreconcilable. The greatness of the hasidic approach is that it doesn't seek to explain the mind of God. The practical–mystical approach of the rebbes is to explain *how* God's world works, not *why* God makes it so. Along the same lines, the rabbinic writings that constitute the Oral Torah open with the laws of reading the *Shema* prayer: "Hear, O Israel: The Lord is our God; the Lord is One" (Deut. 6:4). This very first law leapfrogs over questions of the existence of God and belief in God. The rabbis understood how difficult it is to command people's inner state. Can people be ordered to love and to believe? What human authority can even begin to police the content of people's hearts? But we can demand obedience. The Torah might accept the difficulty of requiring belief; it does, however, require you to behave at all times *in accordance with* the belief in God. "From doing an act not for its own proper sake," say the rabbis, "one will come to do the act for its own, proper sake."[1] Arriving at proper reverence takes a lifetime of practice.

Looking to the behaviors that bind society together, good manners and respect for the rights of others matter far more than such outstanding qualities as the courage to rush into a burning building to save a life. Devastating fires break out only occasionally, but we are afforded the opportunity for common courtesy countless times each day. Smiling and saying "Good morning" to the server who pours our morning coffee, holding the door for others. Simply saying "Please" and "Thank you."

The emphasis of the book of Leviticus on ritual was not even derailed by the death of Aaron's sons, and it continues here unbroken. Last week's portion emphasized holiness: "You shall be holy because I, the Lord your God, am holy" (19:2). This week's portion opens with repetition of the word, now in connection with ritual requirements: "[The Kohanim] shall be holy to God…they shall be holy…he is holy to his God…you shall make him holy…you shall consider him holy because I, your God, Who make you holy – I am holy" (21:6–8). The word *holy* means set aside for an exclusive relationship, a relationship whose boundaries are defined by ritual.

Religion comprises both ritual and ethics, a distinction that is often not fully understood. The objection, "I don't need religion to make me a good person," is a common confusion of ritual with morality itself. Ritual by itself is neither spiritual nor moral; it is a concrete representation and expression of the moral and spiritual content of the Torah's message and expresses the grammar God uses to communicate with us. Nadab and Abihu died because their offering violated the Tabernacle's parameters: they brought "an outsider's fire." It is troubling how the Torah seems to randomly impose the death penalty for what we perceive as transgression of ritual commandments: unauthorized contact with the Ark of the

---

[1] This fundamental principle is articulated in the Babylonian Talmud, tractate Pesachim, page 50b, and repeated prominently by Maimonides, for example, in chapter 10 of his Laws of Repentance. It is a key linchpin of rabbinic thought.

Covenant, Nadab and Abihu's offering, the worship of the Golden Calf, the man found gathering wood in the wilderness on the Sabbath.

But while God punishes ritual transgressions harshly, moral and societal matters are turned over to humans. Pushing back forcefully against the plain meaning of the words, the rabbis interpret the penalties listed at the closing of this portion (24:17–22) – which include the famous formula, "An eye for an eye, a tooth for a tooth" – to mean financial compensation for physical damages, whether to person or property. We are not God. We do not have the right to impose harsh penalties for behavior that, however detestable, turns out to be all too human.

The Torah lists the Sabbath and the festivals, ritual cycles wherein we live and breathe the formal aspects of Torah, to reinforce the centrality of ritual as the container for our relationship with God (23:1ff). We are exhorted to be holy, and though we must also live and breathe the spiritual aspects of religious practice, it's sometimes easier to dispense with the burdens of morality and embrace ritual. The weakness of organized religion is that people focus on the container and often overlook the contents. Worse, they believe the container *is* the contents.

The next passage (24:1–4) hints at this, describing the oil which fuels the eternal light. The Menorah is the rigid structure – the container. But the light itself comes from the oil – the content. Here we have the joint role of ritual combined with ethical behavior and spiritual development. The container is useless without its contents, yet the content cannot perform its function unless properly contained. Harmony.

Suddenly, a blasphemer appears. Out of nowhere, the flow of lawgiving is interrupted as two men fight, and one hurls the Ineffable Name of God at the other as a curse. This perverts both the container and the content; the Name meant to bring peace has been used as a weapon.

The Israelites are commanded to bring the blasphemer outside the camp and stone him to death. But what makes his punishment unique in all the Torah is that first, those who heard him utter the sacred Name lay their hands on the blasphemer and say, "You brought this upon yourself." Maimonides points out that this is the only time in the Torah where the death penalty is combined with a laying on of hands, signifying that society itself is to blame.

Just as the priests need the ongoing support of the entire nation to carry out their task, those who fall by the wayside are equally our responsibility. When we say to the blasphemer, "You brought this upon yourself," we are really acknowledging that we – the society as a whole, and also each one of us – have failed this individual. Had we been more attentive, they might not have been so blind with rage, might not have felt so alienated that they would actually curse in the Name of God. That is our sin, and having others die for it does not bring expiation.

When we focus on the container, we ignore the pain in the heart of the stranger, the outsider. We can even ignore those closest to us. Who will see their pain? Who shall draw them close? For all that we are part of the group today, the time will come when we will be on the outside, too. If not today, then tomorrow. If not tomorrow, our day will yet come. And who will reach out a hand to us then?

## 32

# The World was Created for Me

*The first requisite of civilization is that of justice.*

— Sigmund Freud, *Civilization and its Discontents*

This week's brief portion opens, "And God spoke to Moses on Mount Sinai, saying...." This raises the obvious question: The entire Torah was given on Mount Sinai, as recounted in the book of Exodus; why does this verse, with Sinai in the rear-view mirror, suddenly invoke the revelation? Or: What is so special about this particular reading that the Torah feels the need to remind us of its source? The rabbis bring textual explanations for the Sinai reference here toward the end of Leviticus, but it is the moral ones that prevail.

We have viewed Leviticus as a sort of Torah-within-the-Torah, a focused version of the Torah as a book of laws, with barely any narrative. This portion suggests a correspondence to the Sinai encounter in Exodus, a recasting of the Sinai revelation in a fundamental sense, its message distilled down to its core.

Within the portion are the commandments of the Sabbatical year, the obligation to let the Land of Israel rest every seventh year; and the Jubilee, the fiftieth year in which slaves are freed and debts are canceled. The commandment of the Sabbatical year is voiced in the continuous present tense: "When you come into the land that I am giving you, the land shall observe a Sabbath of rest.... Sow your field and tend your vineyard for six years...and the seventh year shall be a Sabbath of rest for the land" (25:2–7).

The first thing God commands the children of Israel upon their entering Canaan is that, in transforming it from Canaan into the Land of Israel, the land must have a regular year of rest. This is immediately followed by a command to work the land *before* allowing it to rest, mirroring the commandment of the Sabbath itself. The Sabbath is not mere non-action. It is rest *after* labor, a cessation of creative activity. In order to keep the Sabbath, we must first work for six days. Likewise, it is impossible to cause the land to rest without first working it for six years.

So yes; the first thing we are commanded to do when we take possession of the land is to observe the Sabbatical year. As with the Sabbath itself – which is a day of active resting, earned through six days of productive labor – we observe the Sabbatical year by first working the land for six years, then causing it to recuperate.

The Torah then gives the commandment of the Jubilee year, the fiftieth year in which not only does the land lie fallow, but all debts are canceled, all properties revert to the Israelite families that originally owned them, and all Israelite slaves go out free – whether they want to or not.

This is why the Torah here invokes Sinai, the moment we entered into the unbreakable covenant with God through accepting the Torah. At that point, we might have thought that the Land of Israel was given to us absolutely. God gave the land to Abraham and for all time to his descendants through Isaac and Jacob. But God's gift requires active and ongoing acceptance on our part. God gives us the Torah, but it is our responsibility at all times to observe it, to keep it, to uphold it. We take full ownership of the Torah when we live every moment at our utmost peak of ethical and spiritual behavior, both individually and nationally.

By invoking Sinai, the Torah emphasizes the moral requirements that govern our ownership of the Land of Israel. God's gifts – Torah, the Land of Israel; indeed, our very lives – are constantly being given. But do we strive to constantly receive them? There are rules, and God has expectations of us. If we fail to live up to God's expectations, we will lose the land. It has happened before.

The Sabbath is a weekly "factory reset," restoring the balance in our personal and communal relationship with

God. The Sabbatical year restores the balance of the land, while the Jubilee restores society, resetting imbalances and releveling the playing field.

The Torah's fundamental principle of social justice is equitable treatment. It is not "guaranteed equality of outcome," i.e., everyone receiving the same. The Torah recognizes that different people have different capacities, and are born to different circumstances. It does not blame the poor for their poverty, but neither does it praise the wealthy for their assets. The Torah is a document of natural communism – but not anti-wealth. It is a pro-business document – but not a capitalist one. Business must serve the common good; those who create businesses are entitled to become rich, and they in turn are obligated to use their wealth to care for others. This is much more essential than the contemporary notion of "giving back." It is a continual and seamless involvement of the individual with society, and society with each individual. The Torah demands both the sanctity of private property and the absolute obligation of those who have, to share with those who do not.

The tractate in the Talmud dealing with the laws of the Sabbath opens with an elaborate set of transactions depicting the distinction between what the Talmud calls public space and private space. On the Sabbath, it is prohibited to transport objects from public to private space, or vice versa. This prohibition extends to food items, as exemplified in this opening passage.

Two men, identified as the Householder and the Poor Man, engage in an act of charity. The Poor Man stands on the threshold, the Householder stands within, and through different sequences, the Householder gives something to the Poor Man. Either the Poor Man reaches his hand inside the doorway, or the Householder reaches his hand out. The Poor Man takes an object from the Householder's hand, or the Householder deposits it in the Poor Man's hand. Each of these sequences constitutes a different form of a violation of the laws of the Sabbath, because the object is transferred from inside the house to the outside, or vice versa. While the examples clarify the complexities of the laws governing public and private space, the question remains: Why did the rabbis choose these particular characters to act out the message?

This is, in fact, a clear statement of the sanctity of private wealth, and of the obligation of the wealthy to give to the poor – all in the transcendent context of the Sabbath, the day when God's sovereignty is restored to our everyday lives.

The text presupposes that the wealthy Householder will give charity to the Poor Man both freely and generously; there is no need to explain why he is handing something to the Poor Man. What remains unspoken, but strikingly obvious, is that the Sabbath transcends human ownership. During the week, the Householder can satisfy the obligation to share wealth through many forms of charitable giving, including writing a check that then goes into an institution that will feed, clothe, and house the Poor Man. Thus, the Householder can benefit the Poor Man without even knowing he exists. But come the Sabbath, none of this works. There is no way to remain at arm's length and not violate the Sabbath laws; the only way for our rich Householder to fulfill his obligation to the Poor Man is to invite him inside. To share everything in his house.

On the Sabbath, we must invite the stranger in. Our world and God's world merge and become one. In the Sabbatical year, the whole land is given over for anyone to benefit from. Comes the Jubilee, all traces of our societal meddling, our individual strivings – the illusion of ownership, and the wretched power of money we hold over one another's heads – all this vanishes like mist in the morning sun.

"You shall proclaim freedom throughout the land," says the verse (25:10). This verse contains the only appearance in the Torah of the Hebrew word *dror*, meaning "freedom." The Talmud uses this word in an expression equivalent to the modern English, "free as a bird": "A free bird, living in the house or in the field." Moreover, the *dror* is the modern Hebrew name for the sparrow. The sparrow is a highly sociable bird that readily feeds and flocks with other breeds, and lives comfortably among humans, too. Proclaiming *"dror"* throughout the land is our acknowledgment that we share the earth with all other beings, with everything and everyone else that dwells on it.

The Torah forces our awareness that at the end of the day – and concretely, at the end of the week, on the Sabbath; at the end of the cycle in the Sabbatical year; at the end of the Jubilee cycle, in the fiftieth year – the only thing we truly own is our obligation to others, expressed concretely in our commitment to social justice. Without reaching out to care for others, without extending a hand in assistance and friendship, without inviting those in need to share what we have, we fail in our obligation as human beings. Whether it be our money, our houses, or our cars; our family; our personal honor; or even the land we inhabit – the very land God promised to us – we cling to our worldly possessions at our peril. And we relinquish our sense of justice to the peril of all.

## 33

# The Pain of Living

> *Must be hell, living in the world,*
> *Living in the world like you.*
> *Must be hell, living in the world,*
> *Suffering in the world like you.*
>
> – The Rolling Stones, *It Must Be Hell*

Not one, not two or three, but five series of escalating punishments will God visit on the nation of Israel if they disobey the laws handed down at Sinai (Lev. 26:14–43). There will be all manner of terrors, of sickness and suffering. The land will be barren and the beasts of the field shall rise up against the inhabitants. Enemies shall flood the land, plague shall strike, and the cities will fall to utter ruin. The few who survive shall flee in panic and disappear, absorbed into the foreign nations.

If there was any doubt, the Torah tells us in fearsome detail of God's wrathful vengefulness, all pent up, seething, waiting to be unleashed should we falter in our faithful service. This is the final message of the book of Leviticus: Make no mistake, says God; I do not smite randomly, but with vengeance and with rage a-boiling. Numerous scholars point out that these sequences of punishments are actually contractual consequences, fully in line with contemporary royal documents of the ancient Near East: If we abide by our side of the covenant, God will care for us; if we violate our side of the covenant, God will not so much act to destroy us as step aside and allow nature to take its course, with the litany of dreadful outcomes listed here. The scholarly approach is less comforting still, since all these predicted horrors have in fact befallen the Jewish people.

And yet, we must choose to serve and worship this God – the only God there is.

When we come to the book of Deuteronomy, we will again experience this harsh language of rejection, but this time from Moses, who blames Israel for his sorrows, and for their own.

What message does Leviticus, the most bare-bones of the Torah's five books, leave us with? And after the extended language of divine rebuke, how can it casually return to close with a recitation of the laws of gifts to the Tabernacle, of the sanctification and redemption of animals and property, and finally – of all things – of tithing, of actively separating and giving gifts to God, the very God who promises to destroy us and scatter us among the nations of the world?

Let us return to the first – and still unanswerable – question: Why does God tell Adam not to eat the fruit? God tells Adam, "You will die." The serpent tells Eve, "You will become as gods, knowing good and evil." It appears they are both right.

Our text hints that Eden is very much on God's mind as God prepares to threaten us with destruction. Just before the extended rebuke, God says, "I shall *walk* among you" (26:12), using the same verb "to walk" that appears just before God confronts Adam after the eating of the fruit: "And they heard the sound of God *walking* in the Garden." God then challenges Adam: "Who told you that you were naked? Have you eaten from the tree?" (Gen. 3:8–11). God walks among God's creatures, then rebukes them harshly.

God intended Adam and Eve to live forever in joy and comfort. But things break down when free choice enters the equation. The Torah is left to explain, not *why* the world is the way it is, but how to behave within the world to reestablish our relationship with God, to reenter the pure, loving embrace.

Imagine how much more pleasant our lives would be if we had no freedom to choose, did not have to make any decision for ourselves at all but to live eternally in God's care, eating the fruit of the Garden and dwelling in constant bliss. Of course, we rebel at that thought now, but we react this way only after eating the fruit. We face an eternal paradox: we have no way of knowing whether we would be happy if we had never tasted the fruit. In fact, the very notion of happiness can exist only in a world in which good and evil struggle within us; we are happy when we do good, when we experience good. When we cease to do that which is bad – or merely when we cease to experience that which is bad.

Adam and Eve's inchoate state fulfills God's purpose in Creation. It is not total passivity: God gives Adam the job of caring for and tending the Garden, God tells Adam he will have dominion over all the animals and has Adam name them. And noting it is not good for Adam to be alone, God gives Eve to Adam. But neither do Adam and Eve in their unformed state jibe with our post-Eden understanding of human happiness, which comes from striving and the fulfillment of goals.

What is justice; what are the laws of the Sabbatical year, the Jubilee, all of which were just spelled out in the previous portion: letting the land lie fallow, the cancellation of debts, the restoring of ancient and original patrimonies? What are all these, if not a symbolic return to the primordial Eden, to a state where the land produces richly and all may take freely what they need?

But having once been broken, the container can never be whole again. It can be repaired, and will function again as a container, but the lines of breakage and repair will be ever visible.

Our return to God can never be complete. God drove Adam and Eve out of the Garden and made them live in the world. Even after we perform the complete acts of contrition, after we do full repentance, we can never actually return to the Garden. We must live in the world. Says the Torah, You cannot return to the Garden, but God will bring a taste of the Garden to you in every place in which you serve God faithfully and with a full heart. The consequence of the knowledge of good and evil is to live constantly torn between joy and sadness, between bliss and despair, between comfort and the fear of death.

Several commentators wonder why, amidst God's desperate chastisement of Israel, this portion and the preceding one focus on mundane matters of farming, land husbandry, and social welfare. Shouldn't God's threats be balanced by a profoundly spiritual message? But the banal message of daily living is itself profoundly spiritual. It is precisely in the day-to-day where we encounter God. Does God's world contain terrors? Absolutely. And the randomness of violence, whether from people or from nature, is in itself terrifying; the greatest effect is not even in those whom it slaughters, but that it makes each one of us live in constant fear. And God is very direct about this: I will slay you how and when I desire. How are we to know when we have displeased God? If Nadab and Abihu didn't know, how am I to judge my own actions?

The book of Leviticus, the book we have identified as the Torah's crux and core, leaves us with a choice to either accept or reject the world God has created. Which also means to either accept or reject God.

When we reject someone who has hurt or disappointed us, we rid ourselves of their presence, but unless we act to forgive them, we will carry forever the impression of the hurt they caused. If there is a final message and lesson to take from Leviticus, it is one of acceptance and forgiveness. Just as God ends the series of rebuke with an assurance of forgiveness, we must also learn to forgive. Not merely one another; that is simply a baseline for maintaining a functioning society. We must learn to forgive God.

The Torah has exhorted us to emulate God, to walk in God's ways and to follow God's example, and so become a holy nation. And what greater example, what more difficult and yet more powerful aspect, does God reveal over and over than God's own ability to forgive?

Forgiveness is not a onetime action; it is a lifelong process and an ongoing struggle. This is true with regard to our relationship with those closest to us, with ourselves surely, and no less so in our relationship with God. Jewish law and tradition make much of the obligation to ask forgiveness, but the granting of forgiveness is a far more painful process than even the hurt which first gives rise to the need to forgive.

Now, as we leave Leviticus, for all the tragedy we stand to

experience at the hand of God, the Torah reminds us that God is all we have. Yes, Nadab and Abihu died horribly in God's world and in God's immediate Presence. Yes, the Jewish people have been slaughtered in the millions throughout history. How can we turn to God with anything other than anger and fear? How can we not reject God altogether?

The apologetics of some thinkers leave us no better off. To say that all good comes from God, while evil comes from the hearts of human beings, is intellectually pathetic. It dodges the issue, robbing God of omniscience and omnipotence. No, we must blame God for everything. But we also must *thank* God for everything. We must be honest in our pain and disappointment, even in our anger with the Creator. Without that honesty, we will never have a truly intimate relationship. And without the opening for a loving, intimate relationship with the Creator, we have no place to turn with our gratitude.

Truly, we cannot know God's mind, and to attribute motives to God is intellectually farcical and spiritually criminal. Leviticus leaves us with a final message of forgiveness. God says, "I will punish you; I will destroy you. And I will forgive you." Perhaps the hardest work we can do in our lives is that of forgiveness. Of asking forgiveness from others, of forgiving others, and not to leave out the critical work of learning to forgive ourselves. It has been long taught by spiritual teachers, as well as documented in scientific studies, that the two most powerfully positive habits of mind are those of forgiveness and gratitude. When we approach the world with gratitude, we release all sorts of positive brain chemicals. Our physical health improves, and we have a powerful, positive impact on those around us. Forgiveness is the bridge to gratitude; when we work to practice forgiveness, we learn to accept our lives and ourselves. In so doing, we unleash our own spiritual power on the world.

As master meditation teacher Jack Kornfield says, learning to forgive means accepting that I will never have a better past. At the end of Leviticus, God says: I will forgive you. As difficult as it is, as overwhelming as the damning evidence

*Leviticus*

seems against God, if we do not return that forgiveness, we will never free ourselves to accomplish our spiritual task in this life. There is no better, no more compelling place to practice forgiveness than in working to forgive God. God, whose immense gifts, and whose dread acts of destruction, are forever with us. We cannot rid ourselves of God. Rather than fleeing, rather than rage and resentment, let us learn all we can from this relationship. Ultimately, our relationship with God is not for God, but for us, to decide.

God, thank You for forgiving us, and for teaching us by example the gift of forgiveness. I pray that I may learn to forgive others, to forgive myself and, especially, to forgive You.

# Numbers

34 • *Ba-Midbar*        (1:1 – 4:20)
35 • *Nasso*            (4:21 – 7:89)
36 • *Be-Ha'alotcha*    (8:1 – 12:16)
37 • *Shelach-Lecha*    (13:1 – 15:41)
38 • *Korach*           (16:1 – 18:32)
39 • *Chukkat*          (19:1 – 22:1)
40 • *Balak*            (22:2 – 25:9)
41 • *Pinchas*          (25:10 – 30:1)
42 • *Mattot*           (30:2 – 32:42)
43 • *Masei*            (33:1 – 36:13)

# 34

## To Choose or not to Choose

*Everyone has a choice: if you want to follow a good path and be righteous, it's up to you. If you want to follow a bad path and be wicked, it's up to you. This is what it means when God says, "See, the human has become like one of us, with the ability to know good and evil."*

– Maimonides, *Laws of Repentance*

With the book of Numbers, we embark on a new narrative – and on forty years of wandering, homeless, in the wilderness. In this book, our identity will be challenged. Our selfishness will be held up alongside our commitment to creating a harmonious society, and we shall repeatedly fail the test. We will find ourselves homeless when we fail to put aside our own petty interests for the greater goal, when we insist on taking for ourselves now, rather than on building a future for others. As we look with longing to our Promised Land, we must remember that our nation will be defined not by the territory we conquer, but by our commitment to service of God and to righteousness for our fellow human beings.

After the existential turbulence of Leviticus, the fact that we are still reading does not necessarily mean we are reconciled to God's arbitrary nature, nor that we have fully forgiven God and accepted God's world and our role in it. Perhaps we are fascinated by the horror of it all and cannot tear ourselves away until we have seen every last painful detail – determined to go on despite God's seeming aloofness, God's erratic rewards and impulsive punishments. Or maybe it's simply that human beings are hard to kill. We can put up with tremendous adversity, with terrors and suffering that we cannot begin to fathom until we are actually faced with them.

The book of Numbers is a vast biblical road trip, filled with characters both colorful and diabolical, holy and devious, and including some of the Torah's most devastating, as well as some of its funniest episodes. The entire first portion is devoted to an extended census, in which the whole nation of Israel are counted and the arrangement of the camp is specified (and which doubles as the standard military array when Israel will go into battle). This is followed by a detailed sub-census of the clans of the Levites, and an enumeration of their specified tasks in the management of the Tabernacle.

The opening of the book of Numbers, in which the Israelites prepare to enter the Promised Land, echoes the opening of the book of Exodus, which recounts the seventy souls who went down to Egypt with Jacob. There, the Torah counted the people as they headed into exile; here they are counted as they prepare to march to redemption. Little do they know....

In his commentary on the book of Numbers, the great Inquisition-era rabbi, Isaac Abarbanel (Portugal and Italy, 1437–1508), lays out a vision of the Torah's structure. In Abarbanel's outline, we see a parallel in the way the Torah, as a narrative, deals with its own concept of time:

**Genesis** – Gives the ancestry of the world and the forebears of the people of Israel, starting from the moment of the Creation, the world which will receive – and will desperately need – the Torah.

**Exodus** – Introduces the fundamental Jewish theme of exile and redemption, the revelation of the Torah, and the making of the Tabernacle.

**Leviticus**– Holiness finds its home in the Tabernacle; Torah law is sacred, normative behavior.

**Numbers**– The struggle to lead the people. Israel's journeys, their wanderings in the wilderness. Rebellion, delay, and despair. Forty years in the wilderness, leading to the closing of the story of Israel's exile.

The final book, **Deuteronomy**, is a retelling of Israel's narrative from Moses' point of view. Abarbanel seems to read it as an amalgam of Moses' handiwork, spliced in with God's.

It may be that God gave the words, while Moses put them in their final order. Or that Moses wrote, and God approved.

In terms of the Torah's literary structure, the book of Numbers closes the three-book narrative that started with Exodus. It brings to a close the wanderings in the wilderness, setting the stage for Israel's entry into the Promised Land.

The opening of Numbers is very specific with regard to the setting. The place and time of the events are stated precisely: "And God spoke to Moses in the wilderness of Sinai, in the tent of meeting, on the first day of the second month, in the second year of their coming out of the land of Egypt" (Num. 1:1).[1] On a pragmatic level, this portion is about establishing a military draft, and the specificity of the date sets the age range of eligibility for military service. By the end of the book, it will also establish the dividing line between those destined to die in the wilderness versus those who will enter the Land of Israel. From a literary perspective, this will repeat in the opening verses of Deuteronomy, which distinguish between those who will not enter the land and those who will. And of course, God's command to take a census harks back to the sin of the Golden Calf in Exodus 32, where Moses was instructed to take and count up a half-shekel from every able-bodied man.

The half-shekel is omitted this time. In the earlier census, it was an equalizer; God commanded that the rich not give more than half a shekel, nor the poor less. By contrast, this census highlights the differences between individuals, from the array of the tribes and their banners around the Tabernacle to the tasks assigned to each sub-clan of the Levites in the care and transportation of the Tabernacle.

Furthermore, this census is more complex than that first one. Two verbs repeat in the text in describing the action. They are forms of the Hebrew words *nasa* – "to lift," and *pakad* – that complex root whose range of meanings include "to remember," "to visit," "to punish," "to redeem," and "to

---

1   Unless otherwise noted, all references in this section are to the book of Numbers.

command." For our purposes, we shall invoke the idea of remembering.

In Numbers 1:2, God commands Moses to "Lift up the heads of the whole congregation of Israel," with the command *Lift* in the plural – meaning both Moses and Aaron are to perform the count. In the next verse, the command finishes, "Count (remember) them according to those of military age, you and Aaron."

When we analyze these two Hebrew verb roots according to the principle of first occurrences, a fascinating juxtaposition emerges. The root *nasa* appears in the human realm, while *pakad* is in that of the divine.

The first occurrence of *nasa* is Genesis 4:7. God admonishes Cain after rejecting his offering: "Is it not true that if you do well, it shall be *uplifted?*" This is probably best translated as, "Isn't it the case that if you improve, your offerings will be accepted?" We all know the outcome of that scene.

In Genesis 21:1, "God remembered (*pakad*) Sarah," and the impending birth of Isaac was announced. This verb surfaces again at the end of Genesis (50:24), when Joseph is about to die: "And God shall surely *remember* you…and will take you out of this land of Egypt, to the land promised to Abraham, Isaac, and Jacob." In fact, Joseph makes his brothers swear an oath on these very words: "God will surely remember you; and you, bring up my bones from here" (Gen. 50:25).

Not only is that oath passed down; it gives hope for the future when Israel is enslaved in Egypt, and is the remnant that ties Israel to its deep past. The proof that this remained embedded in the Israelites' consciousness is when (Ex. 4:31), "The people believed, and they heard that God *remembered* Israel…and they bowed their heads and prostrated themselves" – though to what exactly, they knew not.

Now, as the Israelites embark on the wanderings of the book of Numbers, they believe that they know.

How wrong they are!

The opening sequence of the book describes the battle array and the order of march the Israelites are to follow as they head off to take possession of the Promised Land. So yes, it appears they have remembered God's promise – to return Abraham's descendants to the land of Israel. But they have forgotten all that came between: the need not merely for strong leadership, but for a cohesive society to follow those leaders; not merely the right to be taken care of, but the obligation to care for others. Not merely the blessings of the manna, the divine pillars of fire and smoke, but the spiritual qualities and ritual observances required to maintain the covenantal relationship. It will take forty years for them to begin to learn.

So it is with us. God continually offers us the opportunity to combine human volition – lifting – with divine providence – remembering. Like Cain, we frequently end up not being equal to the task. Forty years on, though not yet ready, we shall be propelled across the Jordan River.

Still, God's delays are not God's denials. The theme of the book of Numbers is the tension and the balance between the nation of Israel and the individual Jew: balancing our individual destinies with the eternal arc of the destiny of the Jewish people, as well as taking our proper role in the hierarchy of the nation. For the generations that perished in the wilderness, this may seem a bitter lesson – a *remembering*, in the sense of chastisement. For those who are able to regard themselves as part of the overall destiny of the Jewish nation, it is no longer purely bitter. "Is it not the case that if you improve, it shall be uplifted?" Is it not within the power of each of us, individually, to better the situation?

The book of Numbers is a contorted knot of clashing narratives. Starting with a clear description of each person's place in society – both literally, in the configuration of the camp, and more broadly in terms of specific tasks assigned by family and by clan – the book quickly moves on to describe the Israelites' descent into rebellion. People are not content to be who and what they are, but all seek to grasp something that has been assigned to someone else. Above and beyond the standard grumbling over food and water, we shall see the people in rebellion against the leadership of Moses and

Aaron, both by upstart groups of Levites – their own kin – as well as by other groups within the nation. Moses and Aaron themselves will violate a direct command from God. Finally, the entire people will throw off the yoke of Heaven and descend into casual idol worship born of sexual wantonness.

Are these truly the people chosen to bring God's Presence into this world? As we have seen over and over again from the earliest pages of the Torah, the bearers of the blessing and of God's message are not perfect, yet the Torah insists that we strive to perfect ourselves. Chosenness is decidedly not the concept that "God chooses an imperfect vessel to do His perfect work." Rather, it is a two-way street: God chooses Israel to receive God's message. Israel, for its part, must engage with the challenge. And now that the Torah has come into this world, anyone can choose to follow it. Can choose to *become* chosen. As the book of Numbers will demonstrate, it is not an easy path.

# 35

# Breaking Faith, Keeping Faith

*A great embarrassing fact...haunts all attempts to represent the market as the highest form of human freedom: that historically, impersonal, commercial markets originate in theft.*

– David Graeber, *Debt: The First 5,000 Years*

In this, the longest weekly portion in the Torah, the dedication of the altar in the Tabernacle is completed. Before the grand finale, in which the leaders of the twelve tribes bring sumptuous gifts in a lavish procession, the Torah deals with the inevitability of human dishonesty, the devastating power of sexual jealousy, and finally, the need of some people to withdraw from society in search of spiritual experience.

The section of those who break faith – who embezzle or who steal by false oath – is the shortest of these three intervening segments, but with the broadest implications. The Torah's choice of wording is very precise: "A man or a woman, when they shall do any sin against people, to break faith with God, and their soul shall become guilty..." (Num. 5:6). The Torah's choice of the word *when* (in Hebrew, *ki*) is an acknowledgment that people are not capable of attaining perfection. We *will* sin, the Torah tells us, and here is the mechanism for expiation: "They shall confess their sin which they committed, and they shall return the value for which they are guilty, adding one fifth to the principal" (5:7–8).

Commandments and prohibitions fall into two categories: those between individuals or between persons and society, and those between us and God. This passage makes it clear that, while ritual acts are clearly between us and God, the Torah's God-given social structure sees human acts of kindness and charity as the mechanism through which God works in this world. Acts of dishonesty, of violence, or of disregard for others injure God's Torah, which is in fact God's own Self.

What's pernicious here is not the theft itself; the Torah deals with theft elsewhere. It's the cover-up, a violation of God's commandment against swearing falsely. This is worse than simple theft, which harms an individual. Swearing falsely undermines the social contract.

As anthropologist David Graeber points out in his book, *Debt: The First 5,000 Years*, the less people trust one another, the more they require a clearly defined mechanism of exchange. He refers to what he calls a natural communism of so-called primitive societies. Historically, societies that thrive on barter quickly develop extensive and highly sophisticated systems of tracking who gave what to whom, and what they might expect in return. Historian Gordon Wood, in his *The Radicalism of the American Revolution*, describes the minutely detailed records kept in colonial American communities that thrived on intricate barter relationships, a complex set of interlocking transactions spread over long periods of time and accepted throughout the community. The use of an easily agreed-upon medium of exchange – money – becomes necessary when people need to trade outside their communities, when they face others with whom they did not have a communal bond of trust. "In God we trust," reads the sign in the corner grocery store, "all others pay cash."

This concept of trust lies at the heart of all societies: regardless of differences *between* cultures, all participants within a group must have faith in how their group works. Theft is a crime, but it doesn't undermine society. But the false oath about the theft does. As we have seen throughout history, the insistence that one's false oath – the Big Lie of those in power – must be accepted as true is the wedge that rips apart nations from within.

Next in the reading comes what, for modern readers, remains one of the Torah's most problematic passages, that of the wife suspected of adultery (5:11–31). While from our contemporary perspective the process seems unutterably primitive, the rabbis say this is the Torah's ingenious solution to the problem of honor killings. To be both intellectually and morally honest, we can't judge the Torah – or indeed any historical document – strictly by contemporary moral standards. The Torah is a single document setting forth an ethical, religious, societal, and national project, all in one, and all in the context of its time and place. The Torah speaks for all time, but it speaks *from* a world in which slavery was common; in which women were the outright property, first of their fathers, then of their husbands; in which clans carried on blood feuds over generations; and where people killed strangers. If we look into our own time, we will see that very few modern legal systems have confronted societal issues of the magnitude and scope undertaken by the Torah – and with the express purpose not of keeping a ruling class in power, as is typically the case, but of protecting the weak and creating a society founded on equal justice.

This section gives a detailed and disturbingly accurate literary picture of the effects of male jealousy, acknowledging that a man in the grip of sexual jealousy gives in to unappeasable rage, and extreme measures are required to calm the conflagration. Even today, it is common to see sexual anger destroy relationships and families, leading to violence – even murder. The Torah introduces a long-drawn-out and complex process as a counter to the devastating effects of male jealousy, in a world where men bought their wives and could dispose of them as they pleased: casting them out, or simply killing them. The ritual surrounding the suspected adulteress serves as a slowing-down mechanism, requiring many days and many steps along the way before the woman can be formally charged – not even yet punished – for her behavior, thus providing a cooling-off period for her husband's anger. We cannot rewire human emotions. Rather, in order for society to function, we create mechanisms for curbing behavior. The Torah goes a major step further, making sure that the weak are protected from the strong.

The third intervening section in this week's reading deals with the *nazir*, a person who takes a vow of abstinence from drinking wine. The vow of the *nazir* entails other behaviors, notably allowing the hair and the fingernails to grow long, which emphasize that the individual has entered into a period of self-ostracism. The Torah frowns on asceticism. God creates the world as an act of generosity; our task is to make the most of it, not to take the least from it. The Talmud says that when we arrive before the heavenly tribunal, we will be asked to justify every permissible pleasure that we failed to take advantage of during our life. Yet the Torah also recognizes that people sometimes need to withdraw, that sometimes the world can be too much with us and we need to diminish our sensory input – sometimes in search of higher spirituality, sometimes merely to keep a grip on our sanity. The thirty-day withdrawal of the *nazir* is the Torah's way of dealing with this need. Take a break, the Torah says, and we have a way to bring you back, too.

Tying these three sections together is the concept of the vow: the one who breaks faith by vowing they did not steal, the woman forced to vow she was not unfaithful, the one who withdraws by taking a temporary vow of abstinence. All these are tied to notions of faithfulness, of adhering to what is required for a society to run smoothly. Those who steal must admit their act and make restitution. Society must do all it can to reconcile spouses who don't trust one another, who cannot live in harmony. Some people need to withdraw from society, and the Torah offers a mechanism for people to do this without completely severing their relationships.

The vow transforms private troubles into societal concerns. A breach of trust between friends is transformed into an attack on the fabric of society. The family unit is the basic building block of society; trouble between husband and wife is brought not only before the nation, but before God. Feelings of alienation are acknowledged; society permits the individual to separate, then reenter in a ritual that sanctifies their withdrawal rather than condemns it.

Finally, the altar is dedicated. The leaders of the twelve tribes bring their offerings – twelve identical contributions on successive days. As the half-shekel was an equal donation from each adult male for the construction and maintenance of the Tabernacle, now each tribe gives an equal gift to the Tabernacle. The "flat tax" serves not to oppress those for whom it is a hardship, but to raise everyone to equal footing. The Tabernacle and its altar, whose purpose is to seek atonement for the sin of the Golden Calf, must treat each individual equally. This is the most profound of the Torah's social and political messages: that equality in the eyes of God must be reflected in human terms as equality before the altar of God and before the law. Only then will the Tabernacle stand. Only then will the sacrifices be acceptable on the altar. Only then will God speak to Moses from between the hovering golden wings of the cherubim, atop the Ark of the Covenant, out of the eternal emptiness.

## 36

# To Do Better

*You who choose to lead must follow,*
*But if you fall you fall alone.*
*If you should stand then who's to guide you?*
*If I knew the way I would take you home.*

– Grateful Dead, "*Ripple*"

This week's Torah portion begins with God telling Moses, "Speak to Aaron and say to him, When you kindle the lamps, the seven lamps shall illuminate toward the front of the Menorah" (8:2).

The Menorah, the seven-branched oil lamp, is among the very oldest Jewish symbols. It was among the chief vessels that God instructed Moses to have crafted for the priestly service, first in the Tabernacle in the wilderness and later in the Temple in Jerusalem. It is featured prominently in the massive relief carving atop the Roman Arch of Titus, showing the spoils of Jerusalem being carted off to Rome, where it vanished and was never seen again.

This portion comes immediately after an extended section which describes the offerings brought by the princes of each tribe of Israel in the process of dedicating the Tabernacle (ch. 7). The rabbis of old ask, why does God tell Aaron about his task now? Aaron and his sons, the Kohanim, the priestly clan, come from the tribe of Levi, which is the one tribe not represented in the dedication process. This is because the Levites have special tasks pertaining to the construction and maintenance of the Tabernacle. They also take it down and carry it on Israel's journeys through the wilderness. This closeness to God should be enough, the rabbis say. The traditional commentary says that Aaron was dejected because he had not brought an offering, so God told him about his own special task, which was to light the Menorah every day.

Outside of the fact that this makes Aaron seem like a spoiled child, we have to ask why this particular action is singled out. Nachmanides observes that Aaron performed many special acts in the Tabernacle. Indeed, there are many acts that *only* Aaron could perform. So first we can ask, why do the rabbis think Aaron is upset over not having brought an offering? Perhaps more to the point, why is God telling Aaron about this one action, his daily lighting of the Menorah, when he has so many other exclusive tasks? Nachmanides' answer points to the distant future.

The Torah was given some 3,500 years ago, and the story of the Tabernacle follows closely thereafter, within the same year. It would be hundreds of years before King Solomon built the Temple in Jerusalem (the Temple that was destroyed in Nebuchadnezzar's siege of Jerusalem in 587 BCE), and generations more until the Second Temple would be built. In around 170 BCE, Jerusalem was invaded and the Second Temple was looted. The practices of Judaism were outlawed, and the Temple was converted to use for pagan ceremonies. This led to the revolt of the Maccabees, a priestly clan in Judaea.

When the Maccabees and their minions won the military victory, the first thing they did was clean out the Temple and prepare it for the daily ritual offerings that had been suspended. The story is told that they wanted to light the Menorah – a biblical commandment that had to be carried out daily – but they could not find the special, ritually pure oil that was required. Only one flask of oil was found, containing enough oil for only one day. They used the contents in the flask and, so the story goes, miraculously, the Menorah lamps burned for eight days. This allowed the victors to complete the purification of the Temple and to prepare more oil for the daily lighting of the Menorah. This is commemorated in the Hanukkah festival (*hanukkah* is the Hebrew word meaning "dedication," describing the dedication of a new house as well as the consecration of the Temple). Thus, the Temple was rededicated to its proper service.

Nachmanides says God is not telling Aaron to be happy

over his special task. God is saying: Aaron, look deeply into your own distant future. More than a thousand years from now, your descendants will save Judaism, will save the Torah, will save the Jewish nation, and their accomplishment will be symbolized in this simple act which you perform each morning: the lighting of the Menorah. This is not a special gift to appease Aaron. It is an exhortation for Aaron to remember how critically important his job is, how essential every single task he undertakes – a charge to not let his guard down, so to speak. Not ever. *You* think you're just lighting the lamp each morning, says God. What you're actually doing is preparing an eternal spiritual and national practice that your descendants will return to, more than a thousand years in the future, to keep alive the Torah you have just received at Mount Sinai. More than any other symbol or practice in the Tabernacle, the Menorah symbolizes the unity of the spiritual with the societal – religion and nation in one.

But wait. According to the Midrash, there is another aspect to Aaron's displeasure – if indeed he is displeased, which is not at all clear from the text. Characteristically, the Midrash reads the unspoken message glowing between the written lines of Torah text, and here it identifies that Aaron is displeased. Is he sad? Is he angry? That much is not clear. What is clear is that the Midrash finds something troubling about the passage that has gone before, and sees a remedy in this Torah portion. Some wrong has been done, and Aaron is suffering. What could it be?

At the end of last week's Torah portion comes an extended passage describing the offerings brought at the dedication of the altar (7:1–88). There is great pomp and circumstance as the heads of the twelve tribes bring forward twelve identical offerings of silver, gold, flour and incense, and great quantities of livestock for sacrifices. Only the tribe of Levi is left out. The heads of the other tribes appear at the dedication ceremony with wagons laden with gifts. God did not command or request that they bring anything, but now that they have brought their offerings, God instructs Moses to take them and use them for the service of the Tabernacle.

What might be going through Aaron's mind as he stands by watching all this? When his sons brought spontaneous offerings, they died. They were chosen to minister in the Presence of God, to bring offerings on the altar. Yet when they brought additional offerings out of their own depth of spirituality, it cost them their lives. Now Aaron watches the heads of the tribes bearing ostentatious gifts while God tells Moses to accept them. A cynic might say that the spiritual no longer matters, that the religion has been turned over to the wealthy, and that the clergy are no more than the hired help.

This remains the profoundly disturbing reality of life, of the Torah, and of our relationship with God: the world is a place of random danger, and neither moral behavior nor piety guarantees our well-being. All around us the wicked prosper, while the good are crushed and trampled underfoot. The heads of the tribes are praised for bringing identical offerings; like King Arthur's knights, they all are rated equal. By the sheer weight of the description – at eighty-nine verses, this is one of the longest chapters in the Torah – the text places heavy emphasis on the heads of the tribes and their lavish gifts. The rabbis, too, heap praise on the leaders for their generosity, and for working to ensure that each leader's gift is exactly equal to that of the others. What is missing is the connection between God's acceptance of the magnificent wealth brought as freewill offerings and the spontaneous offering of Nadab and Abihu: The heads of the tribes reap God's acceptance and the praise of the rabbis; Nadab and Abihu reap instant death, and condemnation from the commentators. Aaron, with his own bitter experience behind him, must be reeling at God's behavior.

We rush to combat evil. But we accept mediocrity, particularly when it comes bearing silver and gold. We decry business owners over practices such as slavery and child labor, then we praise them and graciously accept their money, even putting their names over the doors of libraries, hospitals, and universities. Look at how much wealth we have! the princes say.

Look at how much we have given to the Tabernacle! It is not blatant evil that endangers society, but the gradual lowering of moral standards. Moses and Aaron are designated to perform their service; the others have purchased their place at the altar. In such a society, it is only a matter of time before the rot eats through to the very foundation. The princes of the tribes bring their gifts sincerely – yet they are shallow, believing that silver, gold, and slaughtered animals are what God truly wants of us. It is inevitable that this society will ultimately tear itself apart. What is not inevitable, and what God now rushes to reassure Aaron, is that the day will come when Aaron's own descendants will rescue God from the clutches of the rich, and will return the altar, not to those who write the biggest checks, but to those who cherish it for its own sake as the place where God chooses to communicate with us directly.

There is a spiritual practice of meditating on the future. We sit and contemplate who we are, where we are. Then we envision our children. It doesn't matter if we don't have them yet; the purpose of the practice is to develop a sense of our own importance in the world, of the very long-term impact we create. The legacy we will leave. Visualize your children. And their children. And *their* children, and theirs, and theirs....

We try to support our loved ones in different ways: often emotionally, frequently financially. It is in this regard that we contemplate God's message to Aaron: If you think what you are doing has importance now, you can't begin to understand how important it will be in some distant future, a future so far away that you cannot imagine it. A future in which your impact will have spread out in the world.

But yes: imagine it. Envision it. Every smallest act we perform today ripples across the years stretching out in front of us, almost to infinity. Certainly beyond any time we normally contemplate in our daily life, when our focus usually stretches no farther than lunch, our afternoon meetings, and the football games we're planning to watch over the weekend.

Give yourself the gift of envisioning a vast future. More, give your future the gift of paying attention to it today. You deserve it. And your future needs you.

# 37

## To See or Not to See

*And it shall be to you for a fringe, and you will see it and you will remember all the commandments of the Lord, and you will do them. And you will not seek after the longing of your heart and the longing of your eyes.*

– Numbers 15:39

This week's Torah portion tells the story of Moses sending spies to reconnoiter the land of Canaan, prior to the Israelites' entry into the Promised Land. In a nutshell, the book of Numbers is about leadership, about the transition from wandering desert tribes centered around a single charismatic leader – Moses – to a functioning society with a hierarchy and a leadership structure. In last week's portion, Moses' father-in-law, Jethro, leaves the Israelites to return to his own people, the Midianites. Jethro was the person who first introduced the idea of a hierarchical division of responsibilities (Ex. 18), which enabled Moses to delegate the responsibilities of leadership. Now, however, the tribes which comprise the desert clan are beginning to coalesce around their own important figures, and a struggle for dominance is emerging. It is just at this point that Jethro announces he is returning to his home, and Moses, almost in desperation, begs him to stay. But Jethro goes off, and the remainder of the book of Numbers recounts a sequence of problems and failures of leadership.

The story of the spies, recounted in this portion, is a defining episode in the history of the Jewish nation. Moses sends twelve men, leaders of the tribes of Israel, to spy out the land of Canaan in order to form a plan for the upcoming Israelite entry and conquest. He explicitly instructs them to list the characteristics of the land and to scout out its people;

in other words, military intelligence gathering (Num. 13:17–20).

When the spies return, they give a straightforward and accurate accounting of their observations, including the difficulties the people will encounter in attempting to conquer the land. They are interrupted when Caleb, one of the twelve spies, jumps up and exhorts the people to go, heedless of whatever difficulties may lie ahead (13:30–33). The other spies shout him down, with the exception of Joshua, who remains silent. This dramatic sequence results in the Israelites' being condemned to wander the wilderness for forty years. God reacts far more harshly to disbelief than to disobedience.

The portion ends with the passage enjoining the Israelites to make fringes on the corners of their cloaks, a practice we continue to observe to this day (15:37–41). One occasionally observes Jews with strings hanging down over their belts. These are fringes tied on a four-cornered undergarment in ongoing observance of this biblical command.

The reason we are enjoined to wear these fringes is so that *"you will see it and you will remember all the commandments of the Lord, and you will do them. And you will not seek after the longing of your heart and the longing of your eyes."* (15:39).

In the Torah, the sense of sight is problematic. At the moment of the splitting of the Sea of Reeds, we are told that the Israelites *saw* the Egyptians dead on the shore, and *saw* the mighty hand that God had raised against Egypt, and upon seeing, they *believed* in God and in God's servant Moses (Ex. 14:30–31). In this week's portion, however, the men who saw clearly, and who accurately reported what they saw, are punished, while the ones who deny the clear evidence of their own eyes – Caleb and Joshua – are rewarded. They are the only males of the generation that left Egypt who will survive to enter the land of Canaan.

The passage from the splitting of the Sea of Reeds and the ensuing Song of the Sea (Ex. 15:1–19) are read in the daily Jewish prayer service each morning. They are uncomfortable reminders that we continually seek concrete proof of God,

## The Weight of Gold

and a challenge to us to recognize that true faith does not rest on factual corroboration.

The Israelites are surrounded by miracles, but no sooner is one miracle performed for us than we turn around and accuse God of abandoning us. We lived through the miracles and the plagues in Egypt; we were saved, and saw the Egyptians dead, at the Sea of Reeds; we were fed manna and given water from a miraculous well in the wilderness. And yet, in this week's portion, we can't believe that the God who brought us this far will help us overcome the obstacles and take possession of the Promised Land.

There are multiple failures of leadership in this portion. Moses doesn't take full control of the discussion when the spies return; the spies trot out all the problems, but fail to offer solutions; Caleb is all rah-rah about the opportunity to inherit the land, but he fails utterly to address the very real specific objections of the other spies. In the absence of strong leadership, we fall apart as a people. (Notably it is Joshua, who remains silent, who will be appointed leader upon the death of Moses, a task for which he will not be fully prepared – and which of us is?)

After all this spying out the land, the portion ends with a warning against believing what we see. In Hebrew, the verb used for "exploring after the impulses of your heart or what you see with your eyes" is the identical verb meaning "to spy." The message is clear: if you need to see in order to believe, you will not succeed. If you need to be shown the truth again and again, you really have no faith. Your mind and your soul are disconnected from one another and so you can learn nothing.

It's difficult to maintain our personal spiritual equilibrium. We find ourselves returning for nourishment. We return to daily prayer, to study, to contemplation, all to reinforce ourselves spiritually. In fact, as the verses say, to remind ourselves of God's gifts to us, and of God's requirements of us.

As people functioning in the world, we need to be able to bring together the concrete reality of the world with our inner spirituality. True success for the individual comes from the ability to hold seemingly contradictory ideas, or at least disjointed ones, and make them work together. Think of it; when we say something is paradoxical, we are actually saying: I don't believe that reality has it right. In truth, when we find something to be a paradox, it is because our mind is not sophisticated enough to embrace it. It's called cognitive dissonance. And the ability to live with it, and to derive certainty from doubt, is what makes individual success possible. The ability to communicate that certainty in ways that help inspire others is what makes for true leadership.

Over and over again, we are exhorted to look at the world from God's perspective. Don't believe what you see, the Torah is telling us. Rather, look into the world and see that which you believe.

Believe in yourself and keep the faith.

# 38

# The Great Undoing

*What we have here is failure to communicate.*

— Cool Hand Luke

Moses has failed.

After the spies' mission, Moses was supposed to lead the nation into the Promised Land. Instead, the leaders of the tribes descend into finger-pointing and the people dissolve in despair. God condemns the Israelites to forty years of wandering, meaning most of those redeemed from slavery in Egypt will now die in the desert. God's promise – to bring the people into the land – remains, but is now unimaginably distant, as those who heard the promise will not live to see it. At the critical moment, when strong leadership was called for, Moses reveals himself as very much "not a man of words," but also significantly not a man of action. His silence while the spies rage at one another, indeed, his complete absence from the scene, are baffling.

Did Moses hope the people would learn leadership through this mission? That the conquest of the land would be the staging ground for forging a cooperative leadership class? But perhaps the spies were emulating Moses, a monolithic leader who announces one law for all. The spies returned with good intelligence about what awaited the Israelites, but they could not speak to one another to create a strategy. They were the leaders of the tribes. Why could they not work together?

Moses conveys God's words to the people, but it turns out that he lacks the powers of argument to inspire them to act. Moses has no gift of persuasion. At two critical moments in this week's portion, Moses shows himself literally incapable of speech. When Korach launches his challenge (Num. 16:4), and again when God threatens to destroy the entire nation

(17:10), Moses' response in both cases is to fall on his face, avoiding all confrontation and burying the very organ of speech, just as Korach will be buried in retribution.

Not all great orators are great leaders, but the successful leader must know how to convince people. At critical junctures, when the existence of the nation is at stake, it is not enough that God speaks directly to Moses. Moses must also know how to persuade the people. Perhaps this is utterly beyond his ken. A man who sits intimately with God, face-to-face – why would we expect him to engage in petty cajoling, in spinning images to try to "sell the program" to his people? Yet for a nation in transition, about to attain its great promise and thus to take on a new identity, communication is called for. Will the elders, those who stand next in line for the leadership of Israel, learn not Moses' wisdom but his failure? Moses' helplessness is the great comeuppance. This is exactly what Moses warns God at the burning bush: "I am not a man of words."

The shock waves continue to reverberate. As Moses withdraws, revolt shreds the bonds of tribe and family, and others rush to step into the vacuum. Challenged by others' words, Moses is unable to respond. Crisis of leadership – a repeated theme in the book of Numbers – expands like a malignancy until the mutiny spurs Moses to wrathful vengeance, and even God seems to go mad, lashing out wantonly and slaughtering indiscriminately with a deadly plague.

Who are these men who challenge Moses and Aaron's leadership? Korach, a Levite, together with Dathan and Abiram, descendants of Reuben, followed by 250 of the leaders of the nation – "men of *name*," a distinction we shall revisit in a later chapter. Korach asserts his claim to leadership as Moses and Aaron's cousin. Dathan and Abiram assail Moses' failure to achieve the national objective, while the Men of Name are the foremost citizens of the nation. From a political perspective, the revolt is led by a royal pretender, seconded by men campaigning for the popular vote, and contested by those who see themselves as the natural ruling aristocracy. For all the public utterances reported in this portion, there is little actual communication. The only ones who actually make a point are Dathan and Abiram (16:13–14): "You brought us up...to die in the wilderness, and now you want to continue to lord it over us? And you haven't brought us into the land flowing with milk and honey!" Still, Moses remains incapable of engaging with those who confront him. Incapable to the point of panic. To the point of murderous rage.

Attentive readers will have seen this coming.

As the Torah lists the names of those sent to spy out the land (13:4ff): "Of the tribe of Reuben, Shamuah son of Zacur; of the tribe of Simeon, Shaphat son of Hori; of the tribe of Judah, Caleb son of Jephunneh..." did we notice that the tribe of Levi is not represented? There must have been great anticipation as the men marched off to scout out the land, and great fanfare on their return. But after they are struck down by God, the Israelites become painfully aware that the tribe of Levi – Moses and Aaron's family – was never at risk.

This week's reading opens with two genealogies: "And Korah, son of Izhar, son of Kohat, son of Levi – and Dathan and Abiram, sons of Eliab (as well as On, son of Peleth), all descendants of Reuben – betook themselves" (16:1). Korach's confederates are descended from Reuben, Jacob's firstborn, who lost his birthright because he failed at the task of leadership. Reuben failed to prevent the brothers from harming Joseph and then failed to save him from the well. He failed to take charge when the brothers traveled to buy grain in Egypt, failed to act as head of the family when they returned to Egypt with Benjamin, and did not step forward when Joseph threatened to take Benjamin prisoner. Reuben was not equal to the tasks demanded of the firstborn. The inheritance of the firstborn was given to Joseph, while the leadership of the family was split, with the political leadership going to Judah and the religious leadership to Levi. Reuben's descendants are uniquely positioned to criticize Moses for his shortcomings. They have also have nursed their resentment over generations, obsessed with the slight to their ancestor's honor. (Indeed, on the eve of Israel's finally taking possession of the Promised Land (ch. 32), the Reubenites will disassociate themselves not only from the nation but from God's covenant, refusing to settle the land together with the other tribes.)

"You have taken too much!" says Korach (16:3). "Since the whole congregation are all holy, and God is in their midst, why do you elevate yourselves above the community of God?" Korach is self-righteous, an iconoclast. But there is nothing convincing in his attack. He claims Aaron's position by arguing, "You're no better than I am!"

Dathan and Abiram level accurate criticism at Moses, but they then turn away and display their anger for all to see. Meanwhile, the 250 "princes of the congregation, those summoned at the appointed times, men of name" (16:2), do not even speak. Everyone knows why they are there. They stand for the hostility and grief of the nation: Moses put the leaders of the people in harm's way while shielding his own family. The men of name know that they could be next.

The calamitous outcome of the spies' expedition has shaken the people's faith in Moses. But a nation does not stand or fall on a single outcome. Even a devastating loss such as the failure to enter the Promised Land – even a signal failure such as Moses' inaction – does not put an end to the people, nor to the dream of nationhood.

What Dathan and Abiram charge is true, and Korach's claim to family lineage is plain. Yet they are no leaders, but mere opportunists. They mislead in the way of all dishonest iconoclasts, because failures of leadership do not undermine the core truth of leadership. If anything, the measure of leadership is to be taken at the nadir, on the heels of defeat. And the people have failed Moses as well, for it is their task to shoulder their own burden within society. To accept their role in the nation's failure. As President Eisenhower said, the true leader gives credit to others and takes the blame himself.

But the Torah's model of leadership also demands wise and dedicated followers. Just as Moses must bear the people's failures, his shortcomings are the responsibility of all. Because failures of leadership are equally collective failures. Up until the spies' return, the people followed Moses blindly. Now their own weaknesses leave them open to resentment. If a society is only as strong as its weakest link, leaders are only as strong as their weakest followers. A commanding officer cries "After me!" and rushes into combat. What if there are no troops to follow?

The confrontation becomes a duel to the death as the tree of resentment yields its shriveled, bitter fruit. Moses, unable to turn the tide with rhetoric, invokes God's wrath, calling down retribution on Korach. Is violence, in fact, "the only language they understand"? Or is this yet more failure of leadership?

Moses challenges Korach to a divine duel, and Korach and his cohort resolutely appear, bearing incense in their smoking firepans. The Torah invokes our horror as they prepare to reenact the tragedy of Nadab and Abihu. It is clear once Moses utters the challenge that Korach and his men will perish. Now Moses appears to panic, calling down destruction on the rebels. It may be that he recalls God's strange command to him and Aaron together toward the beginning of the book of Numbers (4:18), "Do not cut off the clan of the families of Kehath," a charge to protect Korach's family from death at the hands of Heaven. Now, as God does away with Korach and his family at Moses' furious request, Moses recoils in horror as all Heaven breaks loose.

"I will destroy them all!" says God (16:20), threatening not only the rebellious group, but the extinction of the nation. Moses and Aaron panic: "Could it be that one man sins, and You are enraged at the entire assembly?" (16:22). The earth opens, swallowing Korach, Dathan and Abiram, and all their families. Moses intends this to be the end of the matter. But a moment later, fire consumes Korach's 250 followers. Then God goes on a rampage, striking down Israelites right and left until, in a chilling moment, Aaron brings the plague to a halt, waving his own desperate offering of incense "among the dead and among the living" (17:13).

Perhaps the hardest lesson a leader must learn is how to fail and yet not give up hope. To remain determined and committed to the task. The people must also learn this. Assigning blame for failures is the greatest failure of all. The failure of the spies is Moses' own failure – perhaps even God's. It is also a failure of the nation as a whole. But just as the nation yearns to continue forward, the task of the leader is to continue to lead. We can no more replace Moses with Dathan and Abiram than we could replace God with a calf of molten metal. Leaders dare not to step down when plans do not come together – not even when they themselves fail. This is exactly the argument Moses brings to God at the incident of the Golden Calf: "The people You chose," says Moses, "yes they will err, yes they will fail; but You must hold fast to the vision. Because," Moses tells God, "if You abandon us, then what was all this for?"

As Moses continues to learn the lessons of leadership, he models leadership for the next generation of leaders. Perhaps someone will watch. Perhaps someone will learn. If not in this generation, perhaps soon. If not sooner, then perhaps later.

There are moments that make leaders. Even if it takes forty years.

# 39

# "I Am Not a Man of Words"

*Speak softly and carry a big stick.*

– Theodore Roosevelt

At the heart of this week's reading is one of the most troubling incidents in the Torah.

After the death of Aaron and Moses' sister, Miriam, the people once again turn against Moses and Aaron, clamoring for water (20:7–13). "If only we had died in the Presence of God, as our brethren did!" they rail – referring to those who died with Korach.

God instructs Moses to take Aaron's staff from its place in the Tabernacle – where it sprouted almond blossoms after Korach's rebellion – and to gather the people together. "Speak to the rock before their eyes, so that it shall give its waters" (20:8). This designation of a specific rock – "speak to *the* rock" – leads the Midrash to the mystical notion of Miriam's well, a boulder that rolled along with the Israelites on their journeys, and that opened to give them water when they camped. Miriam, whose name contains the Hebrew word for "sea," is identified with water, with nourishment, and with the survival of the nation. When we meet her in the book of Exodus, she watches over her brother from the bank of the Nile, arranging for their own mother to nurse him. But now Miriam dies, and the people are left without water. Moses and Aaron are not Miriam. Without their sister they are helpless and their leadership is defective.

It is a wonder that Moses, who comes on the scene protesting his lack of verbal ability, has done nothing but speak since he returned to his people enslaved in Egypt. "I am not a man of words," he protests at the burning bush. There, God reassures Moses that Aaron will do the talking.

Yet the Torah gives Aaron not one memorable speech, and the one passage which most characterizes Aaron is his stunning, deliberate silence after the death of his two sons. Now God has bidden Moses and Aaron to speak together, to show that their words can fulfill the needs of the people. Moses takes the staff, but he doesn't wait for Aaron to speak. Instead of speaking to the rock, Moses excoriates the people: "Listen, you rebels! Do you expect us to bring forth water for you from this rock?" (20:10). He then lifts the staff and strikes the rock twice, whereupon water gushes forth.

"Because you two did not believe in Me and sanctify Me in the eyes of the children of Israel," says God to Moses and Aaron, "therefore you will not bring this community into the land that I have given to them." This failure to adhere to the letter of God's instruction causes Moses and Aaron to be barred from entering the Promised Land. In fact, Aaron dies shortly thereafter, and his son Elazar is invested as High Priest.

Did Moses really not understand God's command? God commanded Moses to strike a rock with the staff in an earlier episode – could Moses be confusing his orders now? What was so bad about what Moses did that he should not be permitted to enter the land? And what is Aaron's sin? Aaron did nothing – but neither did he speak.

Two weeks ago, we read the story of the spies – the collapse of the nation just as they are about to take possession of the land promised by God. Moses' leadership and the leadership structure of the newly formed Jewish nation implode in disastrous failure. Seeing the people's disarray, and their rejection of the land that was promised them, God withdraws both the promise of the land and the guarantee of divine protection. At the end of the episode of the spies, the Israelites – abandoned by their leaders and by God – are far worse off than they ever were in Egypt.

The episode of the spies contains tragic echoes of the expulsion from Eden: Israel saw the promised fruit and refused it, parallel to Adam's seeing the forbidden fruit and taking it.

As a result, both lost the sacred Land – Adam to expulsion, the Israelites to be condemned to forty years of wandering. Following the tragedy of the spies, the story of Korach revisits themes of Noah and the Flood. The Flood begins not with rain, but with the eruption of a deluge from underground: "On that day, all the springs of the mighty deep were burst apart, and the windows of the sky were opened" (Gen. 7:11). The flood waters come first from the earth splitting open, and only afterward do the rains begin to fall. The rebellion ends when the earth splits open and Korach and his family and close confederates are swallowed up.

One of the key words in the portion of Noah is "name" – in Hebrew, *shem*. It appears several times; and Shem is also the name of one of Noah's sons, the ancestor of Abraham and the name from which the word Semite is derived. The builders of the city and the tower of Babel say (Gen. 11:4), "Let's build ourselves a city and a tower with its head in the heavens, and let's make a *name* [*shem*] for ourselves so we will not be scattered across the earth." In a key literary echo, the 250 leaders of Israel who gather with Korach to challenge Moses and Aaron are described as "princes of the congregation, those at the appointed times, men of *name*" (Num. 16:2).

The book of Genesis opens with God expecting Creation to follow divine intent. But free choice and appetite soon intervene. By the mechanism of choice, and by our humans inability to envision the consequences of our actions, God's program crumbles and God's sadness, God's anger and regret, lead to the decision to destroy the world. At the end of Noah's watery ordeal, God recognizes that human nature will not change: we will never go from being imperfect to being perfect. We will always be ruled by our impulses and appetites. The best we will ever attain is a desire to try to improve, and even that will often falter. Perhaps a pathetic outcome, from God's perspective. But having set this game in motion, God decides to play it out according to its own rules.

This, then, is what Moses faces. Like God facing first

Adam, then Noah, Moses has had two tries at creating a perfect nation. He deputized the heads of the tribes to spy out the land, giving each of them one part of his own authority. Not only did they fail the test, they refused the earthly paradise and destroyed the world that Moses had so carefully worked to create. The confrontation with Korach is born of desire to take that which belongs to others. The Flood is brought because "the world had become corrupt in God's Presence and the world was full of theft." Like the generation of the Flood, Korach and his followers try to snatch what is not given to them. Like the builders of the Tower, Korach's followers are concerned with their name. Like all of them, they suffer the consequences of acting out of their passions, and not out of considering their place in the greater picture.

In response to all this, does Moses in fact sin? For all that has been written on this passage, the commentaries offer little that is definitive. On the face of it, Moses has reverted to type. We should not be surprised. When God first appears to Moses at the burning bush (Ex. 3–4), God tells him, Go and speak to Pharaoh, whereupon Moses says, "I am not a man of words, and I have never been. I am heavy of mouth and slow of speech" (Ex. 3:10). Indeed, when we meet Moses as an adult, the very first thing we see him do is kill a man without speaking a word (Ex. 2:11–12). Moses sees the Egyptian beating an Israelite; he looks about and sees no one, and he strikes the Egyptian and buries him in the sand.

This is Moses, the man who acts. Acts impulsively. Acts, as is spelled out in subsequent passages, to protect the weak from abuse by the strong. But the point is that he acts; he does not speak. He is telling God a deep truth about himself when he says, "I am not a man of words." Much of the book of Numbers is made up of scenes where Moses' leadership is challenged, where he himself is fed up and ready to quit. It seems that at this point, with the Israelites clamoring for water yet again, Moses' famous patience snaps. God tells him, speak to them. In the desperation of the moment, Moses' frustration boils over. And in that moment, a life's work is shattered.

Moses loses control and he lashes out physically. In a jarring depiction of a man tragically aware that he has just committed an irretrievable breach, Moses strikes the rock not once, but twice. The sad image of a man who recognizes an instant too late that he has destroyed something infinitely precious. The first blow was Moses throwing away all he has struggled to create; the second is a blow of defeat, acknowledging that he has brought his own life to ruin.

If we are honest with ourselves, we must acknowledge that we often do things that are against our own deepest principles. We try to justify it by saying it is our nature, but as the hasidic rebbes teach, every human being is composed of an animal soul and a divine soul; raw urges clash with a longing for transcendence. They must learn to live together both in the fecund darkness of our beating heart and in the clarity of our mind. When we fearlessly explore our own animal nature, we create the possibility of understanding ourselves – even of having compassion for ourselves. And we open a door to understanding and compassion for one another. In this way, we, too, can make for ourselves a name.

Nachmanides observes that the rock is impervious to being struck. But, he says, it is equally impervious to being spoken to. It's merely a rock. This begs the question, Why does God instruct Moses to speak to it? Perhaps God, knowing that Moses is near the breaking point, is reminding Moses to calm down before acting. After all, even God had to destroy the world in order to learn that there is no end to the need for patience.

# 40

# Of Prophets and of Fools

*God give them wisdom that have it; and those that are fools, let them use their talents.*

– Shakespeare, *Twelfth Night*

This week we read the story of Bilaam. It's a very weird portion – surreal in some aspects, and shot through with low comedy. All the action takes place offstage, above the heads of the Israelites, who have not the slightest idea what's going on. The main players: the king of Moab and the prophet Bilaam, go at one another at cross purposes throughout the story, then Bilaam abruptly leaves. God speaks with Bilaam, then so does Bilaam's donkey, and Bilaam seems surprised by neither.

Here's the story in brief. Balak, the king of Moab, has just seen his neighbors the Amorites defeated by the oncoming Israelites. Balak gets together with his other neighbors, the Midianites, and together they send to yet other neighbors to summon Bilaam, who is known as a prophet. Balak asks Bilaam to come to Moab and curse the Israelite people "because they are too powerful for me; but maybe I will be able to wage war and drive them out of the land, because I know that whomever you bless is blessed, and whomever you curse is cursed" (Num. 22:6).

At first, God speaks directly to Bilaam and tells him not to go. After Balak's representatives deliver a second request, God allows Bilaam to proceed. En route to meet Balak, God sends an angel to block Bilaam's way, but only Bilaam's donkey sees the angel, leading to a shouting match between Bilaam and his she-ass. When Bilaam finally arrives, he tells Balak to build him a series of altars and offer up sacrifices. After each set of sacrifices, instead of cursing the Israelites, Bilaam lets loose a torrent of blessings, each one more powerful than the one preceding it, and Balak repeatedly freaks out and insists they do it over. After several rounds of this, Bilaam finally walks away.

Bilaam has a unique gift: God speaks to him directly. However, Bilaam also has a flaw: he recounts the words God puts in his mouth, but doesn't reflect on them. Although Bilaam acknowledges that God speaks to him; and though he says repeatedly that he can say only that which God tells him to say and that he *cannot* say anything *other than* that which God has told him to say; and although he scrupulously obeys God's direct orders, Bilaam doesn't have any relationship to God. Bilaam doesn't acknowledge God as the ruler of the world, does not worship God, does not acknowledge God as the Creator, and does not even express thanks for the unique gift he has been given.

At this point in the Torah's narrative, people's awareness of God in the world is still evolving. There are those, such as Moab and Midian, who are aware that the God of the Hebrews was the One who brought the Israelites out of Egypt, and that the God of the Hebrews seems pretty much to win all the battles. But at the same time, Balak enlists Bilaam to turn the God of the Hebrews against the Israelite people, so there is an expectation that, like the idols worshiped by the surrounding nations, God can somehow be convinced – perhaps bribed? – to turn away from the Chosen People, if only long enough for a military victory against them. How does that work?

Throughout the narrative, each time Bilaam is asked to try once again to curse the Israelites, words of blessing flow from his mouth. Oddly – comically – neither Balak nor Bilaam does anything to change the situation. Balak keeps stamping his foot in frustration and saying, "No! I told you to *curse* them, not bless them!" and Bilaam keeps saying, "I told you that I can say only the words God puts in my mouth!" The whole passage reads like slapstick.

It's not just about Bilaam's unique gift of prophecy. Every one of us has a unique gift. Maybe Bilaam's problem is that he never bothered to look deep within himself. Maybe it never occurred to him to search or struggle to find his true calling, to find his unique gift. He never felt the need to seek out a teacher, a mentor, someone to help him, because for him life entailed no struggles. Like Esau, maybe Bilaam never wrestled with doubt. Bilaam is a prophetic *idiot savant*, largely indifferent to the fact that God speaks directly to him – and in this story, to him only. We each have a calling in life, but the calling requires two parties: the caller and the called.

The hasidic masters explain that the greatness of Abraham was not that God chose him, but rather that Abraham chose God. God calls to Abraham and says, "Go forth from your land and from your birthplace and from your father's house, to the land that I will show you" (Gen. 12:1). Many readers interpret this to mean that God chose Abraham, a thought process that leads many to the notion of predestination, which is not a Jewish concept; we each have the opportunity and the responsibility at every moment to choose our course of action. The hasidic approach is to realize that God is always exhorting us – each one of us, and at every moment – to Go Forth to our own particular destiny. Abraham responds to his call from God, and does so over and over.

Literary markers draw parallels between Bilaam and Abraham. They serve to differentiate between Abraham, the one who takes God seriously, and Bilaam, the one who takes God for granted. At times, the comparisons border on the farcical. Far from being grateful for his prophetic gift, Bilaam doesn't even seem to be astonished by it. And when at the end of the story he goes home unsuccessful in his assignment to curse Israel, it is with a shrug that says, Oh well, can't win 'em all....

The problem with Bilaam is that he had the greatest gift a human could possibly have, yet he used it to his own basest advantage, like a carnival trick. He didn't use his unique access to try to draw close to God; didn't bother to ask God, as so many religious people fail to ask, "What can I do for *You*?" And he doesn't try to convince others that their way is wrong, even when placed in a position to do so.

When God offers Abraham an inch, he immediately grabs ten thousand miles and keeps going.

We all have gifts. Bilaam fails to use his for the good, and thus he fails to change the world. How many of our own most precious inner gifts do we utterly ignore or take for granted? How many ways has God given to each one of us to make ourselves better, to influence those around us for the good, to make the world a better place?

God is calling out, calling out to all humanity. Are we listening?

# 41

# Rebel for the Sake of Heaven

*Those who abjure violence can do so only because others are committing violence on their behalf.*

– George Orwell

This week's Torah portion opens with God praising Phinehas, Aaron's grandson, for an extrajudicial killing. At the end of last week's reading, Moses is instructed to punish the Israelites who worshiped the Midianite god, and God brings a plague upon the people. In the midst of this, Phinehas' spontaneous killing of an Israelite man and his Midianite consort brings God's punishment to an end. This earns God's praise and an eternal reward: henceforth all High Priests will be Phinehas' direct male-line descendants.

Set in the aftermath of a series of massive failures of leadership, the narrative of Phinehas hints that the Torah may condone revolutionary violence. That some occasions call for an abrupt overturning of the social order. Rather than bring the offenders before Moses for judgment, it seems Phinehas is rewarded for an impetuous, violent act, for murdering two people only scant verses after Moses, whose transgression was merely to strike a rock in frustration, is denied entry into the Promised Land.

Phinehas' act is also of a piece with the political contest that has ruled for several Torah portions. Korach, the Levite, banded together with descendants of Reuben to challenge Moses and Aaron for the leadership. Now Phinehas kills Zimri, princely leader of the tribe of Simon, and his consort Cozbi, daughter of a Midianite chieftain. What is the context?

Moses rose to the leadership of the nation after marrying the daughter of Jethro, the high priest of Midian. Reuben, the firstborn, lost the leadership of the family and the people, and was superseded by the tribe of Levi, Jacob's third-born son. By rule of primogeniture, the leadership should devolve upon Simon, the second-born. The political machinations are clear: in the aftermath of the failure of Korach and his confederates to wrest power from Moses, the tribe of Simon asserts its claim. Phinehas – a Levite of the line of Aaron – publicly crushes the ember of rebellion. His violent act asserts definitively the primacy of both Aaron and Moses, while sending a clear message to anyone else who might challenge them for the leadership.

Phinehas is held up as the model of the zealot – though the rabbis' discomfort is greater than their veneration. Moses also displayed zealotry; why is he not the model of the one who is willing to lay it all on the line? To be clear: it is not Phinehas' willingness to commit violence, but his willingness to sacrifice himself for the sake of God's cause. This still begs the question of why zealotry is ascribed to him, and not to Moses. Phinehas cannot know what consequences he might suffer for his action; indeed, he should expect to be put to death himself. Yet in the episode of the Golden Calf, Moses shattered the Tablets of the Law in no less an act of zealotry. Moses decides that the Word of God cannot be given over to a people who have rejected God. At the moment Moses casts the stone tablets to the ground, he cannot know that God will bring him back up Mount Sinai and give him a second set of tablets. Moses commands the Levites to kill the Israelites – likewise unbidden by God – and three thousand die. Moses has committed two irretrievable acts, both of which the rabbis later deem as capital crimes: destruction of the Divine Word, and murder on a mass scale.

Why is Phinehas singled out among the sons of Aaron to merit the High Priesthood? Aaron is the man of peace, always seeking to maintain harmony among his fellow Israelites. Aaron, who would not raise his voice, much less his hand, in anger. Perhaps it is not gentleness per se that qualifies Aaron for the priesthood, but rather a wholeness: Aaron is wholly a man of peace – to the extent that he falls silent after seeing his own sons devoured by flames from the altar. The only words that are appropriate to such a tragedy would be words of rebuke, words of anguish, and words of anger. Rather than give rise to any of this, Aaron maintains his peace in the only way possible: silence.

Phinehas comes on the scene armed with a spear. His first act is to kill two people in plain sight. He, too, is true to his own inner nature. Where Aaron was all peaceableness in the service of God, Phinehas is all initiative. Aaron acquiesced to the loss of his sons in the service of God. Phinehas signals his willingness to sacrifice himself for the sake of God, and for the integrity of his nation. We might say that Aaron is all self-control, while Phinehas is all loss of control.

Uniquely in the Torah's narrative, Phinehas embodies in one man the spiritual zeal and unerring focus of the priesthood, together with the swift and definitive action of the enforcer. The event that brings him to our attention is troubling, and perhaps the Torah is teaching us that leadership is a messy business. Phinehas is not elevated because he was right to execute the pair – though his action stopped the plague. It is not that he was overcome by jealousy for God's honor to the exclusion of all human considerations – though this was his mindset, both as explicit in the text and as understood by the commentaries. But Phinehas performed one act for which he stood ready to sacrifice his own life, which is the only aspect of his action that might redeem him. As God will tell Moses, in designating Joshua as his successor, leadership devolves upon those who accept it, even if they appear unready.

The lesson of Phinehas is often misconstrued. The lesson is *not* to kill people who disagree with us or who do things of which we disapprove. It is not that wrongdoers must be put to death – who are we to make that determination? Rather, like Phinehas, we must be willing to lay ourselves on the line for what is right. It is ourselves, and not others, whom we must stand ready to sacrifice. Very little that we do in life will have the weight of Phinehas' deed, but that does not mean we should not approach every situation, every action, every moment, with full and utter commitment.

We read a few weeks ago that Moses was the pinnacle of humility. This week, when God tells Moses of his own impending death (28:12–23), his reaction (vv. 15–17) reinforces that. Moses doesn't plead for his life. He doesn't say, I don't want to die; nor, I don't deserve to die. Rather, he asks, How will the people go on? They will be like sheep without a shepherd! Before You take me out of the picture, says Moses, please make sure there is a strong successor, someone who can lead them as I have. In his own quiet way – privately, face-to-face with God, and out of the public eye – Moses is every bit as fearless as Phinehas. His greatness lies in his willingness to take himself out of the picture, harking back to the great lesson first learned by Joseph in Egypt: that the world's narrative is not about us, but that we live to serve the world into which we are born. How much more clearly can the humility of Moses be expressed than in his willingness to hand over the leadership now, on the verge of completing his God-given task? To step down as he stands on the threshold of the Promised Land?

There is much to contemplate in this portion, not the least of which is the notion that true greatness comes from a combination of commitment to one's goals, seeing clearly one's responsibilities to the group; and of recognizing that it is the task itself which is all-important, and not the one who does it. Both Phinehas and Moses are willing to sacrifice themselves in the service of the task before them.

"Therefore," says God of Phinehas, "I give him My covenant of peace."Peace, says God, not vigilantism. Perhaps this is not a reward. Maybe it is the only corrective God can offer. The Torah acknowledges that there are moments when leaders must act harshly. No less, the Torah recognizes that, try as we might, we will not always be able to curb our worst impulses – we have only to glance back and see Moses strike the rock. Maybe God is saying that Phinehas' act, though dreadful, did put a stop to a much larger problem. When human society seems to spin out of control, sometimes people believe that only extreme measures will do. And who requires God's covenant of peace more than a society whose leadership bases its authority on murder?

It is easy to perform the zealous act when God addresses us. When we have stood at the foot of Mount Sinai and seen the lightning, heard the thunder, and listened to God's own voice. Alas, such clarity is not given to us. How difficult it is to sustain the immediacy and the urgency of our task in the modern world! We must all become a little bit like Phinehas, willing to risk ourselves for the sake of what is truly important. Like Moses – who argues with God, not for Moses' own sake, but for the sake of the nation that God has given into his care. For the sake of God's own plan. Like Phinehas, who was willing to die to restore the integrity of God's people. Our challenges may not ever be on as great a scale, yet we are faced constantly with situations that demand clarity of vision, and a swift and equally clear response. God's covenant of peace must be constantly renewed in the world, and it is renewed by those who take action for what is right, ignoring the consequences to themselves.

# 42

## Nature or Nurture?

*For the mind everything is in the future, for the heart everything is in the past.*

– Andrey Platonov

Three groups do not enter the Promised Land. First, those of the generation that left Egypt, who are doomed to die in the wilderness after the episode of the spies (13:1–15:41). Next, Moses and Aaron, in rebuke for Moses' striking the rock (20:1–13), will join the fate of the first group. Finally, in this week's reading, as we approach the final stages of the Israelites' wandering in the wilderness, two tribes refuse to settle in the Promised Land. Each group is unable to let go of a critical piece of their past. Their identity is tied to their history and not to their destiny, and that traumatic bond costs them their rightful inheritance.

What is identity? How much of myself is *me*, and how much is what I have acquired along the way? We are all amalgams of the people, ideas, and events that have influenced us. We have been taught wisdom; we have been influenced by folly. We have fallen under the influence of teachers as well as of those who would do us harm. We have acquired moral values, but bad habits, too. Where does my experience end and my self begin?

As we saw at Mount Sinai, seeing is not believing. It assures us that something *did* happen, yet holds no guarantee for the future. Like an infant whose mother has left the room, when Israel is not face-to-face with the Divine Presence, it panics. It reverts to type – which is to say, a foundering sense of no-self. And it happens in an instant.

The episode of the spies (chs. 13–15) reveals a society immobilized by old fears and reverting to the unstructured, floundering society of an enslaved people. At a time when leadership is most critical, no one steps forward. The spies bicker over what problems might lie ahead, taking their eyes completely off the goal, and the people melt in despair.

The Torah returns often to themes of our inherent lack of abiding faith; the need to physically see a manifestation of the Divinity, and the inability to carry over reliance on God's promise. To extrapolate future good from past protection. In effect, an inability to grow up.

The incident of Moses' striking the rock occurs in a weekly portion set thirty-eight years after the preceding episode, the rebellion of Korach – thirty-eight years during which God has not spoken to Moses. Suddenly called upon to take charge, Moses, who at his core is a man of spontaneous action and not of words, sees the people in crisis; a crisis so great that God has reentered the picture. Perhaps it is the urgency of the moment, perhaps it is frustration after decades of God's silence. Whatever the reason, Moses acts instead of speaking. He strikes the rock.

In this week's portion (ch. 32), the tribes of Reuben and Gad request that they be allowed to settle outside of the land of Canaan. They possess great herds of livestock, and the lands across the Jordan – that is, to the east of the Land of Israel – are ideal for grazing. They ask to settle there so that they can manage their livestock. The structure of the dialogue is itself revealing; recall the importance of genealogies in understanding biblical characters. Reuben and Gad will forego the apportioning of the land of Canaan into what will become the hereditary tribal portions of Israel.

Reuben, Jacob's firstborn, should be entitled to the double portion of inheritance as well as the leadership of the children of Israel. Instead, he was shoved aside. Joseph, born next to last, was treated as the firstborn, while Reuben lost the leadership of the brothers to Judah. In the narrative of the sale of Joseph, Reuben is so isolated that he doesn't even know that Joseph was drawn out of the pit and sold. Reuben doesn't know until the moment that Joseph reveals himself in

Egypt that his brother didn't perish in the pit. He seems utterly severed from his role in the family, cut off from both father and brothers.

What of Gad? Jacob's wives, Leah and Rachel, are locked in a contest of giving birth (Gen. 29–30). After Leah gives birth to four sons, Rachel offers Jacob her maidservant as a concubine. In response, Leah does the same. The first result of the union of Jacob with Leah's servant is Gad. Thus, Reuben is the firstborn of Jacob, while Gad is the firstborn of his own mother.

As the Jacob story twists in and out of traditional family relationships, Joseph and Judah supplant Reuben as firstborn. The Torah will state in Deuteronomy (Deut. 21:15–17), in a clear reference to Jacob, that the biological firstborn of the father is to be designated as prime inheritor, even if the father doesn't love his wife. Reuben and Gad are both "firstborn" sons – the biological firstborns of Leah, and of Leah's maidservant, Zilpah. Their descendants have acquired excessive wealth in the desert, setting them apart from their brethren. But the text pushes the envelope still further. Though Reuben is the firstborn, the tribe of Gad is mentioned first (Num. 32:2, 6): "The Gadites and the Reubenites came and spoke to Moses.... Moses said to the Gadites and the Reubenites...." Despite his wealth, Reuben continues to live in the shadow of his brothers. Four centuries after the upheaval in Jacob's family, the first still remains last.

At first, Moses objects to the brothers' request: "Your brethren will go out to do battle while you sit here?" (32:6–15). He compares the request of Gad and Reuben to the spies, saying they too dissuaded the Israelites from taking possession of the land; which is why, thirty-eight years later, the children of Israel are still in the wilderness.

The Gadites and Reubenites promise to build pens for their livestock and cities for their children, and to then take up arms and be in the vanguard of the Israelites invading the land of Canaan. The word *livestock* appears four times in the first four verses of this section. Now, "we'll build pens for our livestock here, and cities for our children" (32:16). The rabbinic commentary pounces: Gad and Reuben have put their wealth before their families, and themselves before the rest of Israel. If Reuben and Gad have reverted to type, what "type" is that?

The descendants of Gad and Reuben remember all too bitterly, and cling desperately to, their ancestors' slights: Reuben, dropped from his role as leader of the family, and Gad, born after Rachel's maidservant has borne two sons. The stigma of Jacob's rejection clings so powerfully to their descendants that even now Reuben can't step forward.

Joseph, as the youngest at the time, was forced to remain with the sons of the maidservants: Dan, Naftali, Gad, and Asher, while the other brothers tended the flocks, and Joseph "would bring evil reports" about them to Jacob (Gen. 37:2). Joseph was seventeen years old at the time; the sons of the maidservants were older. As the sons of Jacob's concubines, they did not have rights of inheritance commensurate with the sons of formal wives, and therefore it would not be unusual for the four sons of the maidservants to be apart from the sons of the wives. But why does Jacob keep Joseph back? In the society of his day, a lad of seventeen was fully engaged in the hard work of the clan. Jacob manipulated Joseph, making him spy on his brothers.

The relationship of Reuben and Gad to the rest of Israel is underscored in Moses' valedictory blessings (Deut. 33:6, 20–21). Reuben's is the feeblest of the blessings accorded to the tribes: "May he live and not die, and remain to be counted among the population."

By contrast, Moses inverts birth order, blessing Gad before Dan and Naftali: "Blessed is the One who expands Gad," says Moses. "He chose the first portion...he headed the people, doing God's righteousness and laws with Israel." Gad receives high praise for his past actions and encouragement for his future role.

Moses grants Reuben and Gad's request to settle on the east bank of the Jordan on the condition that they march in the vanguard of the conquering Israelite army. Once the Land of Israel has been conquered and the tribal lots apportioned, they will be permitted to return to their stake. Moses also settles half the tribe of Manasseh together with Gad and Reuben. The text gives no explanation, but the genealogy is revealing.

In last week's portion, five sisters from the tribe of Manasseh come before Moses (Num. 27:1–11). They are the daughters of Zelophehad, a man who died without a male heir. "Our father died in the wilderness," the sisters tell Moses. "He was not among those who rebelled with Korach, nor did he worship the Golden Calf. Why should his name be left out, just because he has no son?" God tells Moses that Zelophehad's daughters should take possession of their father's share in the land. This establishes a new law: that women stand in the legitimate line of inheritance – such a revolutionary concept that the Torah gives it its own episode for emphasis.

Zelophehad's daughters connect not merely with their father's memory, but with a yearning for the Land of Israel. They stand before Moses on the eve of the land's being conquered and apportioned. This invokes Jacob, who instructed Joseph to take him to Canaan for burial, as well as Joseph, who instructed the Israelites to carry his bones out of Egypt for burial in the Promised Land. Manasseh, Joseph's son and Jacob's grandson, is born in Egypt. His name means "forgetting." Joseph named his firstborn in gratitude to God, "who made me forget all my tribulations and my father's house" (Gen. 41:51).

Yet Manasseh has not forgotten the ancestral yearning for the Promised Land. It is Manasseh's descendants, the daughters of Zelophehad, who plead for their own inheritance in the Land of Israel.

Our identity is built of our memories, both the ones we consciously recall and the ones that lie buried. Buried within the ancestral memory of Manasseh – "forgetting" – is the vision of the Promised Land. From this ancestral vision sprouts a passion, and from that passion comes a commitment. Moses divides the tribe most closely identified with the land. Half of them he places within the new Land of Israel, securing their inheritance, but half of them serve to hold their brethren to the greater task.

What is our identity? Where do we return to when we say we are "returning to our roots"? Gad and Reuben show that often our strongest drives, our most powerful motivation, arise from some ancient hurt done to us, some injustice – whether real or imagined doesn't matter – that leads us to react in the present; often wrongly. Today, many people accept the notion that all emotions are legitimate. Since our feelings are part of us, to deny our feelings will only do harm. But to not *examine* our feelings is far worse. Our feelings are real; that doesn't mean they are objectively true.

How do we react in the moment? It is true that Reuben lost his primacy of place, his rightful position as firstborn. It is true that Jacob didn't love Reuben's mother, Leah, and wrongly favored Joseph. It is true that Gad was born of a concubine, and therefore not eligible to inherit. The Torah reinforces this point by having the sons of the concubines babysit Joseph, while their brothers – the legitimate sons of Jacob's wives – tend the flocks that will one day be theirs.

But it is not true that the family dynamic that plagued Jacob's household needs to carry forward like some defective gene, plaguing his descendants forever. History is not destiny. What *did* happen does not foretell what *will* happen. We believe our own fallacies, which leads to impulsive behavior. Leads us to neglect our responsibilities and instead nurse our hurt, the sad child within us. Thus, before we act, we need to understand where our motivation is coming from. In which part of our past does this image reside? What buried pain, what long-hidden anger drives us to act? And when we act out of that long-buried impulse, what dark shadows will we release into the sunlight?

The Promised Land contains everything except the possessions we drag along behind us. Gad and Reuben have great herds and flocks that will not fit comfortably into the new homeland. The situation is resolvable if everyone approaches it openly and with goodwill. But Gad and Reuben, driven by ancestral pain and resentment, are not capable of this. As with Lot and Abraham, no space will be great enough to accommodate the two tribes together with the rest of the nation. Is it because the land cannot accommodate what they own? Or is it that they refuse to share what they have amassed? Are they that jealous of their wealth that they even reject the age-old covenant and promise – here and now, on the eve of its being fulfilled?

As with Lot and Abraham, the physical wealth is not the issue; it is what that wealth represents. Gad and Reuben care about their wealth because they can't see clearly the emotional scars it represents. They cannot separate their attachment to their possessions from their attachment to the slights suffered by their ancestors more than four hundred years ago. When will we ever learn to let go of our pain, of our resentment?

The Promised Land is waiting.

## 43

# Full Circle

*If I am not for myself, who will be for me?*
*And when I am only for myself, what am I?*
*And if not now, when?*

– Hillel

Before there was post-modernist literary theory there was the Torah, whose meta-literary structure reflects its message. The Torah's narrative, poetic, and lawmaking passages are all marked by an astounding economy of language, but also by endless internal cross-referencing, making the Torah both poetically ambiguous and infinitely rich in interpretation.

This week's portion closes the book of Numbers. It is the end of the omniscient narrator story that began with Creation and has brought the Israelites to the borders of the Promised Land. Deuteronomy will enter into a first-person retelling of the story from Moses' perspective.

As we bid farewell to the omniscient narrator, we transition from a group led by fiat and designated leaders to a society where individuals rise to the occasion, fight over authority, and take on responsibility, forming new leadership. This is exemplified by Phinehas, who has the zeal and passion, if not the self-control, to take on the mantle of High Priest; and by the daughters of Zelophehad, who speak up for their rights and win the endorsement of God. The sisters are singled out by name, twice in the portion in which their story takes place, and then specifically at the end of the book of Numbers. Thus, the narrative ends with the names of five women who broke the mold and changed the world forever.

And where are we now, at the end of the narrative? In many senses, we are back where we started.

Moses' journey parallels Abraham's in many ways. The story of Israel begins with Abraham about to leave Haran and enter the land of Canaan. It is Abraham's father, Terach, who actually determines to set out from Ur of the Chaldees heading to Canaan. They pause at Haran – rather too long, it turns out, for Terach dies there, and it is only the further push from God that sets Abraham back on the path.

Similarly, the Israelites left Egypt, headed for Canaan. It has taken forty years, but now they are almost there. Like Abraham, they were sidetracked, putting down roots where they did not belong. Like Terach, those who set out on the first leg of the journey will not live to see its completion. Their children will complete it, but with few exceptions, they will grasp neither the boundlessness of God's blessing nor the enormity of the task.

Contrast this account of the journeys through the wilderness with the passages describing the apportionment of the land of Canaan among the tribes (e.g., Num. 33:54). God leads every step of the way through the wilderness – the pillar of smoke by day, the pillar of fire by night. But once the people enter the land, they are left to their own devices. God will not lead each tribe to its inheritance, but gives Moses a general schematic for figuring it out. As the Israelites in the wilderness mimicked God's Creation by building the Tabernacle, they must now take on the ultimate task of leadership. God no longer leads, but stands by their side instead, watching as the newly formed nation makes decisions that will guide and affect their entire future.

We have seen this theme of handing over authority emerging since the beginning of the book of Exodus, where God exhorts Moses throughout the experience in Egypt to take charge, to exercise his own power; the repeated symbolism of Moses' staff and Moses' hand concretize God's urging and Moses' reticence. Now the Torah gives us a quick recap of the roads we have traveled. Life flashes before our eyes, and it all happens so quickly, in the space of a few tightly packed verses.

As Moses' career comes to a close, God gives him one

final command: to establish cities of refuge for those who kill accidentally (35:15–34). Not premeditated murder, which incurs the death penalty, but manslaughter or accidental killing entitles the perpetrator to a measure of protection. Without a city of refuge to flee to, someone who accidentally kills another person is fair game for the victim's relatives – called "the avenger of blood" – who may kill them in retribution. Once inside a city of refuge, the killer is immune from vengeance and remains so until the death of the High Priest, at which point their guilt is commuted and they may reenter society without fear of avenging relatives.

Moses, too, started his career as an accidental murderer. Perhaps his slaying of the Egyptian was an act of momentary passion, of Phinehas-like zeal. Perhaps it was a reaction he could not control; indeed, as we saw when he struck the rock, Moses is a man of impetuous action and few words, subject to fits where he loses control. And it takes but a moment. The day after the fateful encounter with the Egyptian taskmaster, Moses seeks to intervene between two fighting Hebrews, and one cries out, "Do you intend to kill me, too?" (Ex. 2:11–15). And so Moses flees to refuge in the land of Midian, returning to Egypt only after the death of "those who sought his life" (Ex. 4:19).

The Torah embeds this in the law of unintentional manslaughter: those who kill accidentally face a lifetime of contemplation of their act. All who act impetuously, who lose control and act without foreseeing the consequences, face lifelong contemplation of their actions. Remorse is itself a social value; the compassionate empowerment of remorse has far greater societal effect than the swift exaction of stern justice.

Moses does penance in exile. His early experience – like Siddartha, on his way to becoming the Buddha, Moses goes out of the palace and sees how people actually live – turns him into a reluctant savior and a highly effective leader. Though there are those who will speak of him the way Casca and Cassius speak of Caesar, Moses does not act out of self-interest or to aggrandize himself, nor does he lose sight of the goal, except in the rare moments when his passion gets out of control. He argues with us for God's sake, and with God for our puny sakes, and when God tells Moses his death is near, his only request is that the people not be left without a leader to guide them.

Thus, the final commandment, cities of refuge for those whose passions run out of control, is rendered in his honor: Moses, who was a stranger in a strange land, who fled from one exile into another, then led his ragged people into a national exile from which he was not to enjoy or see the redemption. We, who are not made of the same stuff, are given the mercy of refuge among our own people. And just as we sit behind the walls of our city of refuge and contemplate what we have done, our brethren on the outside must also contemplate what kind of society gives rise to murder, to the killing of another human being and to the spilling of one family member's blood by another.

The Talmud warns us against baseless hatred, saying it was the root cause for the destruction of the Second Temple in Jerusalem. But is there really any other kind of hate? Isn't all hatred ultimately baseless? Doesn't hate stem from refusing to accept others as they are? From believing that we know what is right and other people must be forced to concede? Doesn't hatred arise when we create idols out of our own self-image, when we make our own thoughtless impulses and appetites and egos more important than peace and justice and compassion? When we refuse to accept that we do not control the world and everyone in it?

When will the time come for the creation of the just society which the Torah demands? For all of us to become a nation of priests and a holy people? This challenge is not for Israel alone. You have only to look at the world around you to see how far we are from embracing the Torah's message.

If not now, when?

# *Deuteronomy*

44 • *Devarim* (1:1 – 3:22)
45 • *Va-Etchanan* (3:23 – 7:11)
46 • *Eikev* (7:12 – 11:25)
47 • *Re'eh* (11:26 – 16:17)
48 • *Shoftim* (16:18 – 21:9)
49 • *Ki Teitze* (21:10 – 25:19)
50 • *Ki Tavo* (26:1 – 29:8)
51 • *Nitzavim* (29:9 – 30:20)
52 • *Va-Yeilech* (31:1 – 31:30)
53 • *Haazinu* (32:1 – 32:52)
54 • *Ve-Zot Ha-Beracha* (33:1 – 34:12)

# 44

# Before the Future

*The past is never dead. It's not even past.*

– William Faulkner

Deuteronomy is unlike the four books that precede it. It is unlike them in language, as it abandons the omniscient narrator's voice and instead is told in Moses' own words. It is unlike them in content, because rather than a forward-moving narrative, it is a retelling of the central three books of Exodus, Leviticus, and Numbers. And it is especially different with regard to its audience. Until now we, the readers of this magnificent epic, have lived the Israelite experience: *we* fled Egypt, *we* crossed the Sea of Reeds with Pharaoh and his chariots in hot pursuit. We stood at Sinai and we muttered against Moses in the wilderness. We fled from Amalek, we thirsted in the wilderness and argued against God. We ate the manna, but then we made and worshiped the calf of molten gold – then, when called upon, we slaughtered our own brethren. We made the Tabernacle, watched in bliss as it was inaugurated – and in horror at the death of Nadab and Abihu. We sent the spies into the Promised Land, then rebelled at their word and cast off both God's promise and God's command. We rebelled with Korach, died in the plagues, and in between all our sufferings, we retreated to our tents and wept in solitude, with none to give us solace.

Between the portion in which Korach's rebellion is narrated and the portion directly after it, thirty-eight years have elapsed in which the Israelites have neither heard from God nor, according to some understandings of the text, even moved camp. It is no coincidence that the portion opens with the inexplicable law of the red heifer, whose purpose is to cleanse from the impurity of death (Num. 19:2ff). Consistent with

God's dreadful ruling in the aftermath of the incident of the spies, all the adult males of the generation of the Exodus have died. Aaron and Moses too shall die without entering the Promised Land. The only men of that generation designated to cross over are Caleb and Joshua.

The book of Deuteronomy is addressed to those born in the wilderness, and to those who were children at the time of the Exodus. Most of them will have little or no recollection of the events in Egypt, of the splitting of the sea – or even of the Revelation at Mount Sinai – except what their parents have told them. They are like the children of Holocaust survivors, heirs to a once-in-history, traumatic past, but also removed from the experience, receiving it as filtered through their parents' own trauma. Were those born in the wilderness torn awake at night by their parents' nightmare shrieking? Did they wonder at their parents' odd silences, their sudden bursting into tears? Because even though the Exodus was a redemption, it also, as Nachmanides points out, constitutes the foundational experience of exile that remains the core of Jewish identity. And even though the Israelites escaped Pharaoh and his armies, they then watched as their own brethren died in the wilderness, struck down by God whether by plague or by fire – if not killed by their own family members at God's instruction. The very God who worked mighty wonders to free them from Egypt. The very God who has promised again and again to bring them into the Land of Israel.

All this is foreign to the generation who are about to enter the Promised Land. How is Moses to prepare them? While reading the sometimes incredibly harsh chastisements of Deuteronomy, it is important to remember to whom Moses is speaking: not to those who actually transgressed, not to those who actually forgot God's graciousness, God's miracles, and God's promise, but to their children, those with no firsthand experience of the miraculous. Those for whom the splitting of the sea is perhaps just as distant as it is for us when we retell it each year at the Passover table.

Moses must make a leadership choice. How is he to prepare

this generation to take possession of the land? Should he tell them how wonderful they are, that there is no other people in all of history whom God has so favored? This he does. But he delivers this message bound up in harsh criticism. *You* were responsible for things going wrong! he tells the people. Moses implants in the generation of the conquest an *a priori* notion of ancestral guilt. It is the original Original Sin: despite God's graciousness, God's love for us, God's immense generosity – to say nothing of the miracles wrought on our behalf – our parents constantly wavered in their faith, to the point of outright rejection at the episode of the spies. You dare not let that happen again, says Moses. Let your parents' error of faithlessness be a lesson to you.

And thus the book of Deuteronomy begins.

From Moses' perspective, this is also a case study in the burdens of leadership. Textually, this is the transition from the unfiltered Word of God to our attempts to understand God's will, and to the practical application of the laws enunciated in the Torah. In traditional Jewish terms, Deuteronomy is the transition from the Written Torah to the Oral Torah: from the printed text to the ongoing act of interpretation. And as it draws to a close, Deuteronomy also contains some of the Torah's most powerful poetic passages.

Throughout the middle three books of the Torah, we encounter one brief, ubiquitous verse: "And God spoke to Moses, saying." It always introduces something new. It is tied to God's fundamental act of Creation, accomplished through speech: "And God said, 'Let there be light,' and there was light." God "says" to Moses repeatedly, each time revealing a new legal or religious concept, a new act of Creation.

The verse, "And God spoke to Moses, saying," does not appear anywhere in Deuteronomy. The book opens: "These are the words that Moses spoke to all Israel." The text that follows is visibly different from anything that came before. Instead of God, Moses does the talking. Moses recounts the history of the Israelites' travels, up to the moment, forty years later, when he stands before them "on the other side of the

Jordan" (Deut. 1:1).[1] What is striking about the location, as given explicitly in the text, is that it is "the *other side* of the Jordan." Moses' words are addressed to those who have not yet entered the Land of Israel; they will be read by those who come after them, those who shall be born and live in the land. Even by those who, thousands of years later, shall be flung to the far corners of the Earth.

Moses enumerates the exodus from Egypt, the giving of the Torah on Mount Sinai, and the events that led to the forty years of wandering, to people one or two generations removed from the events – and he is telling it in a framework intended not only for his listeners in the moment, but for future generations. The leader realizes that in order to give us a sense of our destiny, he must paint the complex picture of our history. Otherwise, we are not a people, but merely a bunch of individuals who happened to go through similar experiences. This is simultaneously spiritual instruction, tough love, and the creation of a vision of peoplehood for future generations.

Moses is forward-looking and personally fearless – two essential qualities for a leader. He takes it upon himself to retell the story God has revealed to us at Sinai. He is audacious, he is powerful. Moses is the very essence of a leader and teacher; a philosopher-king. And he does not hesitate to put himself on the line for the cause, for those he leads. We saw Phinehas risk his own life for the honor of Heaven, but that was a spontaneous, onetime act. Moses lays it on the line every day, and in the book of Deuteronomy we get to see the enterprise from his perspective. It's tough going, because Moses doesn't hold back, neither about Israel's failings nor about how difficult it is to be in his position. These are the words, not of God, but of a man who has seen God, who has spoken with God, who has learned Torah as God's intimate study partner, and who now turns to pass on to us what he has learned. Moses' reflections on his own role make this book a paradigm of leadership.

---

1   Unless otherwise noted, all references in this section are to the book of Deuteronomy.

"Moses began to explain this Torah, saying..." (1:5). The Hebrew word translated as "he began" has multiple layers of meaning, including the spontaneous desire to act, venturesomeness, and risk of failure. The root of the word translated as "explain" also means to engrave. Moreover, the verse ends with the word *saying*, the very word with which God created the cosmos. We have become the creators. Indeed, this is our destiny, the purpose for which we are created: to be partners with God in the ongoing creation and perfection of the world.

Indeed, later in the book of Deuteronomy (30:12), we shall read, "It is not in heaven"; the Torah is not some remote, mysterious object to be revered from afar. It is a handbook, a user's manual for the human soul, and we are meant to get our hands dirty with turning its pages over and over, learning how to apply it in our own lives. Unlike what many perceive as a strictly dogmatic approach to religion, the rabbinic model is not, "What *does* the Torah text mean?" but rather, "What *can* the Torah's text mean?" Now. Today. To me and to you.

The transfer, the giving-over of Torah – the engraving on our souls, the explanation – requires someone who is willing to take the initiative to dive in. To be willing to begin, to take the risk of getting it wrong, and to revisit the text over and over again.

Interpreting God's word is an overwhelming responsibility. Most people can't handle it, which is why they look for leaders. More troubling, it is why people look for simple answers. People want the world to be binary, to be purely black and white. In our day we see clearly a massive race to the bottom, both intellectually and spiritually. We are surrounded by people who can't bear the complexity of life. Like children, we are still playing Good Guys and Bad Guys, when we really need to be exploring each other's minds from within, trying to put ourselves in the other person's place. To see the world through their eyes, and ourselves through their eyes. For that is the only way to make peace.

The book of Deuteronomy is not the perfect book handed

by God to Moses. It is one man's version of events. And while Moses is unique, what he teaches us is that each person's unique understanding of God's message is no less important than anyone else's interpretation. This is why Deuteronomy is part of the revealed Torah: it is an exhortation to engage profoundly with this text. To make the Torah belong to us, and us to it. God's revelation is an ongoing process. The rabbis are clear on this point: the giving of the Torah at Sinai is the beginning of a process that continues to this day. Moses is a tough act to follow, but the message is: follow we must. God's Torah is revealed at Sinai, and again through Moses' retelling. And again each day by me, by you, and by everyone who seeks God's truth. It is our job to continue to work on ourselves, to strive to understand those around us, to teach, to lead, and to constantly help others bring out the best that is within them. Only when we all take on the responsibility for making ourselves better will we be able to build a better world for all.

This is Moses' lasting message: spiritual growth requires constant vigilance. It's easy to believe when faced with outward signs of God's favor. It's easy to have faith when things are going well. And it's easier still to lose faith, or – worse – to cast God aside in anger. May we be blessed to continue in vigilance, to grow and learn and deepen in wisdom. To grow as individuals, and as leaders and teachers of others. Each one of us has the potential to become a very tough act to follow.

# 45

# Hear, O Israel!

*Hear, O Israel: The Lord is our God; the Lord is One.*

– Deuteronomy 6:4

Several times in this portion, the Israelites are exhorted to "hear," notably, "Hear, O Israel: The Lord is our God; the Lord is One" (Deut. 6:4). Repeated each morning and evening, this is the core declaration of Jewish faith in the existence and essential nature of God, and in Israel's unique relationship with the One God.

When the Torah exhorts us to "hear," it carries the sense of both "understand" and "obey." Understanding is the ideal toward which the Torah guides us; it is the work of a lifetime, requiring constant mindfulness. Until we come to understand – or when we forget and lose focus along the way – we are called on to obey. This is no different from child-rearing, where the parent balances the need for education with the child's ability to absorb information. At the first stage, the parent says "Do this..." (or more often, "*Don't* do this...") "...because I said so."

At a later stage of development, the child needs to process information for themselves; they resist a simple Do or Don't because the maturing brain no longer acts merely as an extension of the parent's will. Now the parent must add, "Don't do that *because it's dangerous and you'll get hurt.*" Now every admonition requires its reason.

Later still, with the child on the brink of independence, the parent says, "What do *you* think will happen if you do that?" And finally, the child will leave the parent's control and will be in the world alone, making decisions on their own. No parent can watch this without a mix of anticipation and unease: Will my child make good decisions? Did my child learn enough? Did I teach them properly? We experience our children's trajectory as an unbroken commentary on our adequacy or utter failure as parents.

Moses is not a timid father to the Israelites, and here in Deuteronomy the gloves are off. He wades right in, taking a confrontational approach learned directly from God.

Moses' retelling of the wanderings in the wilderness started last week with the appointment of a leadership structure, one ratified by the people. He charges (1:22–32) that the Israelites asked him to send spies to scout out the land of Canaan, and that he agreed. When the spies returned, the Israelites despaired and refused to enter the land, rebelling against God's command. "You murmured in your tents," says Moses, a down-to-earth description of a group where everyone recognizes that they have failed and are casting about, desperate to throw the blame onto someone else. They shut themselves up in their rooms, angry at each other and themselves, afraid and ashamed to go out in public.

Now look back at the event itself (Num. 13:13). God says, "Send men and have them search out the land of Canaan." God unambiguously commands Moses to designate the spies and to send them to reconnoiter and bring back a report. The rabbis are so upset with the outcome of the spies' mission – despair, rebellion, and forty years of wandering – that they too shred the plain meaning of the text (taking their cue from Moses?) and lay the blame on Moses. In the rabbinic reframing, Moses approaches God with the idea, and God resignedly says, "Go ahead."

Now Moses turns this onto the Israelites, saying the tragedy arose because they pressed him to send a scouting party. Worse, as a result of Israel's pigheadedness and rebellion at the incident of the spies, Moses is denied entry to the land. Not only will he not live to enter the Promised Land; unlike Joseph, whose bones he has carried since leaving Egypt forty years ago and whose remains will be laid to rest in Shechem, Moses will suffer the indignity of being buried outside the Promised Land, on the other side of the Jordan in an unmarked grave.

In a perhaps ungenerous, but all too human reading, we might ask: Where did Moses learn this behavior of blaming others? Of shrugging off responsibility? Moses struggles to reach the borders of the Promised Land, only to see it slip from his grasp. Rather than take some share of the blame, rather than calling it a failure of leadership – which it surely was on many levels – Moses blames his loss on the people.

Is this fair? Is it good leadership? What lesson is Moses conveying?

The text itself makes plain the enormity of the Israelites' refusal to go up to the land of Canaan. Moses recounts: "They turned and ascended the mountain and came to the valley of Eshkol and spied it out. They took in their hands of the fruit of the land and brought it down to us...but you did not wish to ascend, and you rebelled against the word of the Lord your God" (Deut. 1:24–26). In the Garden of Eden, Eve and Adam eat the fruit that is forbidden to them; as a consequence, they are expelled from Paradise. Here the Israelites are presented with the fruit of the Promised Land, yet they don't even taste it. They refuse to take what is not only offered but commanded. And thus, the promise is put off until those of the generation which did not go up have died.

If one thing can be said about life, it's that it is unpredictable. Random, as we experience over and over in the book of Numbers. If any one thing can be said with certainty about the Torah, it is that none of us can truly state that we comprehend God's meaning. The Torah exhorts the Israelites to sanctify the world in God's Name, to make of this world a better world, a just world, a compassionate world. In the absence of a clear path to righteousness, in the face of the utter randomness of our existence, we can at least obey the fundamental principles of God's will while we learn, then apply what we learn. Taking this process ever higher, we learn by doing, then do what we have learned – an endless cycle of improvement repeating in our own lives and down the countless generations.

The eternal theme of exile and return runs through the Hebrew Bible. As a historical process, this continues today with the existence of the State of Israel – a concrete, historical return. As a religious and spiritual process, we recognize that the world leads us to lose touch with our spiritual core. Our soul goes into exile. Our spiritual and emotional lives are ongoing cycles of distancing and return; of seeking to come home to our deepest, finest, and most pure spiritual selves.

All the way back at the beginning – Genesis 1:1 – Rashi, the medieval rabbi revered by Jews everywhere as the greatest rabbinical commentator of all time (France, 1040–1105), asks why the Torah, a book of laws, begins with the Creation. We read through the entire book of Genesis, plus the first eleven chapters of Exodus, before we come to the first law commanded to the Israelites. Says Rashi, future generations will rail against us. "You are thieves!" they will say. "You have stolen the Land of Israel from its inhabitants." In reply, we shall point to the opening verse of the Torah. God made the world; the world is God's, and God gives the land to whom God pleases. Whereas once it pleased God to give the land to the Canaanite nations, it then pleased God to take the land away from them and give it to us.

Writing from my desk in Jerusalem, I experience keenly the other side of Rashi's message: our inheritance and safety and ownership of this land are all tied to a moral imperative. Rashi's clear message is that the land does not belong to us forever. God can change God's mind.

God promised this land to Abraham and to his descendants. Thus, the Bible assures us the people of Israel will always return to ownership. But there are conditions. "I will die on this side of the Jordan," says Moses. But, he continues, you will go into the Promised Land. There, after two generations, you will forget your covenant with God; you will become corrupt, making and worshiping idols. Then, warns Moses, you will be destroyed. God will drive you out of the land and scatter you among the nations, where you will worship idols, gods made of wood and stone (Deut. 4:22–31).

The sin of the Golden Calf makes for dramatic reading. The imagery of the molten idol come to life, the wanton, lewd dancing and shouts of mass hysteria – all very cinematic. But Moses dwells tellingly on the episode of the spies. In the sin of the Calf, we did not believe what we did not see with our own eyes; when Moses failed to return, we gave up hope. In the incident of the spies, we refused to believe that which we *did* see with our own eyes: God has promised us this land, God has brought us to the borders of the land, has permitted us to walk the roads and fields and mountains of the land, to taste its fruits, to breathe its air. Yet we refused to enter.

The Israelites made the Golden Calf because they lost faith in Moses. But when they followed the despairing message of the spies, they denied faith in God. Rather than dwell on the sin that caused the loss of faith in Moses' leadership, Moses points to the nation's abandonment of God. That is his greatness; he, of all of us, understands that he lives in service of something far greater than himself.

Seeing, it turns out, is not always believing. Listen, says the Torah. Pay mindful attention. Learn true wisdom, and until you have learned wisdom, follow the basic principles of behavior. When in doubt, says God, do it because I said so.

The price for rejecting God will be exile and the decimation of the people (4:25–28). We – the Jewish people – have certainly witnessed this in the course of history. Rabbi Isaac Abarbanel, in a typically astonishing insight, tells us that above and beyond exile from the land, the decline of our numbers, the living in poverty and misery and terror – beyond all this, the agonizing, constant reminder of our denigration is that we shall worship other gods (4:28). All the while we shall know that God is truth ("Hear, O Israel: The Lord is our God…"), yet we shall turn our backs on God and on Torah. We abandoned God by making and worshiping idols. Now, says Abarbanel, idol worship is not merely the cause of punishment; it is the ultimate punishment itself.

Let us not worship false gods: gods of money, of power over others, of racist ideology or nationalism, of our own rage, of our own close-mindedness. Of our own ego, of our grasping after objects – mere outer symbols of power and success. Like the Land of Israel to the Israelites, each one of us has her or his own particular promise, a deep and unique gift implanted in us by our Creator. Will we, like the Israelites, fear to embrace our particular destiny? Let's not pray for land or wealth or material success, for these pass away. Let's pray for humility and the ability to make that unique gift resonate in the world, lest we lose it.

I have been taught that our task is to make the world a better place, one person at a time. In this lifetime, I pray that person will be myself. I urge you to do the same.

# 46

# The Beginning of Wisdom

*All things are in the hands of Heaven, save the fear of Heaven.*

– Talmud, Tractate Berachot

*And now, Israel, what does the Lord your God ask from you, but to fear the Lord your God…for your own good.*

– Deuteronomy 10:12–13

Words, no less than humans, are communal beings. No less than ourselves, they draw their meaning from their environment, from the context in which they appear. And, similar to the development of human personalities, the meanings of words accrete as they obtain new layers of significance. One such Hebrew word, *eikev*, meaning "because" or "owing to," is the key word in this week's Torah portion.

As Moses' career draws to a close, literary markers invoke Abraham. Two words appear for the first time at the binding of Isaac, directed at Abraham: "And the angel of God called to Abraham again from the heavens and said, 'I have sworn, says the Word of God, that because [*ya'an*] you did this thing, and did not withhold your son…I will surely bless you, and I will surely multiply your seed like the stars of the sky and like the sand that is on the seashore…because [*eikev*] you listened to My voice'" (Gen. 22:15–18).

The words *ya'an* and *eikev* are used in reference to Moses as well. After Moses strikes the rock, he and Aaron are punished with not being able to enter the Promised Land, "because [*ya'an*] you did not believe in Me" (Num. 20:12–13). In this week's reading, Moses says to Israel, "And it will be because [*eikev*] you will listen to these ordinances, and you will keep them and you will do them…" (Deut. 7:12).

For Abraham, the sequence is: *Ya'an*, because you took the action God commanded, and *eikev*, because you listened to My voice. For Moses and Israel, it is: *Ya'an*, because you (Moses) failed to take the action God commanded, and *eikev*, because you (Israel) will listen. From the Torah's perspective, seeing undermines both faith and clear understanding: we demand to see because we do not truly believe; yet when we see the same thing in different settings, we often fail to recognize it. The Torah exhorts us to *hear*, with its dual meanings of "understand" and "obey." Learn and take action.

This week's reading opens, Hear and perform. We are exhorted to be like Abraham, who heard and acted. God rewards him, first for the act itself, and only second for the hearing. Moses and Aaron heard but failed to act. God punishes them for their failure. God will keep God's side of the contract if we keep ours. If we listen.

The fear of Heaven ranges from the simple fear of punishment to the lofty, spiritual awe when we experience our own insignificance in the face of the vastness of Creation. Its pinnacle is the sense of awe we experience when we become aware of our own very great importance – that God has chosen to create us – *us!* – both collectively and individually. And has given us the Torah, whereby we can commune directly with God. When we realize that God has invited us to become partners in the enterprise of Torah and Creation and human history.

The textual echo of Abraham in this third weekly portion of the book of Deuteronomy reminds us that Abraham's journey begins in the third portion of Genesis. Are there other echoes of Genesis? The opening of Deuteronomy evokes the Garden of Eden. Moses recounts the incident of the spies who brought back fruit from the Promised Land. In a reversal of the tragedy of Adam and Eve and the expulsion from Eden, this was the fruit God intended for us, yet we spurned it. We did not eat it, nor did we enter the land. Because of you, Moses scolds the Israelites, I will die here. You have slain me, says Moses. In another parallel to Genesis, the Midrash says

Moses is a reincarnation of the soul of Abel, which has yet to fulfill its spiritual mission.

In the second portion of Deuteronomy, Moses is sent to a mountaintop where God announces his death. This contrasts with Noah, who is saved on a mountaintop in the second portion of Genesis. Moses warns the people repeatedly not to abandon God's law, for the penalty will be destruction, an echo of the Flood. Israel is warned (4:15–18) not to make images of a human, of any animal, any winged flying creature, any creature that creeps on the ground, or any fish – in short, all living beings, all of which (except the fish, who survived on their own) Noah saved in the Ark.

These points are not hammered home; they are subtle literary markers, often elusive. Yet they are clearly there in the text. The Bible is rich with echoes of its own themes, constantly reminding us that, while God and the Torah are infinite, human life is more circumscribed. We keep being placed before the same choices: to fear God, to obey, to do what is right, and to bring justice into the world. And we keep making the same mistakes – which is why we keep ending up back where we began. Says the Buddhist sage Padmasambhava (India, 8th cent.), "If you want to understand your current life, look to your past actions; if you want to foretell your future situation, look to your current actions."

"Take care lest you forget God," warns the Torah, "and you may say to yourself, 'My strength and the might of my hand created all this wealth for myself!'…then you shall surely perish because [eikev] you will not have listened to the call of the Lord your God" (8:11–20).

All of human history, both national and individual, is an unending spiral of exile and redemption. When we are in exile, it is easy to despair. Though we pray for redemption, we lose patience; and with it, faith. What if redemption comes later than we want it to? Or not at all? What if, like the generation of the Exodus, redemption comes not for us but for our children, or even for our children's children? What then? Are we to relinquish our spiritual practices, our faith in God and in ourselves?

And on the other hand, when all is well with us and we are prosperous and feel safe, do we give ourselves the credit? It's so easy to forget God when we have a well-stocked refrigerator, a healthy family, and a comfortable bank account. It's easy to forget our fundamental obligation to constantly bring justice into the world, to reach out to others and relieve suffering – and to give the credit to God. And then when we are suffering, it's easy to forget that there are always others who are suffering far more than we are, and easy to blame God for abandoning us.

How are we to strike a balance? To maintain an equilibrium, to safeguard our partnership with God?

Rashi's message is that we must approach our successes with humility; for we shall surely also suffer reverses. And we must embrace our losses with equanimity, for nothing endures forever but God, and the faith we place in God.

As we saw from the very beginning of Genesis, our dominance and success are not eternally guaranteed. But neither are our failures, nor even our tragedies. Reflect on the message of King Solomon: This too shall pass. Within the constant flow of life, God remains steady. We, as God's partners, are exhorted to mirror that steadfastness. While we live, says the Torah, let us keep faith. Says Solomon, "The beginning of wisdom is fear of God" (Prov. 9:10). The awe when we reflect that God has chosen us, each one of us, to people God's world, has granted us access to God's wisdom and exhorted us to be the agent to bring that wisdom, justice, and compassion to the rest of humanity.

Only this, says the Torah: do not fall victim to pride when things are going well, and do not despair when things go badly. Always stand prepared to do for others, always stand prepared to do for God. Even in the depths of exile, do not forget our allegiance to the purity of God's message. We never know when the moment will arrive when we, and we alone, may be called upon to save the world.

Says Hamlet, "The readiness is all."

Says Rashi, Do not despair, even in the deepest exile.

Says the Torah: "Listen."

# 47

# To Truly See

*All that glitters is not gold.*

– Shakespeare, *Merchant of Venice*

*All that is gold does not glitter.*

– J.R.R. Tolkien, *The Fellowship of the Ring*

The book of Deuteronomy offers a running – yet highly selective – commentary on much of what has come before. Moses' retelling of the last forty years is clearly slanted, and the rabbis understand this book as being largely Moses' harsh reproof to the Israelites for their behavior: they do not stay constant in their faith in God; they complain constantly. When God sustains them in the wilderness with the manna, they complain that they lack meat; When God splits the Sea of Reeds and brings the Israelites through on the dry land, no sooner do they emerge safely on the other side than they look around and, not finding water to drink, immediately complain that God has abandoned them. And so it goes….

This week's portion opens with the word *See*, which to a rabbinic scholar is a signal: where have we encountered this word before? In fact, the act of seeing is one of God's four fundamental acts of Creation: God *spoke*, God *saw*, God *divided*, and God *called*. Look back at the opening section of Genesis; it's all right there.

In the Creation narrative, God's seeing represents God's assessing the extent to which what has been created actually performs as God intended it to. This may not make sense to us; how can a rock be anything other than a rock? And the Torah makes it clear that our capacity for free choice is among the defining factors of being created in the image of God. But God seems to be either testing out the elements of Creation one by one, or at least confirming them once they are in place, like a proud parent praising their child.

There is much to say about the Bible's use of imagery of sight and seeing – as well as of not seeing what is right before one's eyes. I'm thinking of the moment in Genesis where sight is invoked in the created world, the first time a human sees in the Garden of Eden: "And the woman [Eve] saw that the tree was good for eating" (Gen. 3:6). When God saw during the days of Creation, it affirmed the rightness of what had been brought into existence. Now Eve exercises her Godlike power of sight, but instead of seeing the world as God intended her to see it, she sees it from the perspective of her own appetites. Instead of her gift of sight enabling her to treat the world the way God wanted her to, she ties it to its physical source. She thinks it is her own seeing, and that the world is there for her to perceive, to use. To eat.

Later in this week's portion (Deut. 12:29–31), we are warned about the idolatrous practices of other nations: "Beware lest you seek out their gods, saying, 'How did these nations worship their gods? I will do the same'" (12:30). On its face, this seems to be a warning against "going native," against abandoning God and the Torah and fleeing to the embrace of idol worship. To be sure, when we find ourselves in a new situation, there is always the risk that we will relinquish our values and adopt values that are completely foreign, even contrary, to what we believe, all in order to fit in.

Nachmanides has a subtle and profound take on this. He says the real danger is not that we will abandon God, discard the Torah, and take up a whole new religion. Or rather, yes, this threat is always there. But the more pernicious threat, the hidden threat, is that we will allow ourselves to believe that the practices of the idolatrous nations are themselves valid; that by doing what we saw them do, we are merely adopting new ways of serving God, new ways of living the life the Torah commands us to follow.

How many times have we come to the realization that our behavior was completely contrary to our own deepest values? That in the moment, we justified what we were doing, saying, "It's all right. It only *looks* like I've abandoned my moral principles. But inside, I'm really the same person." In the Torah's frame of reference, this is like saying, "All these idolatrous practices, they're just outward motions. It's just another way of doing what God wants." On reflection, after we calm down, our own sense of remorse is unerring in revealing things that we have worked hard to hide from ourselves.

This is something I have witnessed again and again on Wall Street, where the temptations are so massive. We want success, we want money. We want as much money as the next guy – or as the biggest guy. We want more expensive clothing, a more expensive car. A bigger house. A more glamorous wife. Pretty soon, we get so caught up in the externals of life that we have literally turned ourselves inside out: where once we tried to live by our own inner guide, by the principles we believed in, now our whole belief system is based on "How much?" "How big?" "How expensive?" Truly, it's not that there are some rotten apples; instead, it is the barrel itself that is rotten, and we wallow in it at our own peril.

This is but one example of how readily we can go wrong. How easy it is not merely to make the wrong choices, but to doggedly justify those choices, until we come to fervently believe that we have made the right choice.

The portion begins, "See, I have set before you today a blessing and a curse" (11:26); life and what is good, and death and what is evil. By using the word *see*, a word so charged with power, the Torah is not merely calling our attention to two mountains that stand before us (11:29). The Torah is challenging us: when we are faced with a moral decision, do we decide based on what we believe God would want us to do, or based on our own appetites? As the rabbis say, we must weigh the short-term sacrifice involved in doing what is right against the long-term benefit of our proper behavior. And we must likewise weigh the momentary benefit of choices we make based on our animal appetites, versus the lasting negative effect of living with the knowledge that we have failed to be our best self.

We are on a long path, and the ways in which we tread – for good or for ill – will carry forward not only our entire lifetime, but will extend to propel others to continue your journey. Those we teach, those we influence; whether consciously, or by example. Whatever behavior we embrace – whether we seek to find God's will and follow it, or stubbornly insist on our own desires – this is what we teach others. Not least of all, it is what we teach the children we bring into this world.

# 48

# The Doors of Perception

*If the doors of perception were cleansed, everything would appear to man as it is: Infinite. For man has closed himself up, till he sees all things thro' narrow chinks of his cavern.*

— Blake, *The Marriage of Heaven and Hell*

The textual point I want to consider in this week's Torah portion is the opening clause of the first verse. This verse teaches an important societal and moral principle. But the opening words also reveal greater depth when interpreted according to Jewish textual traditions.

The first verse of this portion opens: "Judges and officers shall you appoint within all your gates..." (17:18). This has the simple meaning that each city must establish a court of law. The simple meaning of the words "judges and officers" is those who render legal decisions, and those who enforce. In modern Hebrew, the words for *judge* and *police* are the exact words used in the Torah text.

The word "gates" is taken to mean the city as a whole, because in the societies described in the Bible, the city gates were the meeting place, the place where business was transacted, where public notices were announced, where the king's councilors would meet, and where the local court would sit in judgment. Thus, establishing a court according to the Torah's principles means that each city can rely on a presumption of justice, an objective and universal standard, rather than live in fear of the arbitrary whim of the local warlord.

There's also a hasidic take on it, one that speaks more to the individual. This reading says the "gates" in the verse are not just the actual gates of the city; they are also the individual's gates of perception – in particular, one's moral sense.

Two weeks ago, we read about the sense of hearing: "And it shall be because you listen to these ordinances..." (7:12). The Hebrew word for "listen" also has the very definite sense of understand, take to heart, and obey. Last week we read about the sense of sight: "See, I have set before you today a blessing and a curse" (11:26).

In this portion, say the hasidic rebbes, we broaden the admonition to encompass our entire mechanism of perception. It's not merely the senses of hearing and sight, it's how we understand what enters through the ears and through the eyes – or via taste, touch, or smell.

The Buddhists count six senses: the same five as we Westerners, plus the mind. Including the mind as a sense organ is a brilliant and profound insight because what truly drives our behavior is not the stimuli that our senses perceive, but rather what our mind does with those stimuli as they enter our consciousness. The hasidic approach says, be keenly aware of how you perceive the world, then take responsibility for how your perceptions inform your actions. The world doesn't just "happen to" you.

You object – "But I have no control over what the world throws at me!" True, but meaningless. The one thing over which each one of us might exercise control is how we *respond* to what the world throws at us. Nothing else is of consequence. The events themselves are not of consequence, dreadful though they may sometimes be. We are responsible for analyzing our response to the world. When we allow ourselves to respond automatically – unthinkingly, instinctively, viscerally – we reduce ourselves to the animal at our core. We give up that image of God stamped on our soul. And for what?

We are often told to watch our speech, to watch our behavior. But how often are we reminded to watch how we understand and perceive what is happening to us? Because wrong speech and wrong behavior have a common origin, which is the refusal – or more gently, the inability – to understand the world on any terms other than that of our own, puny ego. When we look at it closely, unafraid of what we will find, we often see that our ego is nothing more than a trembling, frightened, broken-winged bird, a feeble being terrified of the light. No wonder we don't go there.

The hasidic masters have quite a lot going for them. Their level of understanding of human behavior and human psychology is immense, as is the degree of unstinting compassion they show for all humanity. Pay attention to what's going on around you, they say. More important, pay attention to what's going on inside you. When we are passive, the world changes us. When we are attentive, when we explore ourselves deeply and understand how we react to people and events, then we have the capacity to change the world.

May God continue to give us strength as we dive into the uncharted waters of the soul. It's the only way to find the sunken treasures.

# 49

# Captivating Beauty

*And it was towards evening and David rose from his couch and strolled about the roof of the royal palace, and from the roof he saw a woman bathing, and the woman was very beautiful.*

– II Samuel, 11:2

This week's portion has numerous references to marriage and divorce, and to improper sexual relations.

It opens with the case of a woman taken captive in time of war. The Torah describes her as "a woman beautiful of form" (21:11), and tells the warrior how to treat this woman if he desires her sexually.

The Hebrew vocabulary resonates on many levels. The term "beautiful of form" is based on the word *see*, and ties textually to Eve eating the forbidden fruit, to the sexual wantonness of Egypt, and directly to the family of Abraham: three of the four Matriarchs – Sarah, Rebecca, and Rachel – are described using variants of this term, as is Joseph, Rachel's son, whose good looks get him into significant trouble.

These echoes are not mere accidents of the limitations of the Hebrew vocabulary. The case of the captive woman is one of lust: a man sees an attractive woman, over whom he exercises the power of life and death, and he desires to have sex with her. The Torah lays upon him the obligation to wait thirty days, to permit her to mourn the loss of her family, and to then not merely have sex with her, but to take her as a wife. This is striking: the captive woman is not to be raped, abused, or disposed of, and explicitly not to be sold for money if she displeases him.

The captive must marry him; she clearly has no choice. But this is just one example of the ways in which the Torah protects women. In its place and time, 3,500 years ago in the deserts of the Middle East, the Torah was a revolutionary document of social justice. Imagine telling a conquering soldier he is not allowed to rape a woman he has captured? Imagine telling him he is obligated to marry her – which means provide for her and protect her for life. Imagine telling him that if he then decides to divorce her, he is not allowed to sell her for money but must give her unconditional freedom. Imagine: she is not of his tribe, not even an Israelite, yet she is a human being, and her dignity must be preserved as best as possible, given the brutal circumstances under which she came into the community.

Another case in this Torah portion describes a man who has married two wives; one beloved, one hated. He may not favor the children of the preferred wife. There is also the case of a man who spreads a malicious lie that his wife was not a virgin when he married her, and the example of a man who marries a woman and then divorces her, and then wishes to remarry her. Finally, there are a series of scenarios dealing with rape, seduction, and consensual illicit sex.

It is striking that the Torah spends so much time on sex; this is hardly the only section dealing with prohibited and permitted relations. Elsewhere, the Torah prohibits incest, homosexual rape, and honor killings – all common enough practices in certain places and times.

It is said that we use only 5 percent of our brain. If men are honest with themselves, they will recognize that it's because the other 95 percent is taken up with thinking about sex. It is the way males are hardwired. Which means it is nothing to be embarrassed about.

But it is also nothing to act on.

Sex is a powerful force. How often do we listen to our hormones rather than to the voice of reason? Rabbi Shneur Zalman of Liady, the first rebbe of Lubavitch (Belarus, 1745–1812),[1] lays out the psychological process behind this behavior:

---

1   Reverently and affectionately known as the Alter Rebbe ("the Old Teacher"), he was one of the greatest hasidic leaders.

The mind perceives a stimulus. At this point it is a neutral event, mere sensory input. The emotional system then places an emotional value on it. This emotional value gets booted back to the mind, which now believes the emotional reaction to be the objective truth. The mind thinks through how to respond to this misunderstood interpretation, giving rise to concrete thoughts, to speech, and ultimately to action. In this way, we repeatedly ruin our own lives, and often the lives of those around us. By believing our own thoughts to be objectively true, we cast away the unique power God has given us – the ability to sift through chaos and create order. If our creative ability is what defines us as being made in the image of God, the power to create stability in the world around us is among our most important attributes, and one we often ignore.

Wanton sexual behavior is a problem. It is also a powerful metaphor for all the other things we do wrong in our lives – all the times and situations where we act on pure impulse. The Alter Rebbe teaches there are two levels of analysis we must perform before we act. First: where does the impulse come from? Is it from the animal part of me, a purely visceral reaction, or is the impulse to act the fruit of intellectual analysis, of spiritual introspection? In other words, who's in control, my body chemistry or me? My sex organ or my brain?

Second: what effect will my speech or action have on the world? Will my actions make the world better? Worse? Unchanged? As the Rebbe teaches, nothing is ever neutral. And the default position – or doing nothing – usually leads to evil. In order to do good in the world, and to bring good into the world, we must act. And our actions must arise from conscious thought and self-analysis. We must be aware of the power and the potential danger of our emotions and impulses.

## Weighing justice in the balance

Toward the end of the portion, we read about the laws of keeping just weights and measures. The Torah prohibits cheating customers by using improper weights and measures.

The text says, "Do not have two stones [weights used in the marketplace] in your pocket: a large one and a small one. Do not have in your house two measures: a large one and a small one" (25:13). Furthermore, "You shall have a full and just weighing-stone; you shall have a full and just measure" (25:15). The Torah's concept of justice includes the notion of completeness (a "full" stone, a "full" measure). The Hebrew word for "full" has the same root letters as the word for peace – *shalom*, so that maintaining peace in a society is a form of wholeness. In order for society to be whole, unbroken, the Torah requires that we use accurate and standard weights and measures. In the marketplace – and we define this in its broadest sense, meaning in all social and financial dealings – all persons must be treated equally. Using just weights and measures is necessary for peaceable coexistence, for societal harmony. As Peter Tosh sings, "No justice – no peace."

But there is also a deeper message. We are not commanded not to *use* improper weights and measures out in the marketplace. The Torah commands us not to *own* them, not to carry two different weights in our pocket, not to keep two different measures in our house. It is not enough to conform outwardly to the standards of a just society. We must internalize those values. We must live them. We must rid our moral and spiritual house of unjust weights and measures – of our propensity to justify our own desires and passions, our own improper acts. Don't keep unjust measures in your house or in your pocket. Don't act one way in public, while despising everyone around you.

We often go through the process of rationalizing, which is actually the misuse of God's greatest gift to us: the mind. Given the infinite things the mind is capable of, isn't it pathetic how much energy goes into thinking up ways to justify our worst behavior?

When we are out in the world, we generally conform to the standards of society. We are often on our best behavior – and we are swiftly called to account when we slip.

But what do we really think? How do we really want to

behave in our secret times and places – in our pocket, in our house – in our real and private view of the world? There we judge the world by our own standards rather than judging ourselves by the standards of a just society. When we are in public, we think before we act. But if in private our "lizard brain" takes over, then we are not truly part of society. We are behaving under constraint, and not out of an internal sense of right and wrong. Paradoxically, it is when we are most in the grip of this behavior – animal-like and unthinking – that we perceive ourselves as being free.

What does this lead to? I see a woman who excites me. Without thinking of the consequences, I act out my desire. I marry a woman who does not live up to my every expectation. Shall I compromise? No! Better to dispose of her. I have sex with a woman, driven by uncontrolled lust. Once the act is done, she disgusts me, and I can't throw her out of my bed fast enough.

The world is not given to us to take great bites from, then discard like the rind of a fruit, like a despised woman. The world depends so much, so very, very much, on each of us accepting responsibility for keeping the balance.

Living in the world is a challenge. The Torah urges us over and over again to understand our own inner workings in order to control our passions rather than allowing them to control us. Self-control leads not only to a better society, it leads to a better self. What a tremendous challenge it all is. Indeed, the work is the work of a lifetime. The path is the journey of a lifetime.

# 50

# Remembering to Remember

*O taste and see....*

– Psalms 34:8

This week's Torah portion is fundamentally about remembering.

Now, says Moses, "You have seen everything that God did before your eyes in Egypt, to Pharaoh and his servants and to all his land; the great trials that your eyes beheld, the great signs and wonders. But God did not give you a mind to know, or eyes to see, or ears to hear, until this day" (29:1–3). What does this mean?

Remember that the people to whom Moses is speaking are primarily *not* those who experienced the slavery and redemption of Egypt, not those who stood and received the Torah at Mount Sinai. When Moses says, "You did not eat bread, and you did not drink wine...so that you should know that I am the Lord your God" (29:5), what message does this actually convey? Moses is speaking to a generation raised on manna, the food that rained down from heaven. To them, it was their daily bread, not something miraculous.

As the Israelites prepare to enter the Land, their relationship to food becomes a symbol of the transition to peoplehood.

Last week's reading ended with an admonition to remember, and not to forget, the wickedness of Israel's eternal enemy the Amalekites (25:17–19). This week's reading opens with a formula and a ritual practice that reinforces the national act of remembering. In the retelling of the exodus from Egypt, and in the obligation to bring the offering of the firstfruits in annual pilgrimage, the people are told explicitly how to perform the act of remembrance. This lies at the core of how religion binds the individual and the society through shared history and shared values. The *fact* of remembering is not sufficient without the *act* of remembering.

This week's reading also contains an extended passage (the entire, long ch. 28) containing an extensive list of the consequences that will follow when the Jewish nation fails to follow God's word. These are known in the rabbinic literature as passages of rebuke, though in English the word *rebuke* means to harshly criticize someone who has done something inexcusable. In the passages of rebuke voiced by Moses – mostly in Deuteronomy – the rebuke is forward-looking. Moses says, I know that once I am no longer here to keep you on the straight and narrow, you will go off the right path. You will run after foreign gods, you will run after the enjoyments and amusements of the foreign societies among which you live. You will run to pleasures of the flesh. You will not end by rejecting God, says Moses. It is far worse, for you will *begin* by rejecting God – and once you have done so, your descent and destruction are assured.

The rebuke contains the image of us returning to Egypt in despair. We are told that God will bring back upon us our own experience of suffering in Egypt (28:60), which is the suffering of forgetting. In Egypt we forgot who we were, we forgot our relationship with God. Ultimately, our devastation and forgetting were so complete that we could be redeemed only when God stepped in.

We are to remember. That may be the final and fundamental message that Moses leaves us with before closing his narrative. Remember. Just this much: Always remember.

The first taste of milk on the tongue of the newborn creates a lifelong bond. The milk that feeds us in our first days and months also binds us forever to our caregivers – in Moses' case, it was his own mother. Yet as time passes, we become aware of the world expanding around us, we begin to yearn for other experiences.

I remember my own infant son, who had his first taste of solid food at the age of six months; the urgency with which he strained toward the spoon, the trembling expectation as his tongue reached for his first taste of applesauce. The blissful aftermath as he lay back and meditatively reflected on the experience of devouring a mash made of half a baked apple.

When Moses commands the people to bring the firstfruits as an offering to God, he is not only referring to the first of the annual crop. Taking the Torah's imagery to its poetic next step, the fruits the people taste in Israel will be the very first fruits they bring into the world – perhaps the first actual fruits that many Israelites have ever tasted. Whatever other food sources the Israelites drew on during their years of wandering, it is clear that, in the wilderness, the manna was mother's milk to them. Now, like a child about to experience new tastes, new textures – about to experience directly what the child came to know dimly as the smells and colors of food – they tremble with excitement. They can't wait to taste these fruits, to make them part of their own experience.

Every wisdom tradition knows the danger of becoming enamored of the spiritual experience. That is why they all emphasize practice. And Moses also warns us against the danger of spiritual addiction.

Do not take the taste of the fruit, the experience of tasting these foods for the first time, to be the norm. A spiritual life doesn't come in individual spiritual experiences, but in maintaining a connection to the Divine in this world – even in the midst of our most mundane acts. We experience a set of feelings with the performance of an act. Once, and once only, do we have the flood of uplifting, expanding, and mind-altering sensations that come with a new spiritual experience. But we are human, and we expect to be able to experience the same set of feelings and sensations. The same elation. The same expansiveness. And when we do not, we believe there is something wrong with us. Or perhaps that the experience itself is not genuine, or that there is something flawed in the way the experience is taught to us.

Either we are at fault, or our practice is at fault, or our teacher is at fault. Or God is at fault.

Moses says, this is the way most people think. The Torah

is not an experience. It is life. The laws and practices are a way to enter into dialogue with God, speaking God's own language. Prayer is not an experience; it is the way to isolate ourselves with our own selves, to enfold ourselves in God as in an embrace. To give ourselves over to God's will and to God's care. It can be exhilarating; and like all true acts of intimacy, it should also be frightening.

Says Moses, you have seen, but you have not understood. Now, going forward, you must strive to understand, persevering even when you do not comprehend. And understanding comes from remembering our place in the cosmos. From remembering our relationship with God. From remembering the primacy of Torah, especially in the midst of spiritual confusion. When our own spiritual strivings come up short, there is the Practice, handed down to us from Sinai, and standing us in good stead today.

Spiritual practice is like the athlete's daily workout: it's not the game, but you can't step onto the playing field without it. Our relationship with God is not made up of an unending series of spiritual revelations. Rather, we need to devote ourselves to the practice for its own sake. Do your job, says Moses. Don't worry about God – God will do God's part without your help.

Give up your experiences. Make of them, not gifts for yourselves, but gifts for God. If we take the fruits and eat them ourselves, what will happen when we are disappointed by the taste? When it doesn't meet our expectations? Is that not when we challenge God? Is that not when we say: God, you led me to have an expectation, and You are responsible to me for making up my disappointment?

The expectation of reward is its own greatest punishment.

Life is not about us. Or rather, it is about us, but not only about us. It is about us, and our ongoing relationship with God. Remember, Moses is saying – and do not forget. Like the athlete on the practice field, like the person seeking growth who goes dutifully to his therapy session, like the meditator who returns to his silent cushion every day at the appointed time, our spiritual growth comes not from our spiritual experiences but from sticking to the basics. Repeating the formulas, performing the actions. Practice. Sometimes we feel uplifted, sometimes our actions will inspire others to feel uplifted. Sometimes we will feel that we have done everything we could, and to no avail.

When Moses says, "God did not give you the heart to know until this day," he is giving his people a tremendous blessing and compliment – and a challenge.

Now, as they are about to enter the Promised Land, the Israelites finally begin to form an understanding of what came before. This is the transformation which Moses – and dare we say God, too? – so devoutly wished for. A new generation, one which never experienced the miracles, the signs and wonders, the physical Presence of God at the giving of the Torah at Sinai; this new generation of Israel now fully embraces their role as the inheritors of all this cosmic history.

Perhaps they will still not understand it; indeed, never with the comprehension of those who actually lived it. Perhaps they will not always get it right. They will slip, they will become frustrated. At times they will angrily reject what they have come to embrace here today. But as it says in Ethics of the Fathers (2:16), "It is not given to you to finish the work; but neither are you free to desist from striving."

You have lived long enough in exile, says Moses. Now, he urges the people, begin the process of redemption, which rests upon a lifelong process of remembering who you are.

God places each one of us here for a unique reason. Our lives in the world are so overwhelming that it is impossible for us not to forget who we are, why we are here. The Midrash recounts that an angel comes to the womb and teaches the unborn infant the entire Torah. Then, at the moment of birth, the angel strikes – or perhaps kisses – us on the mouth and we forget everything. The philtrum – the vertical cleft running from the upper lip to the nose – is the mark of the angel's kiss. The crease of our forgetfulness.

Hidden in this fanciful image is the underlying message

that our individual truth is still there, hidden away. Right on the tip of our tongue, as it were – hanging on our lip, awaiting the breath of self-awareness. Our work in the world is to rediscover who we are.

We need to stay the course as we continue our daily grind in the confusion of the physical world, the day-to-day of making money and building a business or a career – all of which is important. And at the same time, our daily activities can become a form of exile of the soul, because it is so difficult to keep both our physical and our spiritual necessities before our eyes at all times, to maintain balance.

Hold fast to your inner core of truth. Continue the steady work of remembering, the lifelong practice of becoming the person God intends you to be.

Let your personal redemption begin.

# 51

# All On That Day

*I expect to pass through this world but once. Any good therefore that I can do, or any kindness or abilities that I can show to any fellow creature, let me do it now. Let me not defer it or neglect it, for I shall not pass this way again.*

– William Penn

This week's Torah reading is very short. In fact, the action from here to the end of the Torah covers only one day – the last day of Moses' life.

Deuteronomy features Moses exhorting repeatedly, "This is the covenant I establish with you, and not only with you, but with your descendants." At 29:14, Moses says explicitly that this covenant is "with whoever is here, standing with us today before God; and with whoever is not here with us today."

What is this concept of a covenant? And how can future generations be held to a contract when they weren't even born when the contract was signed?

At Mount Sinai, God gives the Torah to all generations of Israel, those who stand at Sinai and those of us who have come into this world in the 3,500 years since. And we can understand how a gift can be given to a family and its generations – an heirloom, an inheritance. A person acquires real estate, and the property remains in the family for generations. We know of people who have used their great-grandmother's wedding ring for their marriage, of men who carry their great-grandfather's pocket watch or smoke their grandfather's meerschaum pipe.

But a covenant is different. It is a type of contract, and it requires two parties to participate. How does this devolve on generations unborn?

Nechama Leibowitz (born in Riga, Latvia, 1905; died in

Jerusalem, 1997), one of the great Jewish scholars and teachers of the twentieth century, explains the notion of a covenant as a unique type of contract. Normally, a contract requires what lawyers call Offer and Acceptance, and Performance and Consideration. You and I agree that if I do activity X, you will pay me amount Y.

Not so a covenant. If you look through the Torah, you will see God granting a covenant to Noah after the Flood, to Abraham after his circumcision, to Israel at Mount Sinai. But the actual establishment of the covenant depends on the recipient. A covenant, explains Leibowitz, is an unconditional offer. How can this work? Because in order for the covenant to be sealed, it must be equally unconditional on both sides.

God makes an unconditional – and unilateral – offer to Abraham: I will give this land to you and to your descendants. But the culmination of the covenant is when Abraham accepts in similar fashion, unilaterally and unconditionally committing his faith and belief in God. This is what I call the "bi-unilateral" unconditionality that makes a true covenant.

In this week's Torah reading, Moses describes punishments that will be visited on future generations "because they forsook the covenant of God" (Deut. 29:24) and served other gods.

Again: if my ancestors agreed to a contract, how does that make me liable to be punished?

It is a constant principle in society that you can't take advantage of the benefits of an offer without ultimately becoming liable for the associated consequences. If you live in a house, after a certain time you become responsible for its upkeep. If you eat from an orchard, after a certain time you become responsible for tending it. If you cohabit with someone, after a time you are recognized as married. If you bring children into the world, you are responsible for raising them.

So too, we cannot take advantage of God's gifts without acknowledging where they come from. We can't accept the blessings that come into our lives without also taking responsibility for how we treat others; for ensuring that others also have the ability to enjoy God's blessings, that they have the freedom and the resources to live their lives to the fullest and achieve their potential in this world.

The rabbinic commentators have much to say about the notion of individuals losing themselves in the crowd; people who avoid responsibility by hiding behind those who accept responsibility. In a fascinating insight into human nature, the verses describe a person who rejects the Torah, and the consequences: "When he hears the words of this rebuke, he will say to himself, 'I will be all right, though I walk as I see fit'" (29:18, and see also v. 17). How often do we decide to do what we know is wrong, and justify it simply by saying, "But this is what I want to do, so I'm going to do it"? Commentators say this describes a person who says to him- or herself, "God only punishes those who reject the covenant. But I have not even accepted it in the first place! I will be safe!" Or one who says, "Even though I personally reject the Torah, I will be safe, because I am surrounded by those who accept it." In both cases, we see the individual gladly taking the fruit of God's bounty but squirming out of responsibility for the consequences of their actions. More, we see the Torah's insightfulness into the convoluted process of self-justification that we go through each time we make what we know is the wrong decision.

The text tells us, "This commandment that I command you today, it is not hidden, and it is not far distant. It is not in heaven, so that you will say, 'Who can go up to heaven and take it for us so that we can hear and perform what is demanded of us?' And it is not across the sea, for you to say, 'Who can cross the sea for us and take it for us so that we can hear and perform?' But this matter is very near to you – in your mouth and in your heart – to perform it. Behold: I have placed before you today Life and the Good, and Death and the Evil" (30:11–15).

This says it all. God has given us an amazing handbook for the human soul. And lest we think it is all abstract, that it applied thousands of years ago but not today; in these final pages, the Torah rubs our faces in its profound understanding of human nature. You can't wriggle out of it, the Torah is telling us. Life is a gift; do not squander it. God's blessings are given freely – and unilaterally. But if we do not respond in kind, it is as though we have tossed them on the trash heap.

Which kind of descendants of God's covenant are we? What kind of beneficiaries? Do we take what is offered, yet offer nothing in return? Or do we embrace our life in this world as an opportunity to make the most of all that God has blessed us with, and to work as hard as we can to put back into the world more than we ever take out of it?

## 52

## Before the Great Sabbath

*This day I breathed first: time is come round.*
*And where I did begin there shall I end.*
*My life is run his compass.*

– Shakespeare, *Julius Caesar*

This week's reading is the shortest in the Torah, consisting of a mere thirty verses. What it lacks in length, it makes up for in drama.

"Be strong and be courageous," Moses exhorts the Israelites (Deut. 31:6). Moses is preparing to take his leave of his people. For forty years he has led them, taught them, interpreted God's word for them, interceded with God on their behalf – defending them when they were at their very worst and defying God by offering himself up in their place. This is Moses' overriding message. Be strong and courageous. Do not be awed by life's challenges and do not fear, because the Lord your God who is going along with you will not forsake you and will not abandon you.

In the context of the book of Deuteronomy, this exhortation is perhaps more frightening than it is reassuring.

The notion of being the Chosen People is so often misunderstood, perhaps more by Jews than by the non-Jewish world. We are not chosen for special gifts and privileges; we are singled out to be held to a higher standard. The Torah tells us repeatedly that it is our obligation to be a light to the nations (see, e.g., Is. 49:6), a kingdom of priests and a holy people (Ex. 19:6). All the nations of the world will be blessed through our relationship with God (Gen. 12:3). This is a lot to carry, which may be why so many reject it.

In last week's reading, Moses announces that "today" is the day of his birth: "I am 120 years old today, I can no longer go out and come, and God has said to me, 'You will not cross this Jordan'" (Deut. 31:2).

Why is the date of Moses' death important, and why does he die on his birthday?

It is a fundamental religious notion that God's time is not human time. Time itself does not exist until God creates it. The created cosmos is the world of space, time, and motion, all of which require each other in order to exist. Planted at a focal point within the cosmos, we humans are the observers that make all these have meaning. In this way – and with this gift – God makes us partners in Creation. And when God's plan for us is fulfilled, we leave this plane of the cosmos to continue our partnership on another plane.

The notion of God's omnipotence does not clash with the idea of human freedom of choice. We often use the term "free will," which is misleading. It is more accurate to say free choice, because most of the time we face binary, either/or decisions. Our lives are bound by conditions, and our actions are determined by the set of choices we face each moment. And the choices we face in the moment are nothing more than the result of the choices we have made in the past.

God demands that we act now. Not that we *be* perfect – but we are not permitted to cease *trying to attain* perfection. We follow the string of choices in our lives, making a decision-tree pattern as each choice leads to further sets of choices. If we choose correctly, our choice-making can bring us to a result that corresponds to God's plan for us. This must be viewed as a successful life.

What kind of life did Moses live? Let us recognize first that he was born to die. Moses was born in Egypt under Pharaoh's decree that all newborn boys be strangled on the birthstool. When the midwives did not comply, Pharaoh decreed that newborn boys be thrown into the river. Thus, Moses was slated to die on the day he was born. Instead, he is hidden for three months, after which he is committed to the uncertain care of the Nile, where he is rescued by Pharaoh's daughter.

Moses' first act as a mature youth is to kill an Egyptian.

When Pharaoh orders Moses put to death (Ex. 2:11–15), Moses flees to Midian, where he settles and becomes a shepherd. All is peaceful until God calls to him at the burning bush where, oddly, Moses does not object that he can't return to Egypt because there is a price on his head. It is not until after he has not only consented to go, but publicly announced his intention, that God tells Moses he is no longer in danger (Ex. 4:19).

Moses is fearless. Perhaps he possesses the fearlessness of one born with the knowledge that life is but an instant. That the day of our birth may as well be the day of our death; that so many souls never are brought into the world at all. And that so many perish so quickly.

Moses fearlessly defends the covenant between God and Israel in the face of God's outbursts of rage. Stand aside, God says over and over, and I will destroy them. This comes to a head after the sin of the Golden Calf. At Exodus 32:32, in the face of God's threatening to destroy the people yet again, Moses says, "If that's what You plan to do, then please erase me from the book You have written!" And God relents. There are many ways of stating this principle: you have nothing to live for until you recognize what you are prepared to die for.

But Moses goes one giant step further, because he accepts the leadership position that is thrust on him, not because he wants it (he doesn't) and not because, once having tasted power, he relishes it and can't relinquish it. But because, having accepted it, this is now his responsibility, and Moses fully embraces the responsibility he has accepted.

Now, coming to the end of his own story, Moses is indeed vanishing from God's Book.

Moses was given his name by Pharaoh's daughter, who spoke ancient Egyptian, not Hebrew. The name by which our leader is known to us, the political leader who created this nation in earthly terms – as surely as God formed us spiritually – is not his actual name. His earthly, given name is hidden from us, lost forever.

Similarly, we read that Moses is buried in a place in the

land of Moab, "and no one knows his grave to this day" (Deut. 34:6). The request Moses makes of God is fulfilled: he has been erased from the Torah. Why? Perhaps to emphasize that it was not Moses; it was never about him. Rather, it was God who walked at our side all those years – and we never even acknowledged it. We were never aware.

Moses dies on his birthday. It is as though he has vanished. The film has been run backward, from Moses' last day to the hour before his birth. As though he had never been born. It is difficult to imagine that Moses, of all people, did not lead a life that fulfilled God's destiny for him. And so perhaps the manner of Moses' leaving the world at just this moment – perhaps it was a blessing, and not a curse. Perhaps God rewound time for his sake. Instead of perishing, by human decree, on the very day he was born, Moses lives for 120 years, saves the Hebrew people from slavery, brings God's Torah into the world, and forges a pack of miserable slaves into the nation of Israel. But the puny human power to issue a decree is not to be taken lightly. With a gap of 120 years, Moses was one of many newborn Hebrew boys slated for extermination on the day of his birth.

The account has finally come due.

Be strong and courageous, Moses exhorts the people. I shall die, he says, but do not be afraid. In reality, it is God who is walking with you, who has been walking with you all along. I am no more than the middleman.

Moses' greatness emerges in his unflinching ability to put his entire life into the task assigned him. Not a task he chose, and certainly not one that he asked for. But once he saw the duty devolving on himself, he took it up and carried it through with all his might.

One final thought. There is midrashic literature explaining the special significance of Moses dying on his birthday. Because the fixed limit of human existence is 120 years and Moses reached it, the time has come for him to die. But this is his actual birthday, which means he has lived for 120 years and one day. This is a special blessing set aside for those rare righteous ones who merit a unique measure of God's grace.

What we do in this life determines the extent and the quality of the reward we receive in the life to come, but none of us can know what that reward shall be. And thus we fear death. Moses' lifespan, as dictated by the Torah, came to its end the day before, with the completion of his 120th year. His afterlife, his death, will ensue the following day. This extra day is the unique gift of God granting Moses one day when he can experience his reward of the world to come, while still inhabiting this world.

We must strive to fully embrace our responsibilities, the ones we have asked for and also the ones we never wanted. We are measured by how we respond to getting what we want. Are we gracious winners? Do we recognize that blessings come to us, not because of our merit, but in order *that we will strive to merit them*? We are measured too by how we deal with burdens that come unbidden upon us, and which we are nonetheless powerless to dispose of. When the film of our life is run back to the beginning, what story will it have told?

# 53

# Songs of Innocence and Experience

*Great things are done when men and mountains meet.*

– William Blake

This week's Torah portion is the penultimate in the yearly cycle. Last week, God instructed Moses to write a poem as an eternal reminder of Israel's obligation to follow, serve, and obey God, and of the consequences for straying from the path. Our portion presents that song in its entirety, full of powerful imagery and frightening portents.

"Be strong and courageous," Moses charged us on this, the last day of his life. The tone of this intense poem is one of blame and condemnation – a call to heaven and earth themselves to bear witness to the behavior of the Jewish people. At the beginning, Moses reviews the history of the cosmos, as seen from God's perspective. He has also buried a hidden message: as we are God's partners in Creation, God's perspective should be ours as well.

Moses' song begins with a poetic echo of the first six days of Creation evoking the negative association of human behavior. The sins of the first humans – of Adam and Noah, the first leaders of humanity – are sins of appetite. Adam's sin is one of carelessness, while Noah's sin comes from drunkenness – loss of control – which will be mirrored yet again in the story of Lot and his daughters. In this poem, the name given to Israel is Jeshurun (32:14–15), which derives from the Hebrew root *y-sh-r*, meaning straight or upright. *Homo erectus*.

Upright, in the physical sense. Now the challenge is to become morally upright as well. As we come to the end of the Torah, Moses holds out the clear criticism that we have failed, and that we will fail repeatedly.

The section opens with twin images of water: "May my teaching drop like rain, my utterance drip like the dew" (32:2). The Zohar, the central text of Jewish mysticism, says the image of rain represents the Written Torah – which God hands down from heaven; and the image of dew represents the Oral Torah: the teachings of the rabbis, first received from Moses and then passed through Joshua, the Elders, the Sages, and down to our day. Moses is referencing the Written Torah, but also showing us that we can, indeed must, take upon ourselves the work of interpreting it – the Oral Torah.

On a cosmic level, our constant striving to learn and teach and perfect the Oral Torah is the way in which we unite earth and heaven, bringing down the Creator to dwell in the physical world. This is the spiritual task the Torah sets for us.

On a much more urgent level, it is only by constantly examining the Torah, by constantly looking at the world through the lens of Torah, by constantly striving to see ourselves from God's perspective, that we have any hope at all of living properly. Of living a moral life. Of realizing our potential. Of creating a just society: protecting the weak, improving the lives of those around us, and supporting others in their quest to attain their potential in life.

Thus, we are all students and teachers simultaneously. While many of us are aware of being students in life, we often forget that we are teachers, too. The way we live our lives is the most powerful lesson we teach to those around us. We attract people with our words, but our actions prove who we truly are.

It is our task to reunite heaven and earth, yet we must also recall that division and differentiation are among God's fundamental acts of Creation. The task of unification is not that of undoing God's work. It is to drill down to the fundamental level where the underlying unity of God's universe emerges. Torah is one. Not Written *and* Oral. Not Written *versus* Oral. Just Torah. The Word of God is ultimately indivisible, much as this concept is impossible for us to grasp.

Moses' poem tells us that a terrible fate awaits us, and he

doesn't soften the blow. The Jewish people will suffer. We will be scattered and will come near to total extinction. "Don't say I didn't warn you," says Moses. God is demanding. God is vengeful and will turn on you in a heartbeat. I had to tell you this story – all of Deuteronomy – so that you would understand how many times you came to the brink of destruction, only to be rescued at the last minute by my intercession. Now, says Moses, you no longer have me to step between you and the wrath of God. Study this Torah and take it to heart, says Moses, because the tragedy and suffering foretold in this poem will unfold throughout the generations of your future history. And yet, you are not free to walk away from God, nor from the task God has set for you in this world.

In the books of Exodus, Leviticus, and Numbers, Moses took pains to explain the explicit meaning of God's message. Now, throughout Deuteronomy, Moses is teaching us that the only meaning the Torah can truly have is the meaning expressed by the work of our hands. How do we enact God's word in this world? In our lifetime? When others see God expressed in our actions, which God do they see: a peevish, narrow-minded God ready to lash out at those with whom we disagree, or a God who is infinitely expansive, infinitely patient, infinitely caring of others? Who is generous, compassionate, and willing to stand by them to help when life tests them?

Do they see a God who is ready, even at the worst moment, to be reminded of the purpose for which all of us were created – which is to make this world whole?

Moses begins his poem with the recap of Creation because it is up to each of us to re-Create, to make anew. While there is the breath of life in us, we are God's partners in the ongoing act of Creation whereby the world continues to exist. And during those dark times when God seems to have left the scene, we must stand in for God and keep the spheres turning.

And sometimes, like Moses, we must be the ones to stand up and confront God and say, "No! This was not Your plan, not Your promise." "We are made in *Your* image!" we shout. "You put us here to continue *Your* work!"

We will never be able to say for certainty what the Torah means, nor should we desire so narrow an outcome. But we are blessed to be the vessels by which this eternal quest continues to be carried on. Even in the darkest times that have, or shall, come upon us, there is this: the Torah was given for all humankind. But it was given first to Israel. This is our responsibility. The idea of chosenness is not a gift to play with when new, and then to lay aside when we are bored. Those of us whose souls are touched by the words of God's Torah bear a great responsibility, for we must store up the message, and care for it and keep it very much alive until the time comes when the rest of the world will flock to its Truth.

# 54

# The Unbroken Circle

*May God bless and keep you always,*
*may your wishes all come true,*
*May you always do for others and let others do for you.*
*May you build a ladder to the stars and climb on every rung,*
*May you stay forever young.*

– Bob Dylan, *Forever Young*

*Let us rise up and be thankful; for if we did not learn a lot, at least we learned a little.*

– Buddha

And thus we come to the end of the Torah. This final portion is not read in the synagogue on the Sabbath, as is done every week. It comes after the end of the annual cycle of holidays known in the Jewish calendar as the Days of Awe: Rosh Hashana – the new year, on which we coronate God as King of the world; and Yom Kippur – the day of atonement, where we reconcile with God for our failures in the past year and resolve to do better. These are followed by the week-long holiday of Sukkot, the festival of booths. This final Torah portion will be read on the day immediately after the end of the Sukkot holiday, known biblically as the Eighth Day Closing Festival, and referred to as the day of the Rejoicing of the Torah, because on this day we complete the reading of the Torah and immediately begin reading again from the first verses of Genesis.

The Torah is the heart of our life. It governs all aspects of our lives, not merely the few hours each week we spend in synagogue. And although our behavior and our ritual, as well as our social and philosophical and spiritual thought, are guided by centuries of rabbinic writings, we return each week to the source, the received Word of God, unaltered after more than 3,500 years.

In a tangible sense, this holiday is a return to the moment of receiving the Torah on Mount Sinai. The Torah scroll is opened for all to see, then each member of the congregation is called up to read, until the last verses of the Torah are completed. The highlight of the evening is the ecstatic dancing with the Torah scrolls themselves, dancing which often continues long past midnight.

In the Torah's final verses, we read of the death of Moses. This is one of the most emotionally charged moments of the year, as we watch our beloved leader depart this world. Never mind that he will be back on the stage right on schedule with the next year's reading of the book of Exodus. We listen, choked with tears, as the final verses are read.

What is Moses' final message to us?

The key resides in the first word of the portion, which in Hebrew means "and this": "And this is the blessing that Moses, man of God, bestowed upon the children of Israel before his death" (33:1).

The connective particle "and" links this verse to the passage in the previous portion immediately preceding it (32:49–52), in which God tells Moses to go up to the top of Mount Nebo and look out over the Promised Land. Says God, "I will give this land to the children of Israel, but you, Moses, will not enter, because you failed to sanctify Me in the eyes of the nation of Israel at the waters of Kadesh in the wilderness of Zin." This is harsh. Moses has been God's dutiful servant and earthly partner, shepherding an unruly mob through the wilderness for forty years. Not only will he die without entering the land, but in his final moments, God throws this incident in Moses' face.

Moses' "And this" is not merely a look forward to the future of the Jewish people. It is a direct response to what God has just said.

"You are being punished, Moses," says God, "because you failed."

"And this is the blessing I will give to the people," answers Moses. Immediately we recall that the entire book of Deuteronomy comprises Moses' recounting of the multiple ways in which Israel caused him to fall out of favor with God. Yet rather than blame us, he blesses us. The lesson of selfless leadership could not be more powerful.

The Israelites are about to enter the Promised Land, and Moses is the only one who will not cross over. Knowing this, Moses accepts his lonesome and lonely fate, and with his last breath, seeks God's assurance that Israel will remain faithful. Moses begs God to promise that Israel will never stray from the Torah.

This was the very argument raised at the creation of Adam. The Midrash says the angels warned God not to create humans. With their freedom of choice, the angels said, humans would stray from God's commands. They would forget. They would sin. They would rebel. Now God takes the other side of this argument. Moses begs for certainty, for assurances that Israel will remain faithful. But, God seems to reply – gently, perhaps somewhat sadly – they have free choice.

Indeed, even the greatest teacher cannot ensure that the student will learn; the greatest leader cannot guarantee that the people will follow. It is, after all, up to each one of us. As Maimonides repeatedly exhorts us – Will you be wicked? Will you be righteous? It's in your hands, and in your hands only.

Now, at the end of our tale, God the Teacher gently reminds God's own finest pupil: These are the consequences of creation – and of the Creation. These people you have led from slavery to nationhood, from deprivation to plenty, from agony and debasement to spiritual royalty. From blind and desperate obedience to the rule of law. From animality to the creation of a just society: these people are only human. They will choose for themselves; they must. Some will follow, many will strive and struggle, but many will fail. All you can do, Moses, is place your Torah before them and pray that, in whatever measure they are able, they will embrace it.

How do we teach and encourage others to follow the right

path in life? In particular, how do we do it in such a way that they can hear the message and embrace it? Recall the teacher's constant watchword: "It's not what you *say*, it's what *they hear*." These are words to take to heart.

Few things can wreck a life lesson like absolute certainty. How often have we been told, "This is how you *must* behave"? When we were wandering in the wilderness, Moses repeatedly said, "This *is* the law." "This *is* the rule." "Give this to that person – take that away from that other person." And even, on occasion, "Take them outside the camp and stone them to death." Moses speaks with unerring certainty, and we obey with alacrity.

But I am not Moses, nor is there a Moses in our world. Moses took his orders directly from God; none of us does. Yet so many teachers deliver their lessons with a harsh certainty. What a recipe for turning others away! Living a life of Torah is not about certainty. It's about being open to the infinite range of meaning that God's word can bring into our lives, if we will only permit it.

How can it be, we wonder, that you know – that only *you* know, and everyone else is wrong? That you *know*, and what I so deeply feel in my heart is wrong? How can it be that I am not even permitted to question, to ask…to doubt? Is this really what God expects of me? It's no wonder so many people reject God, when all around them they are beset by God's self-appointed representatives.

Even the written word of God's law can be misused, can be perverted – intentionally or, more often, with the very best of intent – and used not as a tool for compassion, but as a bludgeon to force obedience, to enforce conformity. I have no idea, truly, what God wants from all of us, but I am sure that God does not want us to stifle our individuality, our capacity to think and learn and wonder at the ongoing miracle that is life. Because accepting the harsh outlook of our worst teachers – and there are many, alas! – leads us to harshly reject other people. In order to grow we must be permitted to ask, even if – or especially *when* – we interrogate the Torah itself. For it is only by confrontation and struggle that we can uncover the truth about ourselves. And it is only when we truly own our own truth can we turn with compassion to others.

Moses has the authority to speak with absolute certainty. For the rest of us – students, and especially teachers – we need to go through life with the humble awareness that we do not know everything. Indeed, we may not know *anything*. Our job is not to speak, but to listen. Not to tell others how to live their lives, but to learn by watching and listening to others how we might better live our own lives. Not to meaninglessly recite the written words, but to struggle to understand the meaning that lies beneath. We must each struggle with God's word and make it yield its special meaning for us alone. Only then can we truly be said to possess some smidgen of truth.

Through a rigorous process combining intuition with an honest struggle to understand and to continually generate the contemplative and active process whereby Torah becomes ingrained in our very being, and through lifelong dedication, we can bring God's truth into this world day by day, moment by moment. And to the extent we engage in that struggle for ourselves, we may, with God's help, be able to serve as a teacher for others; teaching not so much by the words we speak as by the example of our lives. This is truly cause for rejoicing. It is up to us. If we have learned anything at all about God's Torah, it is this: It is not carved in stone.

Like Moses on the eve of his departure, I leave you with a blessing: May God's grace rest upon you. May God bless and establish the work of your hands and the sincere efforts of your heart, and may you live a life that makes your Creator say, "I did well to bring you here."

Yours for a better world.

# Excerpts

Excerpt from **NEW SPEEDWAY BOOGIE,** Words by ROBERT HUNTER, Music by JERRY GARCIA. Copyright © 1970 (Renewed) ICE NINE PUBLISHING CO., INC. All Rights Administered by WC MUSIC CORP. All Rights Reserved. Used By Permission of ALFRED MUSIC

Excerpt from **RIPPLE,** Words by ROBERT HUNTER, Music by JERRY GARCIA. Copyright © 1971 (Renewed) ICE NINE PUBLISHING CO., INC. All Rights Administered by WC MUSIC CORP. All Rights Reserved. Used By Permission of ALFRED MUSIC

Excerpt from **REQUIEM FOR A NUN** by William Faulkner, copyright 1950, 1951 by William Faulkner. Copyright © renewed 1979 by Jill Faulkner Summers. Used by permission of Random House, an imprint and division of Penguin Random House LLC. All rights reserved.

Excerpt from **AN INTERRUPTED LIFE** by Etty Hillesum, translation copyright © 1983 by Jonathan Cape LTD. Copyright © 1981 by De Haan/Uniboek b.v. Bussum. Used by permission of Pantheon Books, an imprint of the Knopf Doubleday Publishing Group, a division of Penguin Random House LLC. All rights reserved.

Excerpt from **REDEMPTION SONG** by Bob Marley, © Kobalt Music Publishing Ltd., Universal Music Publishing Group. Used by permission of publishers: Fifty Six Hope Road Music Limited/Primary Wave/Blue Mountain.

Excerpt from **A STATE OF SIEGE** by Mahmoud Darwish, from *The Butterfly's Burden*, translated by Fady Joudah. Copyright © 2007 by Mahmoud Darwish. Translation copyright © 2007 by Fady Jouda. Reprinted by permission of The Permissions Company, LLC, on behalf of Copper Canyon Press, coppercanyonpress.org.

Quote from Martin Luther King, Jr., reprinted by arrangement with The Heirs to the Estate of Martin Luther King, Jr., c/o Writers House as agent for the proprietor New York, NY. Copyright ©

1968 by Dr. Martin Luther King, Jr. Renewed © 1996 by Coretta Scott King.

Excerpt from **ZAPISNYE KNIZHKI** (Moscow: NASLEDIE, 2000), 171, by Andrei Platonov, quoted in the introduction to **SOUL AND OTHER STORIES**, Copyright © the Estate of Andrey Platonov, introduction Copyright © 2008 by Robert Chandler. Used by permission of the New York Review of Books.

Excerpt from **MORAL MAN AND IMMORAL SOCIETY: STUDY IN ETHICS AND POLITICS** by Reinhold Niebuhr, Copyright © Westminster John Knox Press, used by permission (conforms to publisher's fair use guidelines).

Excerpt from **THE AUTOBIOGRAPHY OF MALCOLM X,** Copyright © 1965 Grove Atlantic, Inc. © 1993 Betty Shabazz, Myran Haley, Cynthia Haley, William Haley and Lydia Haley.

Quote from Abraham Joshua Heschel, Copyright © Harper and Row 1962.

Excerpt from **THE PRESENCE OF THE LORD**, by Eric Clapton (Blind Faith), Copyright © Warner Chappelle Music.

Excerpt from **JESUS CHRIST SUPERSTAR**, by Andrew Lloyd Weber & Tim Rice, Copyright © ASCAP/Universal Music Corp.

Excerpts from **FOOLED BY RANDOMNESS** and **THE BLACK SWAN** by Nassim Nicholas Taleb, Copyright © Penguin/Random House.

Excerpt from **CIVILIZATION AND ITS DISCONTENTS**, by Sigmund Freud, Copyright © by Hogarth Press, Liveright Publishing Company Ltd.

Excerpt from **IT MUST BE HELL**, by the Rolling Stones, Copyright © Promotone, BV/Sony ATV Music Publishing.

Excerpt from **DEBT: THE FIRST 5,000 YEARS**, by David Graeber, Copyright © Melville House/Penguin.

Except from **THE FELLOWSHIP OF THE RING**, by J.R.R. Tolkein, Copyright © Taylor & Francis.

Excerpt from **FOREVER YOUNG** by Bob Dylan, Copyright © 1973 Ram's Horn Music

www.ingramcontent.com/pod-product-compliance
Lightning Source LLC
Chambersburg PA
CBHW060654100426
42734CB00047B/1651